The Intermediary

Thunder's Eye
father of Isabel
|
William Craig — Isabel
|
Sam Phenney — Adeline Craig
|
Fitch Phinney — Mary
|
Archie Phinney — Grandma Ellen
|
Mary Phinney — Bruce McMillan
|
John McMillan — Justina Clark
|
Zachary — Madison — KC

William Craig in the 1860's; courtesy of Bill Belknap

The Intermediary

William Craig
Among the Nez Perces

Lin Tull Cannell (signature)

Lin Tull Cannell

RIDENBAUGH PRESS
Carlton, Oregon
www.ridenbaughpress.com

Ridenbaugh Press
P.O. 834, Carlton OR 97111
(503) 852-0010
www.ridenbaughpress.com
stapilus@ridenbaugh.com

Composition and editing by Ridenbaugh Press, Carlton, Oregon.
Cover design by Randy Stapilus.

Library of Congress Cataloging-in-Publication Data:

Cannell, Lin Tull
    The Intermediary: William Craig Among the Nez Perces
    Includes bibliographical references.
    ISBN 978-0-9824668-3-4 (softbound)
    1. United States-Northwest-history. 2. Nez Perce Tribe-history. I. Title.

Printed in the United States of America.

December 2010

10 9 8 7 6 5 4 3 2 1

Table of Contents

In memory of my *láwtiwa·*

Carmen Kellar

Acknowledgements

This work is from my pen as a freelance writer and from my heart as a native Idahoan.

While it may take its place alongside those of credentialed scholars, I do not pretend to be a professional historian. Along with the objectivity that is a critical element of historical research and writing, I bring the subjectivity of a native wanting to learn how my little area of north central Idaho got to be how it is. This work is simply an honest effort to capture and share our history.

While there is little hope of thanking all those who have helped with this project—so many people over so many years have had a hand in it—I must mention a few who gave service above and beyond the call of duty or bonds of friendship:

The breadth of information about former mountain man William Craig is due to the hard work of my research assistant, partner, and friend, Gloria Manning.

For the personal encouragement and his Nez Perce perspective, I am beholden to the keen eyes and mind of Steven R. Evans, Ph.D., of Lapwai, Idaho.

For the particularly outstanding help offered, thanks go the staffs at Penrose Library, Whitman College in Walla Walla, the Idaho State Historical Archives and Library—with special thanks to Steve Barrett and Kathy Hodges—and the Washington State Archives, as well as to Jim Magera of Bear Paw Battlefield, Montana.

Melissa Rockwood of Rdesign, Inc. in Moscow, Idaho, has my appreciation for producing, with grace and professionalism, the maps that illustrate this work.

Particularly praiseworthy are the contributions of Craig descendants who have shared with cousin Gloria Manning their research, photographs, and memories. They are Bill Belknap, Fermore Craig,

Bill Freeland, Ryder Heidenrich, Glen Jones, Mary McHale, Glen Hancock, Blanche Moore, Kathleen Randall, Calvin Shillal, and Ann Wooten. Thank you.

To my husband, Merk, goes my unending gratitude and thanks. Without his steadfast belief in me—and my ideas—none of this would have happened.

Lin Tull Cannell
Orofino, Idaho
October 2010

Foreword

William Craig is one of those Idaho pioneer names; read about Idaho in the (very) early days, and it turns up here and there. It's easy to pass by because in many ways, Craig's own story is representative of the time and place.

He was a mountain man.

He lived among the natives, married into an Indian tribe.

He was an early homesteader – probably the first in Idaho, in fact.

But the lesser-known parts of his story are what really grabbed my attention, and what ought to grab yours.

Craig was an intermediary, a go-between, a man trying to broker peace between two societies headed toward conflict. He was the rare individual, in that place and time, trusted by both sides. He was also pressured by and challenged by both sides.

Sound familiar? Do any parallels in our present day suggest themselves?

Craig's efforts at making peace and making his own way in that place weren't easy, and they evolved with time. This man once on the run from society, who came west as a way to stay on the down-low, wound up interacting with officials and armies of various sorts, and even (in the way of the time) trying to shape the contours of a society, even becoming himself various types of public official.

It's one of the great untold – till now – Idaho stories, one barely referenced anywhere in the many books that have to do with early Idaho.

Lin Tull Cannell, who was born in Coeur d' Alene, raised in the Northwest, and has for some years lived at Orofino, became interested in it by observing the landmarks named for or associated with Craig, and wondered what his significance was. What she found out, in the course of more than 15 years of research, was surprising and dramatic. Piece by piece, a new story of the time and places emerges.

It sheds a fresh light on Idaho history, and on the history of the Nez Perce Tribe, which itself has been the subject of several fine studies.

It shifts the traditional focus, from a look through the lens of one side or another – the U.S. settlers and government forces coming west;

the Nez Perce Tribe trying to maintain – and looks instead at how the forces active in the area at the time were interacting. It addresses that · modern question, "Why can't we all just get along?"

Turns out not to be so easy, at least in cases like this. Turn the page, start reading, and you'll start to see why.

Randy Stapilus
Ridenbaugh Press

Introduction

William Craig, a tall, redheaded fur trapper, left the Rocky
Mountains in 1840 and traveled northwest to live with his wife's family
in the Lapwai Valley of what would one day become Idaho. Rising to
the south of the valley were timbered mountains ('*eteyemé·xs* [1] [distant
mountains]) where young Nez Perce people often sought their guardian
spirits. Craig eventually built a house at the base of those mountains
and, as the years passed, people new to the region began referring to
that part of the Blue Mountains as Craig's Mountain. When "Craig's
Mountain" was printed on maps, the written name survived: the
mountain spur is still called that. However, William Craig – the blue-
eyed, redheaded man – has nearly been forgotten.

Perhaps because Craig so successfully hid his past, historians
interested in America's fur-trapping era stopped short of committing
the time and travel needed to research his life. There were, after all,
mountain men who left a more flamboyant—and easier—trail. Idaho's
historians who wanted to learn about the first white man to be granted a
homestead in what is now their state must have been discouraged by
the paucity of information about him. And Nez Perce historians were
not inclined to honor William Craig as one of their heroes, for he was
not *ni·mí·pu·* (Nez Perce people). While he was in many ways their
steadfast friend, his aim was not that they retain their ancestral land and
hold fast to their culture but that they share their land and meld their
culture with his people.

Now, however, more than 140 years after his death, Craig's
activities in the West have at last been identified, documented, and
placed in the context of his times. It is clear that he was a man who
contributed in a unique way to the United States' push to control the
Far West. He was not only a trapper but also a trader and explorer in
the Rocky Mountain fur trade. He married into and lived with the Nez
Perce people, neighbored with the earliest American missionaries to
reach the Columbia Plateau, and, after killings at the Whitman mission,
acted as liaison between the Nez Perces and an encroaching settler
militia. He acted as a middleman between a territorial governor and
some Nez Perce leaders. He interpreted in treaty councils and
participated, along with Nez Perce warriors allied to the United States,
in the resultant wars. He was appointed the first U.S. agent to the Nez
Perce people and he sanctioned the first hanging of a man in what is

now the Lewiston, Idaho, region. He was an entrepreneur—a trader, farmer, stock raiser, innkeeper, ferryman, and guide. Notwithstanding our divergent pasts (and presents), both *so·yá·po·* (white Americans) and *ni·mí·pu·* can agree that William Craig thrived on the Columbia Plateau during a pivotal period in Northwest history.

I was born and bred in the interior Pacific Northwest, but it was not until I had spent almost 30 years working elsewhere and retired back to north central Idaho that I questioned that which I had always accepted. Returning to my childhood home with the "new eyes" of experience, I especially noticed—and puzzled over—the predominance of non-Indian residents (even towns occupied mostly by white people) on the Nez Perce reservation. Curiosity up, I read old treaties between the United States and the Nez Perce Indian tribe: those, and Francis Paul Prucha's *The Great Father*, answered many of my questions about how non-Indians could now be living on Indian reservations.

As I meandered through the hills and canyons around Orofino, I noticed the name "Craig" here and there on the Clearwater River watershed: the village of Craigmont on the Camas Prairie, Craig's Ferry on a sign along the Clearwater River, and, in the Lapwai Valley, a Highway 195 marker declaring that William Craig, a former fur trapper and a "bluff, jolly good fellow," had once lived there. But local libraries yielded little information about Craig. There was no Craig biography other than a magazine article by a local historian, and the usually verbose literature of the fur trade offered but scant paragraphs about him.

In time my curiosity about William Craig led me to do a little research. A person began emerging, one who had participated in important national events and had lived not far from Lewiston, Idaho, where I had attended grammar school. As there was little written about the history of the entire region, I became motivated to learn more about both Craig and the region in which he settled. It soon became evident that telling the story of William Craig and his family would fill a void in the history of the interior Pacific Northwest in general and my little corner of it in particular.

When I was well into the research phase—and discouraged by Craig's trail going cold—assistance came in the form of a slim woman with a serious nature and a strong desire to learn more about her heritage. Gloria Manning is a great-great-great-granddaughter of William and Isabel (Pahtissah) Craig, and she offered to help me with the research. We began an informal partnership. During our years of collaboration, a special friendship developed based upon our common interests and mutual respect. My lifelong ties to the land and its people, along with perennial curiosity, led me to write this book and Gloria Manning, one of William and Isabel Craig's descendants, is responsible for the breadth of information on the Craig family.

Examining the conditions that enabled William Craig to become a landowner was eye-opening. After (probably) killing a man in Virginia, young Craig fled the United States and lost himself in the vast expanses west of the Mississippi River, far from cities, laws, and police. He survived and earned a living in the fur trade. As more Americans—missionaries at first, then others—traveled to the Far West, the possibility of the United States expanding its western border from the Mississippi River to the Pacific Ocean became more than a dream. The fact that Craig and other trappers adopted the "manifest destiny" mindset of the American majority puzzled me: most of the mountain men had loved the Indian way of life so much that they copied it, and title to western lands was recognized by the United States as lawfully vesting in the Indian tribes. Craig was able to build a successful life with his Nez Perce family and friends on their ancestral lands, and yet at first opportunity he assisted his government in its plans to take that land from them. Following Craig's footsteps gives the reader better understanding of the dynamics between natives and newcomers during the period when multitudes of Euroamerican settlers first came to the interior Pacific Northwest.

The lack of personal letters, journals, and diaries made it difficult to get to know William Craig as a man, to hear his own voice. He kept a low profile: he was, after all, hiding out. He did not wax philosophical in any of his surviving business letters, even though some were written during war. My research has unearthed no letters written by Craig to his parents or siblings, wife, children, or grandchildren. To fill that void, I have drawn upon documentation of William Craig's involvement in activities that is found in the National Archives and manuscript repositories. Actions speak louder than words—and by blending the words in Craig's straightforward, non-self-aggrandizing letters with observations about him by others, I have tried to provide some understanding of what a unique person William Craig was.

Since Craig lived more than 30 years among the Nez Perce people, his story is a part of their story, and vice versa. The Nez Perce Tribe's Cultural Resource Program was furnished an outline of the Craig manuscript, and I was directed to Aoki's *Nez Perce Dictionary* for my language-related questions. For a number of years, along with Nez Perce children and a few other adults (both Nez Perce and non-Indian),

I have been a student in a language class, "Tewéepuu Nimiipuutímt for true beginners." Since some of Craig's' descendants live on the Walla Walla Cayuse Umatilla reservation, my research has taken me to the Tamástslikt Cultural Institute near Pendleton, Oregon, where the staff has been gracious and helpful.

In addition to Gloria Manning, other descendants of William and Isabel Craig have contributed to this work. Fermore Craig, Sr., and the late Calvin Shillal of the Walla Walla Cayuse Umatilla reservation shared Craig family information with me in personal meetings, by telephone, and in correspondence. Calvin's artwork rendering the Craig family crest is an important addition to this work. Joann Newell Zipse's genealogical research helped me explore the connection between William Craig and Twisted Hair's family. And Gloria Manning has discovered cousins who furnished vital information and photographs—as well as cousins who have not yet healed from the suffering visited upon their families by mission and boarding schools and who preferred to remain uninvolved.

As we travel (from place to place or from birth to death) it is wise to look back over our shoulders periodically. Seeing where we've been helps us figure out where we're going. The Craig story is a glance back at what came before us on the interior Pacific Northwest. Looking over our shoulders, we see some of the people and events that shaped, in a brief time, the human dimension in this part of America. Perhaps it is fortuitous that professional historians had not gotten around to the comprehensive William Craig, for that left his story to be dug up by one of his descendants—a most meaningful act. Like the spirit of Craig's Mountain, the Craig story may have been waiting for certain people to come, seeking information, finding answers, and in the process achieving wisdom that can only come from better understanding.

Events in William Craig's Life

Abt. 1807	Born in Greenbrier County, Virginia
182-?	Killed a man(?); fled Virginia for the far West
1828-40	Worked as a trapper and trader in the Rocky Mountain Fur trade
1833-34	Accompanied Joseph R. Walker's expedition from Great Salt Lake to the Mexican Territory of California
1838	Married Pahtissah, daughter of Thunder's Eye, Nez Perce medicine man and village headman from Lapwai Valley
	Built and operated Fort Davy Crockett in Brown's Hole on the Green River (Colorado/Utah)
1840	Helped bring the first wagons over the trail (later known as the Oregon Trail) from Fort Hall near the Portneuf River to the Whitman Mission near the Columbia River
1840-45	Lived near Henry and Eliza Spalding's mission on the banks of the Clearwater River
1846	Built a house in Lapwai Valley about eight miles south of the Clearwater River. Filed a notice he intended to claim about 640 acres of land
1847	Sheltered Eliza and Henry Spalding and their family after Cayuse warriors killed Marcus and Narcissa Whitman and other white people at Waiilatpu
March 1848	Served as liaison between Nez Perce leaders and Oregon volunteer militia: Nez Perce leaders pledged their alliance with the Americans
	Appointed Agent to the Nez Perces by Joel Palmer, Superintendent of Indian Affairs for Oregon Country's Provisional Government
August 1848	Filed claim on 640 acres of land
June 1854	Filed notice with Washington Territorial Land Office that he planned to claim land in Lapwai Valley
May-June 1855	Served as interpreter for Nez Perce at Walla Walla Treaty Council held by Isaac Stevens and Joel Palmer
June 1855	Received as a treaty right from the Nez Perce tribe 640 acres in the Lapwai Valley

July 1855	Witnessed treaty made by Stevens with the Flathead, Kootenai, and Pend d'Orielle tribes in the Bitterroot Valley
August 1855	Elected and resigned as representative from Walla Walla County to Legislative Assembly of Washington Territory
October 1855	Interpreted for Nez Perces and signed as witness to the peace treaty with the Piegans, Bloods, Gros Ventres, and Blackfeet on the Judith River
December 1855	Hosted and interpreted council between Isaac Stevens and his Nez Perce allies at Lapwai Valley
	Appointed by Isaac Stevens as his agent to the Nez Perces
	Appointed by Isaac Stevens as aide to Commander in Chief with rank of lieutenant colonel in the Washington Territorial Volunteer militia
1856	Served as Gov. Stevens' agent to keep the Nez Perce warriors allied to the Americans and separated from factions hostile to the Americans
March 1856	Mustered into Company M of Washington Territorial Volunteers to protect Nez Perce Country from hostile war parties
	Approved hanging a Palouse man accused of being a spy and a murderer
July 1856	Disbanded Company M
September 1856	Served as Gov. Stevens' interpreter to Nez Perces at second Walla Walla Valley treaty council
	Nez Perces ordered him away from Lapwai Valley in Nez Perce Country. Set up Indian Agency near Col. Edward J. Steptoe's U.S. Army camp in Walla Walla Valley
	Fought a contingent of young warriors who attacked Stevens' entourage
October 1856	Took the oath of office in Portland as Indian Agent for Washington Territory
June 1858	Appointed Postmaster of "Wailepta" (Walla Walla) and served until October
February 1859	Lost his job as Indian Agent
October 1860	Served as guide for U.S. Army rescue expedition south to Snake/Shoshone Country. [Gold is discovered on the Nez Perce Reservation]
Winter 1860-61	Moved back to Lapwai Valley home from Walla Walla

1861	Built ferry across the Snake River near the mouth of the Clearwater River; built a ferry at Spalding; built a ferry at Greer
1866	Served as a guide on the Lewiston-to-Virginia City (Montana) road-surveying project across the Lolo Trail
Oct. 16, 1869	Died at home near Sweetwater Creek in Lapwai Valley, Idaho Territory

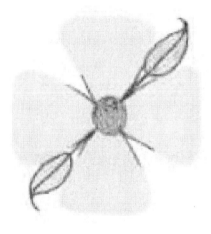

Craig family crest, drawn by Calvin Shillal

1
Mountain Man (1829~1840)

William Craig was a man on the run and the Rocky Mountains were a good place to hide.

Before he settled in the Clearwater area of the Oregon Country (now a part of Idaho) in 1840, Craig spent about a dozen years as a trapper, trader, and explorer in the Rocky Mountain fur trade. The Rocky Mountains—outside the United States and far from his native Virginia and its laws—were a good choice for someone who thought himself a fugitive. With his blue eyes, red hair, and height over six feet, Craig was distinctive in appearance. But while his red hair could have helped authorities identify him, it also may have helped him survive during his flight: Native Americans thought red hair might signify special powers and took care not to harm him. [2]

Craig said he was born in the year 1807 in Greenbrier County, Virginia – and that is about all he divulged about his early life.[3] The fact that he could read and write showed that his childhood had included some education, and a grandson once recalled that Craig tried to disguise his Virginia plantation roots with rough frontier manners:

Old Craig would have spent his life wearing ruffles on his pants if he had not come West...he tried too damn hard to hide it, but even with his buckskin and whiskers, it still would show through...[4]

He was most likely of Scotch-Irish stock (Scots who migrated to Ulster – Protestant Northern Ireland – and then to America) and had been raised a Presbyterian.[5]

Since William Craig (if indeed that was his real name, although there's no evidence to the contrary) successfully hid his background and family, looking at Scotch-Irish characteristics as a group of immigrants to America adds to our understanding of his roots. In North America, the Scotch-Irish were perceived as scrappy, tough, and often the ones leading white settlement westward. They frequently saw the American Indian as a people to be wiped out or shoved aside so newcomers could settle land. Their ancestors had emigrated from Scotland to Northern Ireland and conquered the Catholic Irish, so they were "already hardened to the violent repercussions of taking another's land." As a group they had humor and wit, song and dance inherited from the cultural stew of Scotland, England, Ireland, France, and Scandinavia. They were thrifty and stubborn, commerce often came more naturally than farming, and they were determined to worship as they chose. Some had an affinity for liquor, as evidenced by an old saying from America's Appalachian region: "When English settlers arrived they built a house, the Germans built a barn, and the Scotch-Irish built a distillery." As Presbyterians, Ulstermen placed great importance in reading the Bible, and common citizens thus learned to read; the Scots who migrated to Ulster and then North America had an uncommonly high literacy rate for the time.[6]

William Craig seems to have been rather typically Scotch-Irish, but an event in Virginia changed the course of his life. Several explanations have been floated as to the misdeed in Craig's past, none of which is presently verifiable. Craig may have killed a neighbor with a hoe.[7] He may, while at school, been in a fight over a girl and disgraced his family.[8] A friend recalled that before Craig died he had, over a campfire, disclosed that the traumatic event that changed his life when he was eighteen was a fight with an older man whom he killed in self-defense.[9] For whatever reason, young Craig left his Virginia home and ran toward the West.

Eventually Craig found his way to St. Louis. In the mid-1820s, St. Louis was the town where adventuresome, desperate, or wanted people – mostly men – gravitated to decide on their next adventure. Fur companies had long been headquartered there, and brigades of French and American men left the United States each spring bound for the Rocky Mountain fur trapper's life. Bateaux poled and rowed by French-Canadian voyageurs and loaded with supplies for fur-trading forts always had need of another strong back. Craig threw in with a brigade of men heading up the Missouri River and, after reaching the head of navigation in what is now Montana, joined a company of American fur trappers.[10]

The Rocky Mountain region was where the American trappers mostly conducted business, along with "Oregon Country" (present states of Washington, Oregon, and Idaho). Largely unsettled by Europeans, it was only in these regions that fur-bearing animals remained in any quantity.

Craig was in Oregon Country 1829 at the latest and possibly earlier. Family tradition places him in the Lapwai Valley off the Clearwater River in the winter of 1827-28.[11] The 1829 fur company rendezvous took place in the early summer weeks at Pierre's Hole (near present-day Driggs, Idaho). Craig recalled his exact date of arrival in Oregon as "the 15th day of July, 1829."[12]

In the fur-trade country, William Craig met many and diverse people: Americans like him, Europeans, those of mixed ancestry, and most were Indians. Many became Craig's friends, some he fought and perhaps killed, and at least one—a young Nez Perce woman—he married.

The Nez Perce home territory was west of the Rocky Mountains but the bison that once occupied their country had been hunted out, so some Nez Perce bands regularly migrated east to hunt buffalo among their allies on the plains.[13] Buffalo were numerous in Blackfeet territory, but the plains tribes' loyalty was to the British fur companies and American fur trappers were not welcome.[14] To keep from being overrun by the various Blackfeet bands while hunting in what is now Montana, the Nez Perces formed alliances with, among others, the Flatheads of the Bitterroot Valley and the brigades of American fur trappers.

Craig honed the survival skills necessary to stay alive during long snowy winters and earned the nickname "Old Craig" – "Old" being an affectionate term the mountain men usually gave each other for having shared the trials of mountain life. Trappers hunted game, subsisted almost exclusively on a meat diet, and fashioned most of their clothing from animal skins. The trappers' relationships with regional tribes reflected one of the few times in European expansion across America that bigotry was either suppressed or absent, for trappers, "could and did distinguish between friend and enemy."[15]

While in the fur trade, Craig rode with many men of the Rockies: Bill Williams (Craig believed Williams to be the bravest man he'd ever known), Jedediah Smith, William and Milton Sublette, Tom Fitzpatrick and Joseph Reddeford Walker are but a few.[16] His close friendship with fellow-trappers Robert Newell and Joseph Meek and his relationship with Nez Perce leaders Old Joseph, Old Looking Glass, and The Lawyer lasted his lifetime. Yet he neither sought nor accepted leadership roles—perhaps from fear of becoming well known—and remained one of the almost anonymous men in trapping brigades led by others.

During the fall hunt on the west side of the Rocky Mountains, likely in 1829, Joe Meek, William Craig and a trapper named Nelson were working a creek together.[17] They had left their horses and were moving on foot upstream when they came face to face with a red bear. The men leaped into the nearest trees, Craig and Meek climbing a large pine while Nelson climbed one of two smaller trees nearby. The bear went up after Nelson by putting his back against one of the small trees and his feet against the other, and it almost reached Nelson before the trees bent apart and the bear fell to the ground. This scene repeated itself three times, making the bear angrier each time; finally it ran off into the woods. Joe Meek finishes telling the story:

> *Craig began to sing, and I began to laugh; but Nelson took to swearing. "O yes, you can laugh and sing now," says Nelson; "but you war quiet enough when the bear was around." "Why, Nelson," I answered, "you wouldn't have us noisy before that distinguished guest of yours?" But Nelson damned the wild beast; and Craig and I laughed, and said he didn't seem wild a bit. That's the way we hector each other in the mountains. If a man gets into trouble he is only laughed at...*[18]

The fall hunt lasted from July until the days shortened and the trappers could see their breath in the cold morning air. By September hundreds of fur trappers in the Rocky Mountain area were heading for winter quarters, usually in a broad valley near food for both men and their mounts. While buffalo herds provided winter meat for the men, the creatures grazed out the grass needed for the horses. Many winters the trappers' main occupation was stripping sweet cottonwood bark from trees to feed their horses.

During one winter march, William Craig was in a brigade of trappers led by Jedediah Smith.[19] The snow was deep: there was not enough food for a large group of men and horses. Smith decided to move his trappers to a new wintering place with more graze. It was in an evening's camp during that forced march that Craig lost his precious rabbit. Everyone was hungry to the point of starvation; Craig had caught a rabbit and spitted it on green sticks to roast near the fire. The smell of roasting rabbit must have been too much for hungry companions, for before the meat was cooked, someone figured out a way to separate Craig from his rabbit. Craig was told that the "booshways" (bosses: a corruption of the French word *bourgeois*) wanted to talk to him at their lodge. While Craig was gone, someone took his roasting rabbit. When Craig returned to the campfire and found his meat gone, he flew into a rage and "declared his intention of cutting [the rabbit] out of the stomach that contained it." But the price of finding the culprit was too high and, when no one confessed, Craig went to bed furious and still hungry. More than thirty years later, when both Craig and Joe Meek were nearing old age, Joe—on his word as a gentleman—assured Craig that it wasn't he who stole the rabbit. [20]

The rendezvous of 1832, again at Pierre's Hole, was the largest held thus far by Americans in the Rockies, with about six hundred people, "all kinds of men," in attendance. [21] There were the usual liquor, contests, and gambling and native women. After the rendezvous, a day-long battle with a group of Gros Ventres occurred. In one of the most violent battles of the fur trade era, many Gros Ventres, Nez Perces, Flatheads and trappers were killed or wounded. [22]

The brigades then, as Newell put it, "Scattered in the following courses to our profession." William Sublette left for St. Louis with a train of pack animals and the pelts while his brother, Milton, led his brigade west down the Snake River. Tom Fitzpatrick's brigade (which included Newell) headed north to the Salmon River, then across the mountains to the Three Forks of the Missouri. There, at the head of the Gallatin River, he met William Craig "and some of our hunters we parted with at the Randezvous." [23]

The winter of 1832-33 found the Rocky Mountain Fur Company and the American Fur Company, and a new brigade of white men led by Benjamin Bonneville, in winter quarters along with bands of Flatheads and buffalo-hunting Nez Perces. They were in one of their favorite winter camp areas (on the Bear River, southeast of where Salmon, Idaho, is now located). During the winter Captain Bonneville let it be known that he was hiring additional men, and one of those hired was Craig's friend, "Doc" Newell. [24] When winter camp broke up, Bonneville had recruited a sizeable brigade of trappers.

Captain Bonneville was on leave from the regular army. Rumors persisted that he was a United States spy gathering intelligence on the power of the British and Mexicans, information needed for future United States expansion plans. Earlier, in January 1832 Bonneville had been issued a passport in the name of one of his trusted employees, Joseph Reddeford Walker, so he and his men could legally enter California. [25] After the spring hunt, Bonneville divided his brigade into two groups: he led one group on further explorations of the northwest and sent the remainder under Walker's command toward California.

Both William Craig and Joe Meek were in the Walker brigade when they left the Bear River heading for California.[26] When they headed southwest they had a supply of buffalo jerky—at least 60 pounds per man—on their packs to keep them from starving while crossing the desert and mountains toward California. About 55 to 60 men and more than 200 horses and mules wended their way across the countryside.

Curiosity about the metal traps, firearms and strange-looking men drew Paiutes, through whose country the trappers traveled.[27] Trouble started when Indians stole beaver traps and otherwise annoyed the trappers as they approached Ogden's (also known as the Mary's, the Barren, and today the Humboldt) River. Some of the trappers became short tempered with the constant hounding of the curious Paiutes. The trappers' camp seemed surrounded by hundreds (trapper George Nidever estimated 400-500, Zenas Leonard put the number at between 80-100) of native people. Nidever wrote that "thirty-four...Indians advanced in a body, and 15 of our men, myself among the number, were ordered out to meet them."[28] Walker gave orders for a charge. Mounted trappers surrounded the Paiutes, who were on foot and armed with bows and arrows. The trappers fired, killing almost half of the Paiutes. Walker ordered a few men to "put the wounded out of misery" using the bows and arrows of the fallen. The decisive blow struck by the trappers was rather more than they had intended.[29]

While traveling along Ogden's River, Craig pulled a joke on Walker. At the end of the day's ride the expedition camped beside the river and, as usual, set up their lodges and stripped off their clothes to take a swim. Craig was first to the water and, about to dive in, first checked the depth. The river water had a "milky cast," and when Craig investigated the depth in the eddy he found the water only somewhat more than a foot deep with a soft mud bottom. He waded around and found waist-deep water. Just then Walker arrived and asked Craig how the water was. Craig said the water was "just splendid," so Walker dived "head-first into that four and a half feet of blue mud." Craig scrambled out of the river and hid in brush on the opposite side of the river, getting scratched on some wild rosebushes in the process. He saw Walker pull out of the sticky mud and wash off as much as he could, then walk back up the trail to his tepee. Walker dressed, then "shot his rifle off, cleaned it, then reloaded it," and hollered for Craig to show himself. Craig remained in the bushes the rest of the afternoon, wrapped in a blanket and without his pipe or anyone to talk with. Eventually, Walker sent word to Craig to come to camp, have supper, and leave, that he could no longer travel with the expedition. Craig came in, got dressed, and sat down with his eating partners. The expedition was divided into "messes and each mess was provided with a dressed buffalo hide. It was spread on the ground and the grub placed upon it." Craig, as luck would have it, was sitting directly opposite Walker and noticed each side of Walker's nose still had streaks of blue mud, as well as some around his eyes. Craig found this funny.

"What the hell are you laughing at?" asked Walker.

"Gentlemen generally washed before eating," replied Craig.

With that, all the men around the buffalo hide laughed and Walker, unable to keep a straight face, laughed with them. But Walker threatened to kill Craig if he pulled another trick on him. The spot on Ogden's River was thereafter known among trappers as "Walker's Plunge." [30]

From the sink of Ogden's River, Walker's party rode southwest to the base of the Sierra Nevada mountain range. The high desert country had little grass for the horses and not much game for the men, but it did support a population of self-sufficient Paiute people, who gave the party wide berth. The jerked buffalo the trappers had brought with them was about gone and even though hunters ranged wide each day, they shot only a few rabbits. Once the hunters stole from a brush hut two rabbit-skin bags full of some type of dried food, which they ate in their stew that evening and again for breakfast. The stolen food turned out to be worms and insect larvae. Finally, on the first of October, knowing they must get to the valley on the other side of the mountains so they could hunt and eat, they turned due west.

Crossing the Sierra Nevada in late autumn proved almost too much for even the experienced mountain men. They ran out of food and found no game. As their horses starved one by one, the men finished them off and ate "the best parts." At one point some of the men mutinied and demanded that Walker turn around and lead them back to the plains of the Rockies; he told them to go ahead and turn back, but without the expedition's ammunition and horses. No one left the party.

As they clambered about, discouraged and weak, traversing rock faces and making their way past frozen waterfalls, rocky chasms, and precipices of enormous heights, some of them saw a most spectacular gorge not far below. But the terrain was so rough that they could not get there. Unable to navigate into the valley, they stayed on the rim to the north. Walker and his group of starved men became the first white men to see what is now called Yosemite Valley. [31]

One day a native man, carrying a basket of acorns, was on the trail heading east. Coming around a bend in the trail he spied a white man with a rifle in the crook of his arm, wearing greasy skin clothing and tattered moccasins. The Indian feared for his life, dropped his basket and ran. When the hunter reported back to Walker that night, he brought a basket of acorns and news that lower elevations where oak trees grew could not be far away. The men had not seen acorns since they left Missouri and for the first time in weeks they had hope that they would, after all, get out of the mountains.[32]

Years later, Joseph Walker and Lafayette Bunnell (who entered the valley in 1851) discussed those circumstances. Bunnell related that

Ten-ie-ya [headman of the valley band] had said that, "A small party of white men once crossed the mountains on the north side, but were so guided as not to see the valley proper." With a smile the captain [Walker] said: "That was my party, but I was not deceived, for the lay of the land showed there was a valley below; but we had become nearly barefooted, our animals poor, and ourselves on the verge of starvation, so we followed down the ridge to Bull Creek, where, killing a deer, we went into camp."[33]

Captain Walker and his men were also the first white people to record seeing the giant Sequoia trees, which grow only in a small area on the western Sierra Nevada slopes between 5,000 and 7,800 feet in elevation. In their last days traveling in the mountains they found "trees of the Redwood species, incredibly large—some of which would measure from 16 to 18 fathoms [96-108 feet] round the trunk at the height of a man's head from the ground."[34] Worn down from weeks of fighting for their lives against snow and cold, the men were nonetheless awestruck by the ancient trees, the largest of which were more than three thousand years old.

Once they reached the valley of the San Joaquin, travel was pleasant. They were in country claimed by Mexico since 1822, the year it won its independence from Spain, and occupied by Mexicans and the conquered remnants of groups of natives.[35] As the Walker party neared the Pacific Ocean, they felt that all their deprivation and suffering would be worth it if they could tell their relatives back home that they had stood on the edge of the continent. "The idea of being within hearing of the *end* of the *Far West* inspired the heart of every member of our company with a patriotic feeling for his country's honor."[36] They knew they stood on land the United States of America wanted to claim for its own.

Leaving his men in a fortified camp near the Mission San Juan Bautista, Walker obtained permission from Governor José Figueroa in Monterey to remain in the Mexican territory through the winter, to hunt enough game to sustain his men, and to trade with Mexican citizens. Indeed, Mexico was actually promoting settlement with its colonization law of 1824, which gave land, security, and four-year tax exemptions to foreign settlers.[37]

The trappers settled down to spend the winter in the heart of Alta California. They saw sport made of bull and cock fighting and bear baiting, went to fandangos, admired beautiful women, saw longhorn cattle, and learned from experts how to swing lariats. Some trappers joined a group of Mexicans looking for stolen horses in a foothills encampment of Miwoks. According to later accounts by Bonneville's biographer, the trappers and Mexican men engaged in "hunting the poor Indians like wild beasts, and killing them without mercy."[38]

By February 1834 preparations were complete to make the long journey back to the Rocky Mountains, though some chose to remain and settle in Alta California. The trappers had traded furs for food and ammunition and killed enough game to keep them from starving as they crossed the desert. As they left camp at San Juan Bautista they drove a herd of horses numbering more than 300 (Craig later recalled it as twice that amount) along with 47 head of cattle and 30 dogs. Zenas Leonard rationalized in his journal that horse theft was hardly recognized as a crime since a horse could be bought for as little as one to ten dollars.[39]

Walker led his entourage up the Kern River, where he hired two native men to guide them over the mountains. Crossing with experts to pilot them took only four days of relatively easy travel before they were led out of the mountains (now known as "Walker Pass") into the Owens Valley. Here the party divided, to reunite once again at the trappers' Rocky Mountain rendezvous.

The July 1834 rendezvous was at Ham's Fork of the Green River, near what is now Granger, Wyoming. The Rocky Mountain Fur Company had reneged on its contract with Boston iceman Nathaniel Wyeth (who was aiming to establish a trading fort on the Columbia River) to bring out supplies; to avoid its debts, the owners dissolved the company and sold out to its rival, the American Fur Company.[40] Jason Lee, a Christian missionary, was at the rendezvous; he had traveled west with Wyeth and eventually established a mission in the Willamette Valley where relatively few native people remained. Wyeth, now with unsold goods on his hands, built a post near the

Portneuf River that he named "Fort Hall"; he stocked the fort with the surplus goods, placed a manager in charge and moved on.

The Walker party returned from California to the Ham's Fork rendezvous and found big changes in the Rocky Mountain fur business. Years of trapping had depleted the beaver and the fur brigades were forced to risk more trips into Blackfeet country for pelts. Robert Newell was working for Mssrs. Drips and Fontenelle and had married a young Nez Perce woman to whom he gave the name Kitty.[41] Craig now trapped with American Fur Company brigades, but for two years they pursued an ever-decreasing population of beaver.

The 1836 trappers' rendezvous at Horse Creek (near present Daniel, Wyoming) made history because white women were there. When Fitzpatrick's supply train from St. Louis arrived, it also brought Eliza Hart Spalding and Narcissa Prentiss Whitman, the first white women known to have crossed the Continental Divide. Henry and Eliza Spalding and Marcus and Narcissa Whitman, along with William Gray, had been sent to Oregon Country by the American Board of Commissioners for Foreign Missions (founded by the Congregationalists and Presbyterians) to teach Christianity to the Indians. Over the course of the rendezvous the trappers became acquainted with the missionaries and discussed future plans with them; Craig and Newell talked about settling near them after a station was established on the Columbia River.[42] Could the missionaries have seen into the future, they may have turned back: in less than a dozen years both Marcus and Narcissa Whitman would be dead at the hands of Indians and the Spaldings would seek safety in William and Isabel Craig's house.

Over the years, when winter approached, the Indians and trappers headed towards lower elevations. A perennial wintering place had been a valley of the Green River known as "Brown's Hole"; the border of Utah and Colorado now divides it. In time Brown's Hole became the site of a trading post operated by Philip Thompson of Tennessee, Pruett Sinclair of Arkansas and William Craig.[43] The partners established the trading fort on the left bank of the Green River above the mouth of Vermillion Creek.[44] By the summer of 1836 they had named it "Fort Davy Crockett" after fellow southerner, frontiersman, and U.S. Congressman David Crockett, who had been killed in Texas at the Alamo in March of that year.[45] Kit Carson worked for the partners as a hunter during the winter of 1837-38, providing meat for the post.[46] Both the fort itself and the depressed economy soon had the mountain men calling it "Fort Misery," but the rough log buildings became a hub of American trading activities during the few years before Craig left the fur business.

The 1838 fur rendezvous was set for a broad valley near the Wind River Mountains on Popo Agie Creek, near present Riverton, Wyoming. That rendezvous would be recorded, many years later while Craig was negotiating a U.S. treaty, as the site of an important event in his life – his marriage to Pahtissah, a Nez Perce woman, whom he called Isabel.

A fur-company rendezvous was seldom a dull affair, but the 1838 rendezvous hosted a particularly eclectic gathering. Besides the usual trapping brigades and allied native bands, the 1838 rendezvous included squabbling but industrious missionaries and an insolvent Swiss entrepreneur. John Augustus Sutter, who would soon build a trading post on the Sacramento River in California, lent a European touch to the gathering.[47] Cornelius Rogers, a fledgling missionary sent out by ABCFM, described his impressions of rendezvous in a letter published in the Cincinnati Journal. Trappers and traders, bands of Nez Perces and Flatheads, plus Crows, Arapahos, Shoshones and a new crop of missionaries, attended the rendezvous. Free trappers, Rogers wrote, were "a set of men who hunt on their own responsibility, go where and when they please, and live and act as they [like]. Rendezvous usually lasted several weeks:

...the whole time is spent in drinking, gambling, horse racing, quarrelling, fighting, &c. Alcohol is the only liquor brought here, and is sold at $4 a pint. Some men will spend a thousand dollars in a day or two, and very few have any part of their year's wages left when rendezvous breaks up.[48]

Such was a new missionary's description of the scene where William Craig, many years later, said he legally married Isabel of the Nez Perce people.[49]

In the parlance of the trapper's world, Pahtissah was William's "country wife." Since her Nez Perce band regularly traveled east to buffalo country, Pahtissah and Craig probably met when trappers joined their tribal allies in the Rocky Mountain region. Most likely William and Isabel had lived together for some time, married in the Nez Perce manner that included a trial period and exchanges of food between families.[50] Indian women had for years married or consorted with European trappers and traders, a practice that bonded alliances between their people and increased family status and wealth.[51] Without their liaisons with Indian women, most trappers would not have survived, much less prospered.

It is probable that no formal wedding ceremony following Euro-American custom occurred between William and Isabel; none of the missionaries noted a wedding in any of their diaries. Seventeen years later, when a marriage date became necessary in order to legally claim land, William may have picked a day at the Popo Agie rendezvous as his "wedding date" and Louis (the Mosquito) Raboin, who had attended the rendezvous, confirmed it. Raboin stated that he was acquainted with William and Isabel Craig and that he had "known them to live together as man and wife from the 6th day of July 1838..."[52] Mary Walker, the wife of missionary Elkanah Walker, helped sew a gingham dress for Mrs. Craig while at the Popo Agie.[53]

Isabel was probably not the first woman William had loved, nor even his first Indian wife. The family maintained that he had been expelled from school for fighting over a girl. And later, after Craig surfaced in the Clearwater country, there is evidence that he was connected by marriage to the family of Twisted Hair, the Nez Perce headman at *téwe* (Orofino, Idaho).[54] But, while William may have had other liaisons, Isabel was the mother of the children he claimed and the woman with whom he stayed until his death.

Isabel's village was in the valley of the blue butterflies, *lé·pwey* (Lapwai),[55] between the Clearwater River and the Blue Mountains. Her father was H'inmetú·msilu (Thunder's Eye), the headman of the band, and one of his wives, Weekeween (Feather Earrings).[56] Isabel's extended family included a sister named Toitoinetowiyatoiken and a half-brother, Otkokohl.[57]

Thunder's Eye was not only the headman of the band, but also the *tiwé·t* (shaman or medicine man), a powerful man both politically and spiritually. As buffalo hunters, his band often stayed from six months to several years in the Bitterroot Valley and beyond, participating in the life of the plains people.[58] Known to Hudson's Bay Company traders as *Le Bouton* (The Button), he sometimes trapped beaver for trade with the company.[59]

After the 1838 rendezvous, while Thunder's Eye returned to the Lapwai, William and Isabel wintered at their Brown's Hole post with a large community of local bands and a smaller gathering of trappers. Isabel's tepee was one of several near the rough fort, along with that of Kitty Newell. (Joe Meeks's second wife, also a Nez Perce woman, had packed up her lodge and gone back to her people.[60]) About a dozen trappers, among them Kit Carson and Jack Robinson, were headquartered at Fort Davy Crockett; most trappers had native wives and small children. A later traveler from the United States described the winter gathering:

These remnants of the great trapping parties...commonly make Brown's Hole their winter quarters...old trappers...established themselves there in order to bring around them, not only the means of subsistence...but their tales, jests, and songs, and honest and brave hearts.[61]

Fort Davy Crockett was a pleasant place to be in winter when surrounded by friends and family.

While buffalo herds had declined because of drought, disease, over-hunting, and competition with growing horse herds for critical winter habitat, the beaver were almost completely out of the picture.[62] Traders like Craig, Thompson, and Sinclair, with fewer beaver pelts, adjusted their stock in trade to horses, buffalo robes, and goods from Taos.

In the spring of 1839 Philip Thompson went on a buying trip to Missouri, arranging with Craig to meet the supply train at Fort Vasquez—about fifty miles from what is now Denver—and accompany it to Fort Davy Crockett. Thompson planned to join up with Louis Vasquez and Bill Sublette, who were bringing supplies and people from St. Louis to their fort on the Platte. In July, William and Isabel Craig, with an escort of men, set out to meet Thompson and help transport the supplies to Brown's Hole.[63]

At "Tumbleton Park" southwest of the Yampa River, Craig and his party unexpectedly came upon an old trapper friend named Kelly in camp with some young men from Illinois. Spying Kelly before he spied them, Craig let out an Arapahoe war whoop and galloped, red hair flying, with two of his companions down a hill towards the campers, who quickly prepared for battle. But as the three horsemen hurtled into camp, Kelly recognized Craig, dropped his rifle, and, leaping the stream, ran to meet his old friend. In the words one of the men:

...Kelly seized the hands of three old fellow-trappers. It was a joyful meeting. They had often stood side-by-side in battle...They were

more than brothers, and so they met. We shared with them our last scraps of meat..."[64]

Old Kelly was guiding Thomas Jefferson Farnham, captain of the Peoria Party, and several other men to Oregon. They were the remnants of a larger group who had left Illinois to start a utopian settlement but had a falling-out early in their adventure. It was too late in the year for Farnham to make it to Oregon, Craig advised, for "the grass on the Columbia was already dry and scarce"; Craig invited them to pass the winter at his trading post.[65]

Meanwhile, the Vasquez-Sublette-Thompson train, which the Craigs were to meet, had left St. Louis with thirty-two people and four wagons pulled by six mules each. Among the people was a New York architect, E. Willard Smith, who kept an interesting journal of the trip from St. Louis to Fort Vasquez.[66] The train and its outriders arrived safely at Fort Vasquez, an adobe building on the South Fork of the Platte River. The Craigs and their party joined Thompson's camp about a mile and a half from the fort. The men at the fort traded with some twelve lodges of Cheyenne people who were camped nearby and danced, caroused, gambled, and "got drunk on alcohol."[67] Finally on September 16, 1839, Craig, Thompson, and their entourage broke camp and started west across the mountains. There were eight men, two women and three children in the party. One of the women was Isabel Craig; the other was Philip Thompson's wife. One or more of the children may have been Craig's.[68]

Four days of travel brought them to the Rocky Mountains proper. As they climbed steep hills the nights turned frosty, the surroundings more rugged. Craig and Thompson rode out ahead of the main party and hunted for meat, coming back to camp with three buffalo on one trip and three deer the next. On September 23 they entered The Park, a very large valley where about 2,000 buffalo grazed, and two more days of travel brought them over the Continental Divide. As they progressed down the western slopes brushed with sage and bunchgrass, they passed the scene where a battle had recently been fought—there was a log breastworks and nearby the skeletons of four horses.[69]

On the evening of October 1 the party arrived in Brown's Hole and was welcomed by Pruett Sinclair. The next day Kit Carson told the travelers about the fight he and other hunters had just had with about twenty Sioux—it was Carson and six other hunters, along with two women, who had fought the Sioux, erected a log barricade, and had four horses killed.

Travelers coming through Brown's Hole delighted in describing the place. Thomas Farnham described two waterfalls tumbling down from the cliffs off to their right as they entered the valley, with Fort Davy Crockett in the center of the valley:

...on the winding bank of the Sheetskadee (Prairie Cock)[now Green] River. The dark mountains around it rose sublimely, and the green fields swept away into the deep precipitous gorges more beautiful than I can describe.[70]

Another member of the Peoria Party described the fort itself as:

... the worst thing of its kind...a low, one-story building, constructed of logs and clay, wth three connecting wings, and no enclosure. Instead of cows the fort had only some goats. In short the whole establishment appeared somewhat poverty stricken...[71]

The winter of 1839-40 at Fort Davy Crockett was desolate. The European demand for beaver had fallen even faster than the trappers had eradicated the animals. Men's' beaver hats were out of style: silk top hats were now the vogue. The mountain men knew they had to find a new way to make a living.

In January 1840 Walker encountered Joe Meek, who hadn't eaten for five days, trying to make his way from Fort Hall to Fort Davy Crockett to pick up his (third) wife, Virginia.[72] Walker fed Meek and brought him, weak from starvation and with tattered clothing, into the fort. Sinclair, William and Isabel Craig, Doc and Kitty Newell, the Thompson family, Kit Carson, Caleb and Fanny Wilkins, and some members of Farnham's party were among the several hundred people in the valley that winter. There was barely enough to eat. Times were hard throughout the Rocky Mountains and people were getting desperate at Fort Davy Crockett.

One commodity was readily available: the horse. Stealing horses was part of life among the Plains tribes, but there were certain rules to the game that were understood. It was acceptable, even expected, to steal from enemy tribes, but not from friends. In the case of Craig and the other mountain men, that meant they could steal horses from, among others, the Blackfeet, Sioux and Bannocks—or the Mexicans in California—but not from Flatheads, Nez Perces, or friendly Shoshones.

The Sioux got away with 150 horses from Brown's Hole in the fall of 1839 and, unable to recover them, some of the trappers stole horses from the Hudson's Bay Company at Fort Hall. The same trappers, with Philip Thompson at their head, stole about forty horses from the friendly Shoshones, an act that Craig and the other trappers feared could turn friends into enemies. When the Shoshones complained to the people at the fort and requested restitution, Meek, Craig, Newell, Carson, and 25 others, under Walker's command, rode out to retake the horses. They found the herd on an island in the Green River. Walker tried to drive the horses off the island and across the ice without arousing the suspicions of Thompson, but they were discovered. Thompson and his gang charged and tried to recover the herd, but Walker and his men outflanked them and herded the horses into the fort. Craig and the others were stationed around the perimeter and stopped Thompson's men from entering.[73]

Thompson negotiated with warriors in a nearby Ute camp, promising them a reward of horses if they would help, but the Utes—who feared both the trappers and the Shoshones—stayed out of the squabble. After a day of threatening negotiations, Craig and the rest of Walker's men drove the herd out of Fort Davy Crockett and Thompson and his men backed off: the horses were, in time, returned to the friendly Shoshone people.

Times were hard when trappers stole from allies and turned partner against partner; the economy was forcing many fur trappers to think of new ways to make their livings.

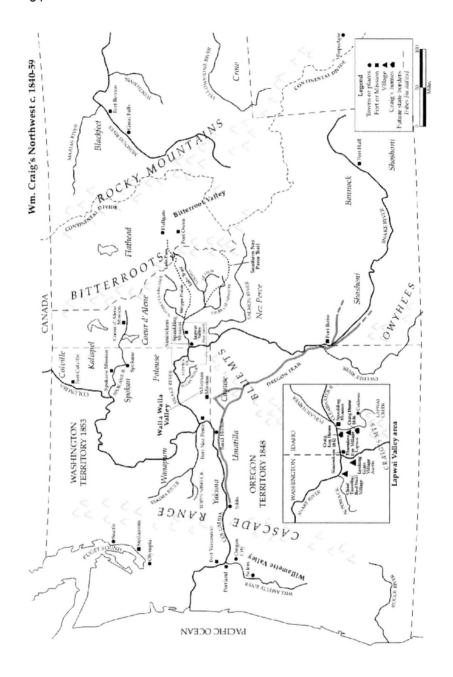

Wm. Craig's Northwest c. 1840-59

2
Missionaries, Nez Perces, and Mountain Men (1840-1847)

Big changes occurred in the American fur trade in 1840. There was a rendezvous of sorts that summer at the mouth of Horse Creek on the Green River, but it was the last year the American Fur Company planned to bring supplies to the Rockies. The Americans were basically out of the fur business. The partnership among Craig, Sinclair, and Thompson broke up, too, after the horse-thieving incident.[74] Unemployed trappers began to scatter in all directions—some to their old hunting grounds, others to Missouri, the southern trade in New Mexico, the warmth of California, and new possibilities in Oregon Country.

Craig and his companions likely discussed over winter campfires the possibility of bringing the Far West into the United States; if trappers joined the American missionaries who had already settled in Oregon Country, Americans might outnumber the British and tip the scales in favor of the United States. George Ebbert had left the mountains in 1838 and, with his Nez Perce wife and their children, had joined a growing white settlement in the oak-studded land of the Willamette Valley.[75] Craig, Newell, Wilkins, Meek, and others had also married Nez Perce women; they had in-laws in the Oregon Country, and it would please their wives and children for them to settle near their Nez Perce families. Moreover, since Henry Spalding had built his mission in the valley of Thunder's Eye's people, there had been disquieting reports from some of the *ni·mi·pu·* about changes not to their liking. Craig wanted to see what was going on between the missionary and the people in Isabel's village.[76] For trappers who could no longer make a living in the fur business, Oregon Country was a tempting destination.

The 1840 rendezvous was a rather dull affair, for times were hard with no beaver.[77] Although many new travelers were present, there was little drinking or gambling among the old-timers.

Three missionaries and their wives, heading west from Illinois, had traveled with the supply train to the fur rendezvous. The Reverends

Harvey Clark, Alvin T. Smith, and P. B. Littlejohn were now looking for someone to guide them the next 300 miles to Fort Hall. Newell was hired and asked Craig to help with the piloting.

For his guide services, the missionaries paid Newell one wagon and a double harness, and an idea germinated in Doc Newell's mind to take the wagon all the way to the Columbia River. When Newell met Meek at Fort Hall, he convinced Meek to drive that wagon west. Two other wagons were made ready, their wheels greased, their beds loaded. William Craig said he would go along, as did Caleb Wilkins and his family, who were headed for the Willamette Valley, and Jack Larrison. An Indian man of the Shoshone (Snake) tribe served as herder for the cattle. On August 15, 1840, the first wagons rolled out of Fort Hall toward Oregon.[78]

Most of the trappers, while ready to start new lives in Oregon Country, were less than enthusiastic about trying to get wagons through. There was but a narrow trail across the arid country; sagebrush hung up in the wheels and dragged across the bottom of the wagon beds, exhausting the draft animals. Newell was sorry he had thought of such an undertaking, for "continued crashing of the sage under our wagons, which was in many places higher than the mules' backs, was no joke." When the animals began to fail, the men took everything out of the wagon beds and loaded the loose pack animals. They then removed the beds from the axles and abandoned the beds. The expedition struggled across the lava and sagebrush desert of what is now southern Idaho, breaking a road with the wheels and undercarriages of bedless wagons.[79]

When the wagon train arrived at the Hudson's Bay Company trading post on the Boise River, Francois Payette, the class-conscious factor of the post, welcomed the party but managed to insult Craig and Meek. He invited Newell to join him in the fort. To the remainder of the people in the party who were camped outside, Payette sent a piece of sturgeon for their dinner "with his compliments." Affronted, William Craig and Joe Meek sent the gift back to Payette "with their compliments."[80]

After Fort Boise, the trail became somewhat less troublesome but the expedition ran out of food. The hunters brought in little game, and they "were too proud to eat anything but dried salmon skins after our provisions had become exhausted."[81] Their route later became known as the Oregon Trail, and their bedless wagons made tracks for thousands of covered wagons to follow within a few short years. The group sweated and strained over the Blue Mountains until they finally descended to the Umatilla River (about where Pendleton, Oregon, is now). Crossing the Umatilla, the party followed the well-traveled trail to the right (through what are now Adams, Weston, and Milton-Freewater, Oregon) across the rolling hills to the Walla Walla River and Dr. Marcus and Narcissa Whitman's adobe mission at Waiilatpu.[82]

Newell and his entourage were hungry and rough looking from the weeks on the trail; the doctor and his wife fed them and made them welcome. When Newell told Whitman he was sorry he tried to bring wagons, the doctor disagreed; Newell had "broken the ice, and when others see that wagons have passed, they, too will pass; and in a few years the valley will be full of our people." The Cayuse people, in whose country the Whitmans lived, called the strange wagons "horse canoes."[83]

In the years since the Whitmans had built a mission at Waiilatpu, a number of Cayuses, Wallawallas, and other families had gathered there for instruction, rallying to their teachers as a source of new knowledge and its expected powers. The Whitmans, however, were preparing for their countrymen to join them in the Far West and were working to save Indians from what they believed would be certain extinction by converting them to Christianity while teaching them to farm.

At Waiilatpu, Newell's expedition split up. The Newell, Wilkins, and Meek families[84] along with the Shoshone herder turned west down the Walla Walla River to the Columbia. There Newell left the wagons with Pierre C. Pambrun, trader at the Hudson's Bay Company post known as Fort Nez Perces.[85]

The trading fort, nestled alongside the eastern shore of the Columbia, was dwarfed and surrounded by powerful landscape. Thousands of years earlier, ice had dammed glacial meltwaters, backing the waters up into deep lakes, then bursting open as cataclysmic floods that scoured the land to bedrock. All this occurred time after time, in an area that had been covered millions of years earlier by molten lava—now referred to as the Columbia River Basalts (the largest volcanic landform in North America). Northeast of the fort was dramatic, semi-arid, landscape, almost devoid of topsoil, with coulees and waterworn basaltic columns and escarpments chiseled by ancient rivers, known as the "channeled scablands."[86]

William Craig and Jack Larrison followed the well-trodden trail east, topping rolling hills before descending to the Tukannon River and then, after crossing grassy knolls of loess deposited by Cascade volcanoes, into the deep valleys of the *pikú·nen* (Snake River) and *himeqisníme* (Clearwater River) that was Nez Perce country.

Craig would soon see his newborn child. William and Isabel's first child of record, Joseph William Craig, had been born September 10, 1840, in the Lapwai Valley home of his mother's family. If tradition held, Isabel's mother and grandmother helped with the birth and the child had a good start in life.[87]

On November 20, 1840, Reverend Spalding wrote in his journal, "Cragg & LaRison, two mountain men, have arrived, probably to spend the winter. I have seen enough of Mountain men. It rains almost constantly day & night."[88] Isabel had erected her lodge for William, herself, and their family near the mission buildings on Lapwai Creek, joining the lodges of other Nez Perces who had moved from outlying villages to learn from the Spaldings. Thus began a period of uneasy neighboring between the Craig family and the Spalding family in the valley of the blue butterflies.

It had seemed to some Nez Perce leaders after years of trading for rifles, ammunition, metal tools, and woven blankets that the white people had some power greater than theirs. They noted that the white men all had books. Men in the Lewis and Clark party had scratched on paper, recording experiences in their journals. The men of Hudson's Bay Company trading posts used marks on paper to keep track of business, and the American trappers passed winters hearing tales read from books. Common to most visitors was the book the Nez Perces came to know as the *talapó·sanm tí·mes* (Bible). In 1831 leaders had sent a delegation of Nez Perce men to St. Louis to ask Superintendent of Indian Affairs William Clark how to become literate and how to help their people with a better way to worship.[89] Their visit was misinterpreted: a letter appeared in the March 1833 *Christian Advocate and Journal and Zion's Herald* erroneously describing them as emissaries from a western tribe who were desperate for conversion to Christianity.[90]

The American religious community responded promptly to what it thought was an appeal for Christianity. In 1834 a 56-year old representative of the American Board of Commissioners for Foreign Missions, Reverend Samuel Parker—accompanied by Dr. Marcus Whitman—journeyed among the plains and plateau tribes to determine which tribes had suitable mission sites. Parker's and Whitman's journey was in keeping with United States governmental practice, as it had for many years (to spread "civilization") accepted Protestant missionaries as partners, and the most important Protestant missionary society was the ABCFM.[91] Parker was impressed with the Nez Perces and they were impressed with him; Parker's words, like those of Lewis and Clark before him, were well remembered by the people who heard him preach.

Parker, according to his interpreter (a Catholic named John Toupin), told the headmen he had come to find a place for a mission but that he did not "intend to take . . . [their] lands for nothing," promising an annual "big ship loaded with goods" to be given to them each year.[92] After Methodists sent Jason Lee out West in 1834, the ABCFM authorized three missions in the Columbia Plateau country.[93] Dr. Marcus and Narcissa Whitman built their mission in the Waiilatpu country of the Cayuses, Henry Harmon and Eliza Spalding with the Nez Perces in the Lapwai Valley; a year later Elkanah and Mary Walker and the Cushing and Myra Eells established a mission at Tshimakain, among the Spokanes.[94]

By inviting the Spaldings to teach them from the Bible, many Nez Perce people expected to add the new information to their existing beliefs and traditions. Like their neighbors, they were spiritually one with the natural world, having entered into a covenant with the Creator to take care of the land, water, plants, and animals that sustained them.[95] On Mother Earth, they believed, natural objects as well as humans had souls; humans were helped by a guardian spirit, or *wé·yekin*, sought by each individual as a rite of passage prior to adulthood; and wealth was the result of proper religious balance.[96] They were always on alert for new ways that would enhance the returns on their religious practices.

But the Spaldings' teachings were aimed at a different target: that of transforming the people—not only converting them into Christians but also convincing them to change their hunting and gathering lifestyle (for had not God commanded that land be cultivated?) in order to survive future American settlement. The missions at Lapwai, Waiilatpu, and Tshimakain were western counterparts of many eastern missions that had for years been carrying out the government's aim to teach Indians to be Protestant American farmers.

The Spaldings had first built their mission about two miles up the Lapwai Valley from the Clearwater River.[97] But in summer, with steep hills blocking the wind, mosquitoes plagued them. After about two years Henry Spalding coerced (using threats and a whip) Nez Perce men to build him a new house further north, near the mouth of Lapwai Creek in the canyon of the Clearwater River.[98] By the time William Craig came to settle, the mission site contained the Spalding house, a church, a school building, gardens, fences, a building for a printing press, and the first house built for a Nez Perce family. There were fields of wheat near the Spaldings' old house, orchards and irrigated gardens at the new house near the river.[99]

Craig was not the first ex-trapper to locate near the Spalding mission. Next door to Craig lived mountain man James Conner and his Nez Perce wife.[100] Conner had guided William Gray and a party of Oregon mission reinforcements from the 1838 trapper rendezvous to the Lapwai and stayed to build Spalding's mill and millrace.[101] George Ebberts and Richard Williams, with their Nez Perce wives, had moved on to the Willamette Valley. A French Canadian trapper, Charles Compo, and his Nez Perce wife went back and forth between the missions at Waiilatpu and Lapwai.[102]

Mission policy dictated that the native people be "settled" or "civilized" as a precursor to being Christianized, for missionaries found it difficult to teach people who never stayed long in one place. Since the Indians traveled around the country to collect food in its season, the missions tried to replace their traditional food with domestic animals and farm produce. Cows, sheep, pigs, chickens, as well as wheat, corn, potato, and other vegetable seeds were made available by the missions so Indians would stay put.

Some Nez Perce men became allies of the Spaldings from the beginning and helped them carry out their teaching. One was Lawyer, a son of Twisted Hair, who learned English and was later to be elevated (artificially, by Isaac Stevens, first governor of Washington Territory) from the position of village crier in the Kamiah area to a "head chief" of all the people.[103] Tiwiteqis, whom Spalding re-named Joseph, came to the Lapwai Valley from his home in the Wallowa country and was accepted into the Spaldings' church.[104] (Old Joseph, many years later, threw away Christianity and kept clear of white people in his country.) Tamootsin, re-named Timothy, celebrated his new religion by calling his village on the Snake River "alpowa," a derivative of *halahpawit* (Sabbath rest).[105] Timothy was to remain a stalwart Christian and lifelong friend of the white people. Thunder's Eye, who had invited the mission into his home valley, initially gave full attention and support to the teachers.

But Thunder's Eye was questioning Spalding's actions before his son-in-law, William Craig, moved nearby. Not only was Spalding often tyrannical; each year Thunder's Eye saw more land taken up for farming, and the *ni·mí·pu·* received no gifts to offset the use of grass, water, wood, and labor. The ongoing presence of a teacher who whipped his students, erected buildings and fences, and dug ditches

was offensive to the headman of the Lapwai band. Thunder's Eye
worried about Old Joseph and Timothy's bands staying nearby to learn,
for too many people taxed the region's resources.[106] It was highly
unusual for any band to live for extended periods in the traditional
territory of another.

Adding to Thunder's Eye's discomfort was the fact that people were
not requesting his *tiwé·t* (medicine man) services as often as they once
had. He had great power as a medicine man, so much so that children
would cover their eyes with blankets at times rather than look into his
eyes and come under his power.[107] But now Henry Spalding was being
asked to doctor the sick—much as William Clark had done in earlier
times—and was responding with simple medications and bloodletting.
It is logical that the Nez Perce people would seek medical help from
Spalding, since he was seen as an outsider with special knowledge as
yet unknown to them, but by treating them Spalding had unwittingly
cut into Thunder's Eye's professional activities as medicine man.[108]

Thunder's Eye's family became so resentful of the Spaldings that
two young men painted their faces and bodies with war paint one day
and rode their ponies right up to the schoolhouse door just as Eliza was
opening the day with prayer. They tried to talk their people inside into
quitting their teachers. Henry was unable to make them leave, and
Thunder's Eye supported them, as they belonged to his lodge. With
only three men offering their support, Henry turned to prayer. In the
privacy of his room he beseached God: "O Lord has it come to this?"[109]

Henry, while taken aback by the animosity, was also worried about
the fundamental success of his and Whitman's missions. Rumor was
rife that the Catholics had entered the Northwest and were competing
with him for Indian souls. He wrote that night in his journal:

> *Our own sins as a Mission has doubtless brought this & similar*
> *chastisement upon us ... a Catholic priest has been in the mountains,*
> *baptising great multitudes of Flathead children & also Nez Perces*
> *children...*[110]

Protestant missionaries also suspected that Great Britain was using
the Catholics to keep the Oregon Country from the Americans.
"American expansionism and Indian salvation thus began to become
synonymous, because only an American Oregon could produce
Protestant Indians."[111]

Spalding was right in thinking the Catholic priests were involved in

Thunder's Eye's dissatisfaction with him. Spalding's harsh, puritanical teachings were not as appealing as the "baptize-first-teach-later" approach of the Catholics. Catholicism's rituals and use of icons did not require the Indian initially to give up many of their ancestral customs.[112] By 1841, Jesuit Father Pierre Jean DeSmet reported 80 Nez Perce conversions to Catholicism while he was working among the Nez Perces' Flathead relatives in the Bitterroot Valley.[113] No Cayuse converts had been baptized by Marcus Whitman.[114] Spalding, over a longer period of time, had baptized very few Nez Perce people.

Even before he came to live among them, some Nez Perce people had discussed Spalding's actions with William Craig, their old friend from the buffalo country who was *himíyu* (relative or in-law) to some.[115] His advice was even weightier since he had once lived in the "country where the sun comes up" (the United States) and was, like Spalding, a *so·yá·po·* (white man).[116] Craig reported that ministers in the East did not rule the white people like chiefs and they paid for land, work and food like everybody else. To his way of thinking, it was not right for Spalding to cultivate the Nez Perce land and require the Nez Perce people to work without offering pay for both. Nor was it right for missionaries to set themselves above the people they came to teach and punish transgressors by whipping them: a missionary was not a *miyó·xat* (chief).

Within four days of their arrival William Craig and Jack Larrison went to work for Henry Spalding, for the Spalding mission was a source of needed supplies. Spalding indicated they would be paid in beef: a "Colville ox" had just been killed, yielding 163 pounds of good meat.

But trouble soon erupted when Spalding tried to organize a work party of Indians and ex-trappers. Planning to go up the Clearwater to cut timber for more building, Spalding asked James, Jacob, Old Joseph, and Timothy to go and requested each bring six men for the logging crew. He asked Craig and Larrison to accompany the party, which would then total over thirty men. Spalding offered pay in the form of "some pork, orders on Vancouver [Dr. John McLoughlin's Hudson's Bay Company trading post] or such clothing as I have to spare." Craig had been told of used clothing offered as payment for work; he and Larrison wanted Spalding to show them the "striped shirting just from Boston," so they could inspect it before making the deal.[117]

The following day Thunder's Eye told Spalding the Nez Perce men had been warned not to work for Spalding unless he paid them. According to Spalding's December 1, 1840, diary entry, Craig "tells them I am making dogs & slaves of them. I ought to pay them for going after timber."[118] (Used as beasts of burden, dogs lacked status in Nez Perce culture.) Furthermore, Craig and Larrison said if Spalding wanted them to work for him he must let them pre-approve the goods they were to receive, for they weren't going to tolerate payment in second-hand, donated clothing from the mission barrels. The mountain men were challenging the missionary. The crew was organized, however, and just before Christmas a group of men that included Larrison, but not Craig nor Thunder's Eye, left to cut timber.

An active trader even though far from Fort Davy Crockett, Craig, along with Jim Conner, spent New Year's Eve with Pierre Pambrun at Fort Nez Perces (near present Wallula Junction). They covered the 180 miles back home before the weather turned cold. In mid-January 1841 the mercury registered 26 degrees below zero. Many of Spalding's potatoes froze and Craig could see that, without buffalo or elk nearby to keep a family in meat, winter living near missionaries was going to be different from winter camp with fur trappers.

Since William Craig seemed to thwart him at every turn, Spalding decided to confront Craig and settle their differences. On an early evening in February, five white men arrived at Isabel's tepee to have a talk with Craig. Missionaries Alvin Smith and Cornelius Rogers, as well as Jim Conner and Jack Larrison, came to help Spalding challenge Craig with the grievances against him. Isabel and Otkokohl (Spalding renamed him Thomas) were also present. Craig was given an opportunity to "clear himself...of the charges alleged against him."[119] Otkokohl remembered that when William (the Nez Perces called him only William) learned that Christian missionaries were coming to the Nez Perce people, he was happy. But when he came to live near the mission, he saw Spalding live on Nez Perce land without paying them for it, require the Nez Perce people to stay at home, not to hunt for their food and clothing, and to work for him in return for religious instruction and the necessities of life. Craig accused Spalding of once selling frozen potatoes to the people: Spalding retorted that the people had picked up potatoes thrown out of the root cellar despite being told not to do so. Isabel spoke, recalling that William told her people he would set things right when he came to live with them. Spalding was sick at the "discovery of such a dark plot," believing Craig wanted him sent away so that Craig himself could take over the mission property.[120] When the meeting ended Craig's and Spalding's viewpoints were further apart than when they started.

The next day Thunder's Eye led men who tore down the dam that supplied water for the mill. The Spaldings spent the day watching the demolition, fasting, and praying. Spalding wrote of Craig in his diary, "How is it possible for a man born of Christian parents (his parents are members of the Presbyterian church) to be guilty of such deeds of darkness!"[121]

Tom Hill, a Delaware Indian, had—like Craig—married into the Nez Perce tribe and become one of them. Hill had lived with the Nez Perces in buffalo country and distinguished himself fighting the Blackfeet; his advice and counsel were heeded when, in 1845, he returned with his Nez Perce band to their home in the Clearwater country. Hill—whose Delaware tribal councils passed down the history of generations of violence and broken treaties—advised the Nez Perces not to trust missionaries, for they were often the precursors of land grabbers with guns. When it came to missionaries, Craig reported, Hill preferred Whitman to Spalding; but in the year Hill spent in the Lapwai, his teachings against missionaries in general never varied.[122]

One of the structures being built near the mission school was a house for Timothy and his family. In June Spalding helped Timothy prepare lumber for his house, and for more than a week he helped build Timothy's house. This took Craig aback, for Timothy's family lived miles away—with Red Wolf's band on the Snake River. That the first house built for a Nez Perce family was located in the Lapwai Valley but occupied by people from the Alpowa area shows how little Spalding understood traditions of the people with whom he was living.

The day after seeing the milldam destroyed by Craig's family and friends, Spalding made an evening visit to Isabel's tepee to "converse on the subject of religion, converse & pray with him, leave a testament, a sermon & tract."[123] Spalding was unsuccessful in convincing Craig that he was not taking advantage of the Nez Perce people.

On February 14, 1841, a week or so after the trouble at the dam and millrace, Thunder's Eye stood up in church and accused Spalding of making the Nez Perces miserable—of ruining them. Thunder's Eye reiterated the convictions Craig had shared: that if Spalding were a true teacher, he would not be spending so much time building houses, getting wood, irrigating, and cultivating the land. Later that night in his diary, his pen fueled with righteous indignation, Spalding ended his diatribe against Craig:

Such is the management of a selfish, lawless, self-ruined scape goat from the States who having rejected the offer of mercy hates above all things to any body else in a way to be benefited. How much injury he will do here I know not, but pray the Lord to turn his counsel into foolishness, if it can be made any more foolish & absurd than it is.[124]

Meanwhile, the number of Catholic converts increased and competition between the Catholic and Protestant missionaries heated up. Two years earlier, Thunder's Eye had delivered a letter to Spalding from Asa Gray at Waiilatpu, telling how the chief of the Wallawallas had not permitted his son to be baptized by the *samaq cimúˑxcimux* (black dress, black robe, Catholic priest) now at Fort Nez Perces. The reason the chief declined the invitation was the condition attached by the priest—the boy must promise never to go into the house of an American missionary. Rumors ran wild among the Protestants. As time passed, they received news from the Willamette country that Catholic priests were re-marrying couples earlier married by the Methodist missionaries and re-baptizing those who the Methodists had baptized. Both Whitman and Spalding lectured their Indian pupils on the evils of Catholicism.

It was easier by far to be accepted into the Catholic church than into the Presbyterian, and the Catholic baptismal ceremony was much more colorful than its Protestant counterpart. Some Nez Perces had been trying for several years to pass the tests required for acceptance into Spalding and Whitman's churches. When the first two Catholic missionaries, Fathers Francis Norbert Blanchet and Modeste Demers, arrived at Fort Walla Walla and later baptized one of Young Chief's (Cayuse half-brother of Old Joseph) children in a ceremony full of splendid ritual, the Indian people were impressed.[125] When the Spaldings learned that one of their earliest students, Rotten Belly (Takensuatis) and his wife had become Catholic, they were deeply hurt.[126] Whitman and Spalding defended their puritanical practices, however, and believed it entirely too easy for the Indians to become Catholics.

In mid-February, Spalding supervised the milldam repair with the help of three of his faithful friends: Timothy, Luke, and Jacob. Two leaders were absent, Old Joseph and Thunder's Eye. Spalding had sent a written invitation to William Craig, Jack Larrison, Dick Williams and Jim Conner, but it is unclear if they came to help with the repairs.

Meanwhile, in the Willamette Valley, Doc Newell, Joe Meek, Caleb Wilkins, and their families had spent the first winter in their lodges, attempting to stay warm and dry in the cold, damp climate. The Hudson's Bay Company had been the primary non-native establishment in the region for many years and, although McLoughlin was a generous host, it was clear to the mountain men they were neither welcome nor able to trap beaver for a living. (Hudson's Bay Company trappers had exterminated beaver south of the Columbia River in an attempt to keep the United States from settling the region.) By Christmas 1840 the ex-trappers had their lodges set up on the west bank of the Willamette River (present-day Hillsboro, Oregon) and called their little community "Rocky Mountain Retreat."[127] They would try to start farming in the spring, but now they were short on both funds and food and prospects were dim for staying healthy.

On March 2, 1841, Craig and Larrison rode out of the Lapwai Valley heading for the Willamette Valley, responding to a message that an old trapper, Ewing Young, had died. (Spalding was a relieved man, noting their departure in his diary, stating that he hoped "to see peaceful times soon."[128]) Young left a large estate and Craig's friends were among the people trying to figure out what to do with his land, buildings, furnishings, livestock, and crops. Helping with Young's property, Craig worked four days with his horse and Joe Meek worked three—rounding up cattle perhaps—each earning two dollars a day wages.[129]

On October 7 Craig and Larrison returned from the Willamette Valley and, as was the usual practice, they brought mail to the Spaldings. According to a letter sent by Whitman to Spalding, the Cayuses were becoming hostile and the Whitmans had been "treated basely, life endangered, door broken in."[130] The Whitmans—seen by some Indian people as arrogant empire builders—were being warned that they were no longer welcome to live among the Cayuses.[131] The Whitmans expected to retreat to Fort Walla Walla for their safety, and they asked Spalding to meet them there.

When Spalding rode to meet the Whitmans, Thunder's Eye was one of the Nez Perce men who accompanied him, but their truce did not last long. At a large meeting at Spalding's church upon his return, Thunder's Eye took exception to the sermon about faith, rose from the congregation, and defended his people's belief in their guardian spirit. He said he had received his *wé·yekin* as a young person and cherished the power it gave him over winds and clouds and rain; that he could cause the wind to blow and the clouds to give rain whenever he pleased. Timothy defended the Spaldings' faith, but Thunder's Eye refused to listen. The next day, Thunder's Eye visited Spalding and told him it was Craig who had advised the Nez Perces to demand pay for their lands and Craig who had told them the previous winter to tear down the milldam. Then Thunder's Eye bade Spalding goodbye and

rode to *siláylo·* (Celilo, Wascopam, The Dalles); he was finished with
going to Henry Spalding's church.

Dissention among the plateau missionaries led the ABCFM to order
the missions at Waiilatpu and Lapwai closed.[132] During the winter of
1842-43, Whitman traveled east, convinced the board to rescind the
closures, and returned to Waiilatpu leading a wagon train of more than
1,000 immigrants bound for the Willamette Valley.[133] Traveling west
with Whitman was his 13-year-old nephew, Perrin Beza Whitman.[134]
Perrin Whitman would be closely associated with the Nez Perce
people—and with William Craig—in the years to come.

Another group of Oregon-bound emigrants had passed near
Waillatpu in September of 1842. Among them was Dr. Elijah P.
White, the newly appointed subagent for Indian relations in the Oregon
Country. White had no authority over the Nez Perce people in their
own land. Yet he had developed, probably with Spalding's help, a list
of laws that he said would govern both whites and Indians: laws that
demanded hanging, whipping, and damage payments as penalties for
murder, arson, theft, and trespass.[135] Nez Perce leaders, who believed
White's laws would result in white men finally being punished for
murdering Indians, had agreed to them.[136] The Nez Perces expected
fair laws to bring amicable relations with the newcomers that would
result in profitable trade and wealth; they had, after all, good relations
and good trade with the Hudson's Bay Company men and were wealthy
as a result. But, although Nez Perce leaders began immediately to
carry out the laws, white men did not. When a white man at Sutter's
Fort in California murdered Elijah Hedding, the Christian son of
Yellow Bird, chief of the Wallawallas, the white man remained
unpunished. The murder of Elijah Hedding was added to a growing list
of unredressed wrongs perpetrated by the white men—and the Nez
Perces and their neighbors forgot none.

By the time White entered their country, the plateau Indians had
been trading with foreigners for many years and had worked out ways
to get along with each other. The foreign traders had business on their
minds – something the Indians understood, excelled at, and welcomed.
They had lived together, traded with one another, and tried to meet
their trading partners' needs without letting go of their own; an
unwritten code of conduct had developed.[137] As settlers came to the
Northwest, the mountain men (who understood the code) acted to
educate their fellow Americans and serve as liaisons between
newcomers and residents. However, the American newcomers had an
agenda far different from that of the British traders. White's laws laid a

foundation for American settlers whose goal was to take control of the land and its people—and one way to do so, already proven effective, was to install their own legal system.[138]

However profound the impact of American settlers would be on the Oregon Country's original residents, it was White's change to their political system that was to haunt the Nez Perces for years to come—and be instrumental, by 1861, in the tribe's disunity. White proposed that the Nez Perces elect one person, a high chief, to speak for all the bands. The Nez Perce headmen accepted and acted on White's proposal and—although disquietude prevailed over the foreign concept—finally elected Ellis, the grandson of Red Grizzly, who could speak English.[139] The Nez Perce people, however, continued to operate as they always had—with independent and autonomous villages led by chosen headmen—and it was only when dealing with white men that they did so through one person the Americans called a "head chief."

Meanwhile, at the Spalding mission—although both Craig and Thunder's Eye disagreed vehemently with much of Henry Spalding's behavior—necessity dictated that neighbor help neighbor in the daily business of living. Late in January 1842 Spalding sent to Dr. Whitman a translation from English to Nez Perce of some of the Bible, and Craig delivered the document. A week later Craig returned from trading at Fort Walla Walla (Fort Nez Perces), bringing news that there was deep snow in that region and rumors that England had declared war on the United States. (The rumors were not true as it turned out, but years of posturing between England and the U.S. resulted four years later in Oregon Territory below the 49th parallel being annexed into the United States.) Thunder's Eye rode in from The Dalles just three days later, bringing letters from the Willamette Valley to the people in the Lapwai Valley.[140]

There are earlier instances of such cooperation as well. In 1841 Craig had helped Spalding put a roof on the Spaldings' new house, which was finished early in 1842. Working alongside Spalding, Craig helped him prepare wood for "stocking" plows, since iron plows had been sent from the United States without wooden handles to save money and space. Craig also planned to erect a building of his own; he spent five days upriver with a crew felling timber and floating the logs down to the mouth of Lapwai Creek, where they were sawed into lumber. Craig then built a house about 600 yards downriver from Spalding's new house, west of Lapwai Creek's mouth on the Clearwater River.[141]

Even though the Craig's house was finished, when the time came for the child they were expecting to be born, Isabel likely went to a special tepee with her helpers for the birth. On February 20, 1842 (*alatamá·l*: February, the season of a hard time to build a fire), doubtless with the help of knowledgeable women and traditional methods, Isabel gave birth to a girl. Isabel and William named their child Martha.[142] Henry Spalding's diary makes no mention of the event.[143] Of all the Craig children, Martha was destined to be an active participant in Idaho Territory's growth and transitions, for she would become the widow of a wealthy Boise City developer and later the wife of an outlaw.

While Henry Spalding was dictatorial and difficult, Eliza Spalding earned the respect and friendship of the Nez Perce people with her gentleness, bravery, strength, and faith. Eliza sized up Craig as a good man, judging him to be "very kind & friendly," when he first settled in 1840 just below Jim Conner near the mouth of Lapwai Creek. After Thunder's Eye disagreed with devout Timothy and left in a huff, it was Eliza who welcomed Thunder's Eye back in her school and furnished him with a copy of the Ten Commandments she had printed in the Nez Perce language. Thunder's Eye memorized the Ten Commandments and added them to his traditional faith. "Poor old man," Eliza judged, "his medicine business seems to be his delusion—Yet I feel to pray for him..."[144]

Meanwhile, on the eastern side of the continent, the federal government in Washington City was trying to understand just what resources were in the West that its citizens might exploit. If the U.S. was going to establish control from the East to the Pacific shore, government needed to know about topography, climate, Indians and especially what natural resources could be extracted.[145] The government in 1838 had sent out its first U.S. Navy expedition, commanded by Lt. Charles Wilkes, to explore the Pacific coast. Several ships came up the mouth of the Columbia River and dispatched exploring parties inland.

One of these parties, led by Lt. Robert Johnson, paid a visit in the spring of 1842 to the Lapwai mission. Spalding furnished Craig with sinew from a butchered animal so that a pair of moccasins might be made for their visitor.[146] A sociable host, William Craig had no doubt welcomed the visiting sailors to his house beside the river and offered to provide their leader with moccasins made either by a Nez Perce woman or a mountain man: a fine gift no matter the Craig who made them.

Even though he resisted their teachings, William Craig continued to be a familiar presence in the daily lives of the missionaries in the Lapwai and Walla Walla Valleys. In the summer of 1842 missionary Asa Gray's wife, Mary—then living at the Lapwai mission— complained that Spalding "has given cattle to Craig to dispose of for half the profits, which were promised to Mr. Rogers [volunteer Cornelius Rogers came west with the missionaries in 1838] by the Mission…"[147] Within the next few days, Craig and a Mr. Tompson (probably Philip Thompson, Craig's former Fort Davy Crockett partner) came to the mission; a few days later Craig and a couple named Newbanks, with Thompson's wife and children, came to the mission, stayed for dinner, and listened to a sermon.[148] Philip Thompson later served briefly as the agent at the Utilla (Umatilla) Reservation.[149] When he was at the Whitman mission, Craig would have seen Joe Meek's young daughter, Helen Mar: Meek had left the three-year-old in the care of Narcissa Whitman when he moved from the fur trade to the Willamette Valley.[150]

In May 1843 Craig was again working for Spalding, and more buildings were being constructed at the mission site. The mill was operating, and Spalding and his followers had started construction of a meetinghouse as well as five houses for Nez Perce families.[151] Shortly thereafter, Joel Palmer, Oregon Country's Superintendent of Indian Affairs, directed Philip Thompson to visit Craig to see if the Nez Perces had been hit by the smallpox epidemic then making its rounds through the country.[152] In August 1845 Craig accompanied Spalding and an Indian fellow to The Dalles to pick up barrels of donated goods sent from Boston for the mission; they packed sixteen horses with ploughs, books, clothing and barrel staves and traveled the 295 miles to the Lapwai mission without mishap.[153] The following year, Craig and a deaf-mute man—probably Mustups, who lived with the Spaldings— helped the Spalding family go to Whitman's mission, a four-day trip during which the Spalding's baby was sick with a fever.[154] As they rode west they met large groups of Nez Perce families returning after trading their buffalo robes, hemp rope, parfleches, halters, game and *síkem* (horses) for the prized pounded salmon of the river people.[155]

Yet Craig continued to be troubled by many of Spalding's practices. Timothy's house near the Spaldings remained a sore subject. Timothy was a faithful convert and a close friend of the Spalding family, but Craig thought Timothy should be farming in his own territory. Craig also supported his father-in-law's view that Spalding should not be selling for profit grain raised on Thunder's Eye's people's land.

The Spaldings and Whitmans met as often as practicable to discuss their work. Whitman heard of Spalding's "severe trials with regard to the action of the Indians in taking away the cultivated lands from Timothy" and understood that Spalding had many enemies.[156] Whitman believed Craig to be the perpetrator of the movement to kick Timothy off Thunder's Eye's land, the prime advocate of bringing Catholic priests to replace the Protestants and thought Craig had kept "busy in trying to excite the people against the laws as recommended by Doct White..."[157] Whitman was likely correct on all counts.

Although many of the Nez Perce people learned farming and embraced the new faith taught by the Spaldings, others were interested in learning about the black robes' teachings. A priest was teaching about his religion in the Coeur d'Alene country; some Nez Perces heard him and reported back to their people. After council talks, the Nez Perces sent a contingent of four men to find out more.[158] Thunder's Eye was one of the men in the 1845 delegation to seek Catholic instruction, as was a younger man named Youmukmuken.[159] Thunder's Eye converted to the Catholic faith during this period. At least one other in Thunder's Eye's family—his daughter, Isabel Craig—also became Catholic.[160] No documentation has been found showing where or when Isabel converted, but she would remain a Catholic for the rest of her long life.

When Spalding and Whitman learned that some of their close students had turned from them and embraced Catholic teachings, their distrust of Catholic priests overwhelmed them. It gave rise to unfounded suspicions that the Catholics plotted to displace the Protestant missionary community entirely.

How William Craig felt about the religious disagreements seems clear: like his Nez Perce family, he had little patience with the interdenominational fighting of the Catholics and Protestants. Henry Spalding's work to change the Nez Perce people was unacceptable to Craig, but he didn't seem to feel the same way about the efforts of the Catholic priests. The perception that Spalding and Whitman were becoming wealthy at the expense of the people to whom they were dispensing religious education—and the lack of personal wealth among the Catholic missionaries—could be partly responsible for Craig's reaction. Whatever the case, when William's wife and children became Catholic, he neither blocked their path nor joined them.

No longer trapping beaver or hunting buffalo—although sometimes absent on trading trips—Craig was basically living a stay-at-home life for the first time since his childhood. And his family was growing. On May 5, 1845, Isabel gave birth to a girl they named Adeline.[161] How were Isabel and William to know when they looked at their tiny daughter that she would one day be the grandmother of the renowned scholar Archie Phinney, the first person of Nez Perce heritage to earn a Ph.D.?[162] Little Adeline was simply an infant snug in her *tiké's* (cradleboard) as the pine trees drifted yellow pollen onto the waters of the Lapwai and Clearwater.

International events were unfolding that soon affected the people of the Pacific Northwest. In 1846 a treaty was signed between Britain and the United States in which Britain ceded Oregon Country south of the 49th parallel. Many settlers immediately filed claims on the "U.S." land. With no system yet in place to handle such early claims, most progressed no further. Whitman was alarmed about the possibility of mission stations being taken by United States land claims, especially after he learned of "a secret effort of Mr. Craig a neighbor of Mr. Spalding to get a claim recorded so as to include the [Spalding] Mission premises."[163] It may have pleased Craig to think he could oust the Spaldings and their mission from Nez Perce land; and it is certain that, when he saw an opportunity for the first time in his life to be a landowner, Craig was in the vanguard of land-grabbing Americans.

On September 15, 1846, the Craig family moved to a new location.[164] The site they selected, undoubtedly with the consent of Thunder's Eye, was a prime parcel of tillable land some eight miles south of Spalding's mission and just south of Thunder's Eye's village. At about the same time Craig filed paperwork to claim hundreds of acres of Lapwai Valley land.[165]

In a rugged, mountainous region where tillable soil was limited to some high prairies and the bottomlands of a few deep, timber-lined valleys, the land the Craigs selected was uniquely suited to both farming and grazing. Streams that rose in the high country fed the narrow canyon that was sheltered to the east and west by steep hillsides punctuated by pine groves and basaltic rock formations. There was a spring of good water on the site, and it was at the spring that William and Isabel built their new home. The trail through the valley then climbed to the *qémes* (camas) prairie thousands of feet above. To newcomers, the mountain southwest of the place where Isabel and William built their new home (*'eteyemé·xs* [distant mountain], or *wá·yatinwa·s* [place to receive guardian spirit]), became known as "Craig's Mountain."

Spalding continued trying to turn *ni·mí·pu·* into prosperous, stay-at-home farmers in the belief he was saving them from becoming a vanishing race. In the summer of 1847 Spalding paid Craig $100 to keep the mission's cattle and horses at Craig's place and out of the Nez

Perces' fields. While Spalding had little patience for people who had not fenced off their fields (he judged them to be "too reckless to raft down timber & build good fences"), he nonetheless wanted their farming efforts to succeed. But the cattle found their way back to the mission through the Nez Perces' fields and enraged someone enough that the ears and tails were cut off two of Spalding's animals. Spalding believed the person who mutilated the cattle was Craig's brother-in-law, Thomas, who was upset about a sermon on the evils of gambling and sorcery.[166]

Both the Spalding and Whitman missions suffered dangerous undercurrents of mistrust. Each year, more white people traveled by the Whitman mission on their way to the Willamette Valley; many were sick and passed diseases on to the Cayuse people. Tom Hill had warned the Nez Perces about missionaries: First the white people send a few missionaries, said Hill, and then many white people come. They talk, they treat, and then they take your land. Before he left the area, Tom Hill advised killing the missionaries. Missionaries were, indeed, an important part of federal policy.[167]

When some settlers from an 1847 wagon train pulled into the Whitmans' yard, they hastened the mission's doom by not continuing on to the Willamette Valley. Arriving at about the same time was a French-Canadian-Iroquois man named Joe Lewis, who was remembered by some Nez Perces as being connected with the Mormons.[168] Joe Lewis hated white people, especially missionaries, after seeing what had happened to the Iroquois in the East. An epidemic of measles spread through the people around the mission: the Whitmans nursed the sick immigrants from the wagon trains as well as the sick Cayuses, but the infected Cayuse people began to die in alarming numbers while most immigrants recovered.[169] Whitman had been warned that his medicine did not work for Indians as it did for whites; he had also been warned that it was the Indians' practice to kill medicine men whose medicine did not work.[170] Seeing the Cayuse people sicken, Lewis spread the rumor that Whitman had been poisoning them in order to take their land. Some Cayuse warriors decided that the Whitmans must die before they had to bury all of their people.

It was late November 1847, and in the Lapwai Valley the Craig household was snug and ready for winter. Their children were well and growing—Joe was seven, Martha almost five, and Adeline two years of age. Craig may have thought to check in on Eliza Spalding down at the Clearwater, for he knew Henry had taken their ten-year-old daughter,

Eliza, to the Whitman mission to enter her for schooling. But Eliza's brother, Horace Hart, was at the Spaldings' home, along with a man named Jackson and a white girl from a wagon train who was helping Mrs. Spalding with the housework, so Eliza had both company and assistance. It's likely the sound of a horse galloping into their dooryard was the Craigs' first indication that something was amiss.

Just after noon on Monday, November 29, at the Waiilatpu mission, some men of the Cayuse tribe used guns and tomahawks to kill Marcus Whitman, his wife, Narcissa, and nine other white people.[171] Thirteen white people were killed over the course of two days for once the carnage started it was slow to stop. And then the warriors went looking for their other primary target, Henry Spalding.

Amidst the confusion of the attack at Waiilatpu, an immigrant managed to escape and brought the news to the Lapwai Valley. Eliza Spalding then sent a Nez Perce friend to the Craig house to inform them of the trouble and also asked two trusted friends, the Eagle and Timothy, to ride fast to Waiilatpu to save little Eliza. The following day a Nez Perce messenger brought news that Henry Spalding had evaded the attackers. The reaction of the Lapwai Valley people, both native and newcomer, was one of shock.

At first light Sunday morning, Craig saddled up his horse and joined warriors from Thunder's Eye's village for the ride to the Spalding mission. Eliza Spalding heard Craig out as he urged her to collect her children and some clothing and come to his house. But she refused— she would not travel on the Sabbath. Craig and the Nez Perce protectors stayed at the mission until the next morning; when, the Sabbath over, they made ready to transport Eliza, her children, and the other white people to the Craig house.

But before they left the mission, a group of warriors arrived. They, like the Cayuses, believed the missionaries were doing them harm. Knowing what had taken place at Waiilatpu, they were determined to also rid themselves of the whites at Lapwai. Finding the whites guarded by Craig and a large number of Nez Perce warriors, they waited until the party moved off toward Craig's place, then looted the mission.

Henry Spalding evaded the searching warriors and made it back to the Lapwai mission. He lost his horse so he was afoot and traveled only at night most of the long, cold journey. Henry and Eliza Spalding were reunited in the Craig home, where they stayed under the protection of the Nez Perce warriors for about a month. Then, in late December, the warriors escorted the Spaldings to Fort Walla Walla, where they were reunited with their daughter.[172] Young Eliza Spalding, along with the other hostages, had been recovered after weeks of captivity through the efforts of Peter Skene Ogden of the Hudson's Bay Company, who paid a ransom for their return. The Spalding family then settled in the Willamette Valley.

The killings and other violence at Waiilatpu emptied the Protestant mission site at Lapwai immediately and the Tshimakain mission on the Spokane prairie in less than half a year. The Eellses and Walkers stayed with the Spokane tribe until March 1848, when they were provided an army escort out of the area; they too went to live in the Willamette Valley. The events at Waiilatpu not only ended the lives of Marcus and Narcissa Whitman (and, because she had no caregivers, Meek's daughter, Helen Mar) but also closed forever the other two Protestant missions in the interior northwest.

Isabel Craig, 1860's. Courtesy of Bill Belknap.

3
Volunteer Army Hunts the Cayuses (1848-1852)

When they learned of the violence at the Whitmans' mission, the Willamette Valley's white settlers feared an attack on their settlements. The Oregon provisional legislature met immediately and called for volunteers to form an army for protection. Henry A. G. Lee (kin to Robert E. Lee) took command of about fifty volunteers, was given the rank of major, and set off to establish a military base at Wascopam (The Dalles).

Over the next six weeks the Oregon provisional legislature authorized formation of a volunteer army; about 350 men responded to the call.[173] The men elected a settler from North Carolina—a veteran of the Blackhawk War and a former Missouri congressman—Cornelius Gilliam, to lead them. Reflecting the sentiments of most settlers, the editor of the Oregon City newspaper called for destroying the Cayuses: may "their name and race be blotted from the face of the earth."[174]

Robert Newell was then speaker of the Oregon provisional legislature, and that body also created a three-man commission to negotiate for peace with the tribes east of the Cascades. Henry Lee, an 1843 immigrant who had spent time at the Spalding mission and learned the Nez Perce language, was one of those appointed, along with the Quaker Joel Palmer and Robert Newell. They were directed to treat with the Nez Perces and other tribes in order to "avert a general war...and to prevent a union among the tribes..."[175] By late January 1848 about 400 armed and mounted white men—three of whom were responsible for diplomacy—had traveled east of the Cascade Mountains to Wascopam and were poised to march up the Columbia and Walla Walla Rivers to Waiilatpu.

The Oregon Country was not an organized territory of the United States, but the United States had encouraged its citizens to settle there—and the federal government had been responsible since colonial times for controlling Indians who might get in the way of settlement. Based on their understanding of U.S. policy, the men in the Oregon legislature decided to seek federal help for the war they were about to wage. They prepared a memorial to the U.S. Congress requesting the "Immediate influence and protection of the U.S. Governor in our internal affairs" and authorized Marshal Joe Meek to carry it and other documents across the continent to Washington City.[176]

There was fear on the side of the Indians as well: Columbia Plateau tribal leaders were afraid that the Americans, more numerous and better armed than they, would send an avenging army. Trying to avoid a war, they sent messengers to the white men, requesting councils.

Earlier, as an aftermath of the attack on the Waiilatpu mission, a hostage situation had developed in which Thunder's Eye had played a key role. Entire families from the wagon trains had survived the attack for the warriors' targets had been only those they believed they needed to stop in order to protect their families. After the killing stopped, survivors were taken hostage. Some Cayuse leaders—like Tamsucky (one of the prime instigators of the attack)—wanted to kill the captives and be done with them.[177] Traditional practices in tribal warfare called for killing enemy men and capturing women and children to become slaves, who were then assimilated into the tribe. A number of tribal leaders were summoned to a council to decide the hostages' fate.

Theentheenmeetsa (brother or cousin of Umapine, a Cayuse stockman whose daughter would one day marry young Joe Craig) intervened on behalf of a few of the white men whom Cayuse leader Teloukaikt (Crawfish Advancing) and his son, Clark, wanted to kill.[178] Thunder's Eye—known to the captives as "Old Jimmie, a weather shaman and a Catholic"—offered a different idea.[179] He proposed keeping the prisoners alive and using them to guarantee that no white army would be sent to attack the Cayuse. The other leaders agreed. If, by spring, no avenging army entered their country, the Cayuses would send the hostages downriver to safety. The leaders directed that Henry Spalding write Oregon governor George Abernethy, outlining the Cayuse/Nez Perce proposal. The Nez Perces would protect the Spalding party—and overlook the fact that Elijah White had not punished the killer of Elijah Hedding—in return for the Americans not sending an avenging army.[180] Nez Perce riders delivered Spalding's letter to Bishop Francois Norbert Blanchet at St. Anne's mission on the Umatilla River; but before the proposal could be delivered to Governor Abernethy, the Hudson's Bay Company intervened.

The HBC sent Peter Skene Ogden to talk with the affected tribal leaders. On December 23, he held council with Yellow Bird of the

Wallawallas, Young Chief, Crawfish Advancing, and some young Cayuse men as well as Nez Perce delegates.[181] For the Waiilatpu hostages, Ogden offered a ransom payment of 50 blankets, 50 shirts, 10 guns, 10 fathoms of tobacco, 10 handkerchiefs, and 100 powder and ball charges; for the Spalding party at the Craig place, he offered 12 blankets, 12 shirts, 2 guns, 12 handkerchiefs, 5 fathoms of tobacco, 200 ball-and-powder loadings, and some knives.[182] Ogden had brought boats loaded with the ransom goods. He gave the Cayuses six days to deliver the captives and sent a letter to Henry Spalding at the Craigs' home, urging him to hurry with his people to the fort.

Although not all the responsible Cayuses thought it wise to give up the hostages, Crawfish Advancing finally prevailed, and the captives were delivered before the deadline. Nez Perce warriors escorted the white people from the Craig home to Fort Walla Walla, and Ogden paid the ransom. On January 2, 1848, Hudson's Bay boats carrying former hostages pulled away from the fort and took them to the Willamette Valley.[183] By giving up the hostages, Thunder's Eye's plan to keep an avenging army out of the interior was short-circuited.

As the Indians feared, when the worst of winter was behind them and the hostages were safe, the Americans prepared to enter Cayuse territory. Since they were sending a "peace commission" along with a retaliatory army, they needed interpreters. Former HBC and mountain men had Indian wives, spoke some tribal languages, could communicate in Chinook jargon or sign language, and were familiar with the tribe-trader code of conduct. It was likely Robert Newell's idea to call on William Craig and John Baptiste Gervais, already with the Nez Perces, and Philip Thompson, George Ebbert, and others living in the Willamette Valley, to help keep the interior tribes from all-out war.[184] Thomas McKay and Philip Thompson were asked to accompany the peace commissioners.[185] These men knew the etiquette of successful councils: rituals of giving gifts and sharing pipes cleared the way for serious business. If ever there was a time for acceptable protocol, it was now.

But conflict occurred before councils could be arranged. In early February Henry Lee's troops, while waiting for the rest of the army at Wascopam, skirmished with some nearby Deschutes warriors. The Deschutes were rounding up cattle left by immigrants when Lee's volunteers captured about sixty of their horses.[186] Word quickly spread up the Columbia River that an army of white men was coming.

When he learned the Willamette Valley militia was collecting there, William Craig rode to Wascopam and met with Lee. Both knew that alliances often changed and the Nez Perces could go either way—with or against the Americans—depending on how the Americans behaved right then. "The operation of a single hour may fix our doom for weal or woe," Lee said as he tried to keep Col. Gilliam from rushing to fight before sitting down in council.

"[M]*arching the army…without a previous interview with the Nez Perces will involve us in a general war with all the tribes. …I have long since asked the Col. [Gilliam] to allow me to take Mr Craig as interpreter and go to see them…"*[187]

But Gilliam, who preferred the smoke of gunpowder to that of council pipe, ordered the combined forces of peace commissioners and the volunteer army to march eastward together. The situation worsened when one of the volunteers, Hiram English, shot an Indian under circumstances that caused Newell to announce it was "a most shameful thing."[188]

Lee sent a message to the plateau tribal leaders: the whites wanted to stay friendly with everybody other than those who committed the murders; that the Americans were slow to anger, but that when they started fighting they never stopped until their enemies were dead. Lee pointed out that the Americans were "very numerous in our own country—like the trees on the mountains, we will never be done coming."[189]

In a move designed to limit the hostiles' ability to make war, the Oregon legislature had prohibited introduction of firearms among Indians and set fines for anyone who provided munitions of war to Indians.[190] (It was the desire to have this arms embargo lifted that would eventually drive some plateau Indians—now dependent on rifles and ammunition to hunt food for their families—to help Americans punish the Cayuses.)

The country to the east of Wascopam was semi-arid, in marked contrast to the dramatically green landscape of the Pacific coast at the mouth of the Columbia River. Traveling to Wascopam from the west took one through the rugged Cascade Mountain chain, well watered, covered by timber, and punctuated with dramatic waterfalls. At Wascopam the rainfall lessened, and eastward from that point the vegetation (predominantly sagebrush) was sparse and the soil sandy;

basalt outcroppings sculpted by ice-age floods guarded the course of the Columbia River. It was a country through which wise travelers kept to the river, where there was water for themselves and their mounts.

The American militia traveled with the peace commissioners into the Columbia River Basalts. They did battle with some Cayuse warriors at Sand Hollow (about twenty-five miles west of present Umatilla, Oregon), where Five Crows was badly wounded, another Cayuse leader killed, and the white men cut off from water for a day.[191] Couriers traveled between the armies, for both Indians and whites were working to arrange a council.

By the third day of March, the peace commissioners and volunteers were camped near the ruins of the Whitman mission. Using adobe bricks from the mission, they started building a wall so they could defend themselves against the Indians moving in their direction; it was rumored that the Nez Perces would join their Cayuse brothers in war against the whites.[192]

Neither the Nez Perce warriors nor the untrained militia operated as unified armies, but for different reasons. Many new immigrants to the Oregon Country viewed all Indians as enemies, and their volunteers not only were undisciplined but had just come from their own racial and regional struggles in the states; the Nez Perce warriors were guerilla fighters from many bands, and traditionally no one leader commanded them.

On an early-spring day of rare fine weather, Yellow Bird, some Nez Perce men, and Gervais brought good news to the peace commissioners: the Nez Perce people were coming to meet them and hold a council. William Craig, also at the Americans' encampment, left the next morning with Gervais, promising to return in a day with the Nez Perce contingent that included "all the warriers 250 men."[193]

Joe Meek and his Washington City-bound party left Waiilatpu in the dark of night to begin their mission. They were dressed in the Scotch caps and red belts of the HBC trappers, for the Indians were not angry with the Hudson's Bay men and the disguise might facilitate safe passage. One hundred Oregon volunteers (one was Captain John W. Owen, who would come to know William Craig well) rode as Meek's escort to a point below the Blue Mountains' snow line.[194] Meek's party would not only carry the Memorial to Congress but also deliver news of Oregon's "Indian war" to the East. Thus it was that the Cayuse attack on the Waiilatpu mission accelerated the creation of Oregon as a new territory of the United States.

On March 6, with Craig as their vanguard, the Nez Perce contingent – about 250 warriors along with their women, children, and elders – arrived as promised. They made a grand entrance into camp and were welcomed by the volunteers, who shot off some of their scanty supply of ammunition in salute and cheered the impressive Nez Perces. The salute was returned by the warriors, all of them riding in grand parade. After the niceties were over, the Nez Perce women dismounted and set up camp near the Americans.[195]

A general council was held the next day between leaders of the Nez Perces, Cayuses and Wallawallas, the peace commissioners, militia officers and William Craig. Among the participants were the Cayuse war chief Old Man Chief, the Wallawalla chief Yellow Bird, and eleven Nez Perce leaders, including Old Joseph, Red Wolf, Timothy, Kentuck, Thunder's Eye and his son Thomas. Cornelius Gilliam, Thomas McKay, D. W. Cook, Joel Palmer, Henry Lee and Robert Newell represented the Americans, and in the absence of Ellis, who had "gone to buffalo," Old Joseph was appointed "head chief." It was a compelling collection of leaders who sat down together.

After, as Newell wrote in his journal, "the pipe of friendship had passed around till our hearts were all good and our eyes watery," the talking began. With Craig translating, Palmer read to the delegates Gov. Abernethy's letter that set forth the Americans' position.[196] They demanded that the killers of the mission whites be denied shelter among the other tribes and be delivered to the troops.[197] Robert Newell gave a speech warning the Indians to "never go to war with the Americans," and, further, that "Mr. Craig will tell you that we are your friends, he loves you, so do we like him, he has told us many good things of you."[198] Without exception, the headmen said they had not known in advance that the Cayuse planned to kill the Whitmans and they wanted no part of war against the whites.

Americans and Nez Perces had been allies and friends since Lewis and Clark came through Nez Perce country. Nez Perce leaders chose an alliance with the Americans—who often traded guns (and the black powder to fire them) for *ni·mí·pu·* horses—as a means of keeping up with the weaponry of their Shoshone and Blackfeet enemies.[199] In other words, they set up a trade alliance with the Americans to trade what they had plenty of for what they needed most. More generally, Indian-European alliances were often the result of a tribe's long victimization by tribal enemies. Indians allied with Europeans because together they were strong enough to fight even stronger enemies.[200] Their loyalty was defined not by race but by community.

Within twenty years of the Lewis and Clark party sitting in council with Nez Perce leaders, American fur traders were beneficiaries of the Nez Perce-American alliance. Over the course of America's participation in the trapping business, Nez Perce warriors and American mountain men had, together, fought common enemies. "I have not come here to make peace with you, we never have been at war," Newell said. "I have fought with the Nez Perces, some of them I see here, but we were on the same side; we have lost friends on the same day and in the same battle together..."[201]

But while the Nez Perces and the Americans were allies, the Nez Perces and the Cayuses were *himíyu* (relatives). It was a harsh dilemma, for if the Nez Perces chose to protect their Cayuse friends and relatives—as their hearts told them to do—they would risk endangering their own wives and children in a war with the Americans. If they agreed to the Americans' terms to give up the men who had attacked the white people, war could be avoided. They obviously decided to take a middle ground: they would publicly agree to remain allies of the Americans but privately, behind the scenes, keep the fugitive Cayuse safe from them. Newell recorded that they said they would "not join the murderers to fight" the Americans.[202]

Accord reached at least on the surface, Joel Palmer—the new Superintendent of Indian Affairs for Oregon Country's provisional government—appointed William Craig his agent to the Nez Perces and promised that Craig would teach them to farm. Borrowing from treaties used in the East, Palmer promised as soon as "the present difficulty was settled" he would provide them a blacksmith and a schoolteacher and that no other white man should settle upon their lands without their consent. If they had trouble with the whites, Craig was to inform Palmer, who would fix it. The Nez Perce leaders agreed to Palmer's proposal.[203]

William Craig was also appointed caretaker of the Spalding mission and abandoned property. Palmer wrote a letter validating Craig's appointment as "Agent for the Superintendent of Indian Affairs among the Nez Perces" and further instructing Craig that, in order to continue the friendly relations between the Americans and the Nez Perces, he was "to take possession of the premises heretofore occupied by the Reverend Mr. Spalding (but now abandoned by him) and occupy the same." Craig was instructed to inventory Spaldings' mission property, keep the property safe, and keep an account of expenses connected with preserving the property.[204]

The council ended and gifts were exchanged. After receiving a large American flag and a supply of tobacco, the Nez Perces honored the Americans with a war dance. Newell critiqued the dance thus:

[the dance] *amused and delighted us much; and we do them but bare justice when we say the performance was well timed, the parts well acted, characters represented to the very life, and the whole first rate.*[205]

The next day Craig rode south with Nez Perce warriors to talk with the Cayuses. Their mission was to persuade those Cayuse people who had not participated in the murders to pull away from those who had, leaving the attackers exposed and without protection. But their talk was unsuccessful: the Cayuses gave up no one to the Americans.

On March 9, Col. Gilliam led his army towards the Cayuse camp with intent to attack. The attack was averted when Stickus, an influential Cayuse who had been a friend of Dr. Whitman, along with a Nez Perce and two other Cayuse men, held a lengthy council with Gilliam, Newell, and others. At one point in their talk, Gilliam offered to take Joe Lewis for five of the accused murderers named on a bounty list drawn up by Henry Lee, but no agreement was reached. At the behest of the peace commissioners, Gilliam turned his army around and did not attack the Cayuse camp, but again the Cayuse men were not surrendered to the Americans. Newell noted that the volunteers rounded up stock, and that eight beef cattle had been killed for food with "no respect paid to who they belong."[206]

The commissioners, angry with Gilliam and discouraged by the Cayuses' refusal to surrender the guilty men, gave up and decided to go home. The volunteers had often been beyond Gilliam's control. When the commissioners pulled out of the Waiilatpu camp in mid-March, Col. Gilliam was readying his discordant troops to search for Cayuses.[207]

Finally, three Cayuse families—those led by Stickas, Camaspello, and Theentheenmeetsha—left their relatives and allied with the Nez Perce-American coalition.[208] William Craig and others began referring to them as the "friendly Cayuse." Soon, to keep them from being harmed by volunteer soldiers, they had to identify themselves with a marker so they would be recognized as "friendly."[209] And, although he refused to come talk with the Americans, Young Chief also pulled away from the fugitive Cayuse; he went to the mountains with only his lodge.[210] Young Chief was a Catholic and a half-brother to Old Joseph of the Wallowa Country. Five Crows, another of Old Joseph's half-brothers and the only Cayuse to have been baptized by Spalding, stayed out of reach. Craig and the Nez Perce contingent went home, while the fugitive Cayuse families kept on the move with Gilliam's volunteer troops determinedly, if unsuccessfully, on their trail.

Henry Lee's initial assessment of the volunteer troops—that what was needed was "military talent more than men"—proved to be true.[211] On March 20, 1848, while camped near the Umatilla River on his way to The Dalles for more ammunition and supplies, Cornelius Gilliam died from the discharge of his own gun.[212] Rumors persisted that the event was not accidental. As the Oregon militia hunted for Cayuses, those that did not move into the Blue Mountains for protection went to visit the Nez Perces, who gave them a great feast.[213] Couriers kept Craig and the Nez Perce leaders informed of the Oregon volunteers' whereabouts, and the majority of the Nez Perces avoided obviously taking sides. It was only due to the shortage of ammunition that there were no more deaths in the "Cayuse war," perhaps more aptly called the "Cayuse chase."

Following Palmer's orders, Craig visited the Spalding mission site, spending four days there and reporting some Spalding property had been returned but most of the grain was gone, stolen either by "Telyer" and "Jervis" (Gervais) or by Nez Perces.[214] In early May, he and some Nez Perce warriors traveled to Waiilatpu to again talk with the Americans. Nez Perce horses were missing, and in at least one case the volunteers refused to return them. Finding the officers absent, Craig wrote a letter on behalf of the Nez Perce men and sent it off by courier to "Col. Lee on the road":

There is some of the Nez Perces here waiting for your arivel with great impatience. They wish to see you and some starts home this Day. They have come from the mountains and wish to have a talk but there is no one here that wishes to talk with them. The news was false about them going to join the Cayuses. They have had no thought of it. They appear verry well satisfied with the treaty. I wish your return verry much for there is a great deal of talking about horses that has been taken. There is one horse belonging to an Nez Perce that was lost in the spring, when they came here the whites brou't him in and will not give him up. They say of them they was told that such property would be given up to friendly people.

I have been up at Mr. Spalding's station [and] find things as well as can be expected. The cattle troubles them verry much about there crops. They would like them to be taken away as they have to guard them all the time. ...

believe me to be Sir your most Obt Servant
W Craig[215]

By mid-May Craig was on the Columbia River at Fort Walla Walla, waiting with a few Nez Perce warriors to accompany an expedition to The Dalles. He wrote to Superintendent Palmer:

I have a few minutes to spare and I embrace the opportunity there is nothing strange, with the exception that the little cheaf of the Nez Perces has come from the mountains, and have joined the army with five other Nez Perces, and we are fixing to start after the cayuses. The Old looking glass sais that there will a great many join the first chance the[y] all appear anxious to have the murderers taken. Col Waters will take one part and Lt. Col. Lee will take the other after Tealock [Teloukaikt]. This Day the[y] are starting for--Dalls Leutenant Denyard commands. I will write to you again after we return. I will let you know all about it.

Allow me to ackowledge to bee Sir your most Obt Servant
Wm Craig
The waggons are starting[216]

The Oregon volunteers, Nez Perce warriors, and Craig tracked the band of Cayuses over the rolling hills, up and down pitched draws, and across rocky scablands. At one point the posse crossed the Snake River and climbed northward out of the canyon, following the trail up a narrow defile (now known as Steptoe Canyon) to the high grasslands of Palouse country before they lost the Cayuses' trail and decided to turn back.[217]

The Oregon volunteers had alienated most of the bands on the plateau by killing Indian people at random, slaughtering and eating cattle wherever they were found, and indiscriminately taking horses. They had shown the people of the plateau that all white men were not like "King George men" or the American fur trappers, that many of the Willamette Valley "Bostons" hated Indian people. Henry Lee, when he succeeded Joel Palmer as Superintendent of Indian Affairs, urged evacuation of all white people who had settled east of the Cascade

Mountains. Leaving a small militia at The Dalles, volunteer officers pulled their troops out of the interior Columbia River country and returned to the Willamette Valley. A militia detachment had in March escorted the Walker and Eells missionary families out of the Spokane country; a similar detachment escorted William Craig, who brought along what he had retrieved of Spaldings' property, out of the Lapwai Valley.[218] Isabel and the children seem to have remained in Clearwater country.

After the volunteer soldiers went home, the lives of the plateau people returned almost to normal—except that many of the Cayuse people were homeless. Henry Lee, with Abernethy's concurrence, declared the Cayuse land forfeit and opened it to settlement—hoping to entice enough settlers to remain on the plateau and man the forts in the Walla Walla Valley and Wascopam. While the mission land was reserved, Lee published in a mid-July *Oregon Spectator* a notice to attract settlers to the Walla Walla Valley, stating that all the basics were there for starting a settlement, including mills, blacksmith tools, fields of crops, and iron tools. The Oregon City newspaper's editor endorsed the land confiscation and wrote a glowing report of the area but with the Cayuse band at large few settlers took up claims.[219]

Catholic priests and Protestant missionaries had been expelled from the interior for their safety, but some, Bishop Blanchet included, quietly remained.[220] Blanchet lived among the Cayuses in their camps as they wandered in exile and was able to continue Catholic services and instruction.

Although militia had escorted William Craig out of the Clearwater country, he was not away from home very long, nor was he idle during his absence. In August 1848 Oregon Country became a United States Territory, the boundaries of which spread from the Pacific Ocean to the Rocky Mountains and encompassed all of the present states of Washington, Oregon, and Idaho and part of Montana. Craig had in June filed a claim on 640 acres of the land in what was then Clackamas County, Oregon Territory, on "Parsha" Creek.[221] There are two possibilities as to the claim's location: it may have been at "Pataha" Creek (in the vicinity of present-day Pomeroy, Washington) or Craig may have tried to claim the land on which the Whitmans built their mission (the Cayuse word for the stream now known as Mill Creek was something like "Pasha" or "Pasa."[222]) In either location, the tract Craig attempted to claim contained excellent farming and grazing lands; was well watered and covered with bunch grass, wild rye grass and some timber; and was located west of Alpowa on the road to the trading center at The Dalles. But, as with many claims filed in the early days of territorial organization, Craig's claim was never finalized. He soon returned to his family in the Lapwai Valley and continued farming.[223]

In the next few years the number of white people settling in the Far West increased dramatically. Euro-American immigrants came west primarily for the Indians' land. It was estimated that by 1848 more than 14,000 immigrants had already traveled westward on the Oregon Trail.[224] Most of the immigrants were farmers heading for the Willamette Valley.[225]

Lawyer, who replaced Richard as "head chief" of the Nez Perces, was becoming a political influence to be reckoned with. After Oregon became a territory, Lawyer made a trip downriver to see its new governor, Joseph Lane, in the Willamette Valley.[226] The purpose of the visit was to cement relations between the new governor from the East and the allied Nez Perces, for a contingent of U.S. mounted riflemen had been seen traveling east to west across the plateau.[227]

Lane, with the U.S. military at his disposal, was anxious to punish the Cayuses who had participated in the killings at Waiilatpu. He had sent letters to the Nez Perces and Cayuses, urging that the perpetrators be given up for punishment. If the guilty men were not turned over, Lane promised war.[228] Some Nez Perces and Cayuses, hoping to have the arms embargo lifted, agreed with Lane. Generally, too, they wanted to see the "Cayuse problem" settled in order to avoid war with the Americans, as well as for the sake of keeping young men of their own bands in line. In October 1849 the HBC trader at Fort Walla Walla, William McBean, wrote to William Craig (who was in the Willamette Valley at the time), stating that the Wallawallas, Cayuses, Nez Perces, and Palouses were ready to go after the wanted Cayuse men and either capture or kill them.[229]

In the winter of 1849-50 a posse of 60 Cayuses, 21 Nez Perces, and five Wallawalla warriors set out after the elusive Cayuse band. The posse caught up with them in the upper John Day country east of the Cascades, and the fugitives—after sending their women and children to safety—erected a fort for defense. In the two-day fight that followed, Tamsucky was killed, along with Crawfish Advancing's son, Edward, and four others were captured. After the posse returned to Young Chief's Umatilla camp with prisoners, horses, and other booty from the routed Cayuses, there was a difference of opinion over division of the spoils, and the Nez Perce warriors went home. Fifteen Nez Perce chiefs communicated to Governor Lane that they had done their duty and cleared their country of the murderers, but they were angry that Young Chief had kept the booty, especially the captured guns.[230]

That spring five Cayuse men surrendered to U.S. military at The Dalles to answer for their alleged crimes at Waiilatpu. The wanted band had not gone far, for their families were without food and they had been unable to journey to the mountains or buffalo country. Those placed under arrest by the military were Crawfish Advancing (Tiloukaikt), Little Chief (Tomahas) and his brother Frank Escaloom, Clokamus, and Panther Shirt (Kiamasumkin). Only two of those arrested, Crawfish Advancing and Little Chief, were on the 1848 list of five ringleaders issued by Henry Lee.[231] Of the other three on Lee's bounty list, Joe Lewis had escaped and the Indian posse had killed Tamsucky and Edward.

The prisoners were taken under armed guard more than 200 miles to Oregon City, where Joe Meek served as territorial marshal, and they were imprisoned on an island in the Willamette River until a trial could be held.[232] The Americans prepared an indictment charging the Cayuse men with killing Narcissa Whitman, "not then and there being an Indian."[233] Two militia officers and the Secretary of Oregon Territory were offered 50 horses for defending the accused men in court while U.S. Attorney, Amory Holbrook, prosecuted the case. Called to testify for the defense were Stickus and Dr. McLoughlin, both of whom testified, in part, that it was the Cayuse practice to kill medicine men if their patient died. Among those appearing for the prosecution was Henry Spalding. Associate Justice O.C. Pratt, who presided over the trial, instructed the jury that the Cayuse nation had surrendered the defendants, "the nation knowing best who those murderers were."[234]

On May 24, 1850, the jury found the defendants guilty and Judge Pratt pronounced a sentence of death. Henry Spalding was circulating among the hundreds of people who came to town to witness the hangings and he stated his belief that the tragedy at the Whitman mission was the result of a plot between Catholic missionaries and the Cayuse Indians. Marshal Joe Meek, on June 4, hung Crawfish Advancing, Little Chief, Clokomas, Frank Escaloom and Panther Shirt for the murder of Narcissa Whitman at Waiilatpu.

Back in July of 1848, William Craig had submitted written testimony as to what he believed to be the reasons behind the killing. It is unclear if his statement was read into the court record. He understood the Cayuse men's reasons for killing the Whitmans: it was traditional to kill the medicine man who did not effect a cure, and the deaths from disease among the Cayuse people had been staggering.

Ten years earlier he had seen the Blackfeet people perish from smallpox, and the tribes and trappers had believed the rumor that the Blackfeet had been purposefully infected in order to kill them off. The Cayuse men were doing what they thought was necessary to stop the dying before they had no families left alive. [235]

But the Indian way was no longer the way things were done on the plateau. The European fur traders and now the Americans had made enough inroads into traditional behavior that the Indian way was now secondary to that of the whites. Apparently, in order to pave the way for five men to give themselves up for certain hanging, Governor Joseph Lane had made a side agreement: he had promised immunity from punishment to the others involved. A newspaper article a week after the hangings indicated that the world did not know everything that transpired in the case:

Wm. Craig…says that he gave Governor Lane the names of eight other Indians who were equally guilty with the five who have been executed, but that the Governor only insisted on the delivery of the five… [Perrin] Whitman reports Mr. Craig as further saying that the understanding among the Cayuses is that the other eight are by the treaty which the Governor made with them, exempt from inquiry or prosecution. How is this?[236]

Indian anger over the hangings was to affect their relations with Americans for years to come: Albert H. Robie would, in 1856, listen as angry Nez Perce leaders recalled those hangings and others since that time. Only when white men were hung for wrongfully killing Indians would plateau tribes accept that American laws were just. The Cayuse people, to this day, continue to honor the sacrifice made by "the Cayuse five" (at least one of those men was probably not involved), and many Cayuse people continue to distrust laws and courts.[237]

Although revenge had been exacted on a small tribe of plateau Indian people, the Americans who had settled in the Pacific Northwest believed themselves guiltless. One historian has concluded:

Few white Americans went west intending to ruin the natives and despoil the continent. Even when they were trespassers, westering Americans were hardly, in their own eyes, criminals.[238]

And William Craig, although believing himself a true friend to his wife's people, exemplified Americans' thinking at that time. He came to the West to improve his chances for a good life, not to hurt others' chances for the same. It would take a number of years—and two treaties between the United States and the Nez Perces—before he distanced himself from his government's methods.

Meanwhile, Craig turned his attention back to the farm. It was spring and there was no end to the work waiting. He had broken more land to the plow and piled rocks into barriers to keep out wandering cattle. The family worked at plowing, fencing, watering and weeding and put more land under tillage each spring; visitors in later years reported they raised wheat, corn, potatoes, peas, tomatoes, squash and melons. There were fruit trees, and fenced pastures for cattle and their many horses. The Craig family was prospering.[239]

If Isabel Craig was typical of native fur-trappers' wives—and it seems that she was—she adopted some of her husband's people's ways while holding fast to many of her family's traditions. Native women taught their children to prepare animal hide clothing and containers, and sewed, beaded, and decorated the articles as their grandmothers and mother had taught them. A plateau floral design was beaded on special clothing and it became recognized as the Craig family crest; the four-petal design was worked in yellow and looked much like a buttercup.[240]

Isabel Craig was known for her intellect and strength of character. Long after her time on earth, a court of law included this description in its findings:

Isabel Craig, while an Indian was a woman of superior intelligence and conducted a home for him [William] similar to the homes of white men of that day, where they had the usual furnishings of such a home and where she prepared meals to which he invited his friends at which his friends were seated at the table with himself and wife..."[241]

With all that he accomplished in his lifetime, it is noteworthy that William was described as a man of unusual intelligence and activity while Isabel was described as a woman of superior intelligence. For an American court of law to make such designations leads to the conclusion that Isabel's legacy was one of great wisdom—she must have had more brainpower than her more prominent husband. Perhaps because she was particularly smart, one of the items in many American households that Isabel chose to avoid was alcohol—"Isabel did not drink such intoxicating liquors."[242]

Craig was, by nature, generous and helpful.[243] It was among his duties, as agent, to help his Nez Perce neighbors learn to farm. Because the Craigs prospered on their Lapwai Valley farm, they must have served as an example to interested Nez Perces of how to make a living while staying in one place and raising their own food.

One can only surmise about the day-to-day activities of the Craig household. It's highly likely that the older girls learned from their mother, aunts, and grandmother about root digging, preparing traditional foods, tanning, and handiwork—along with keeping house, cooking, and serving meals like their father's people did. Joe, now ten, probably shadowed his father at work in the fields and with the horse herd and other livestock. Isabel and the children—now including Mary, born August 24, 1850[244] —followed the teachings of the Catholic priests. All of the Craig children were likely fluent in the Nez Perce and English languages and Chinook jargon, but they probably spoke only *ni·mi·pu·tímt* around their elders.

Craig had continued his trading business since coming to live in the Lapwai Valley. He may have traded initially without a license, but government was making itself known in the Northwest. In April 1851, Craig received a license to trade with the Wasco, Columbia River, Deschutes, Yakama, Cayuse, Nez Perce, and Klickitat tribes. Francis (Frank) Newell, son of Doc and Kitty, was one of his two employees.[245] Craig's partner, George T. Allan, was a former HBC clerk with years of trading experience in the west and Hawaii.[246] Their business plan, as advertised in the *Oregon Spectator*, was to trade articles such as clothing, agricultural tools, and provisions that would benefit "the Indians or Emmigrants" at Wascopam.[247]

When he issued Craig's license to trade, Anson Dart was Oregon Territory's Superintendent of Indian Affairs, stationed in the Willamette Valley. A political appointee from Wisconsin, Dart would hold councils with tribes throughout the region. In the summer of 1852 he organized a trip to Nez Perce country, hiring Elkanah Walker and Perrin Whitman as interpreters.[248] The purpose of the trip was ostensibly to assess damages owed by the U.S. government to ABCFM for property loss following the killings at the Whitman mission and the looting of the Spalding mission buildings.

The Dart party's journey from the Willamette to the Lapwai Valley was without apparent danger. After passing through the deserted Whitman station at Waiilatpu, the party wended its way to the

Tucannon (*tuké·nen*, Nez Perce word for "digging") River, then across
the high, grassy hills before descending to Alpowa in the Snake River
canyon, where Dart noted apple trees in fruit and a field of corn, the
work of Red Wolf's and Timothy's families. Dart's party traveled up
the Snake and Clearwater rivers to the site of the Spaldings' former
mission and camped three miles above it. There they "met William
Craig, who was married to a Nez Perce woman, and who had remained
in the valley during the years following the Whitman Massacre."[249]

On June 26 a large number of Nez Perces came to meet and talk
with a representative of the United States government. The first band
came to the council grounds late in the afternoon and announced their
arrival with war whoops and drums. Walker described about 150
warriors galloping their painted horses back and forth; "the sight of
them look[ed] formidable. This was Joseph's band, led by himself."
The little group of white men stood in a tight knot in a clearing as the
warriors whooped, shot their guns, and circled their horses a number of
times before stopping in front of them. After honoring the group of
Americans, each band making a grand entry, the Nez Perces further
welcomed the Americans by performing their war dance.[250]

The men got down to business after passing the pipe. Nez Perce
leaders, with Craig interpreting, heard Dart's proposal from the
Americans that they wanted to make a treaty for land, and when the
time came to sit down and make such a treaty, "the Government was
willing to reserve their own lands for them" as reservations. The
meeting between the Nez Perce people, Craig, and Anson Dart's party
was full of pageantry, pipe smoke, and good talk—after which Dart,
highly satisfied, left the interior.[251]

There were a number of reasons the *ni·mí·pu* headmen did not reject
a proposal from the *so·yá·po·* leader in the East to buy land from them.
First, they had for many years traded with (and their women married)
British and American fur traders. As a result, the tribe's overall wealth
and status had continued to increase. Additionally, the idea of more
white men arriving in their country was not new. The Nez Perces and
their neighbors had long anticipated more white men coming after
making alliances with some who were already there. They expected to
profit from them in the future as they had in the past. Moreover, they
were well aware of the fates suffered by the Mohegan, Creek,
Cherokee, and other eastern people: many women and children had
died; still the Americans took their homelands from them. In talks
about the coming *so·yá·po·*, the Nez Perce headmen listened to Craig's
words. He was not afraid to fight an enemy—he also had a family to

protect—but he did not advise killing the white men. Craig and other former fur trappers told them that for every white man in Nez Perce country there were thousands more where the sun came up. The Nez Perces numbers were too small to win a war with the United States. Craig advised them not to fight but to keep their alliance and grow even wealthier from the new trade opportunities the Americans would bring.

After the Dart party returned to the Willamette Valley, life for the Craigs and the Nez Perces returned to the regular routines of making their living from fishing, farming, hunting, trading, and gathering. Large horse herds grazed the steep hills, and now cattle, sheep, and other livestock were to be found in the valley pastures.

Craig traded at Fort Walla Walla and with the Yakamas, Klickitats, Wascopams, Deschutes, and other downriver bands as well as with the Cayuses, Wallawallas and Palouses. The Hudson's Bay Company Fort Nez Perces/Walla Walla had long been a source of trade items. The trail was well worn between the Lapwai Valley, the HBC fort on the bend of the Columbia, the traditional trading center at *siláylo·* (Wascopam, The Dalles), and the Willamette Valley.

In the fall of 1851 Robert Newell wrote for Craig a letter of introduction to the proprietor of a store at The Dalles where Craig wished to trade. Newell wrote that his friend, "Mr. Craig, a partner at the Dalles," needed to buy some groceries and asked the merchant to let Craig have the supplies "on reasonable terms as you would Old Doc."[252] It was good to have friends to help make connections with the Americans coming West on the Oregon Trail, and the new business trading with the immigrants was very welcome.

1855 Sohon sketch of William Craig (Washington State Historical Society)

4
White Expansion into Washington Territory (1853-1855)

In 1853 the U.S. Congress created Washington Territory, including what is now Idaho, from Oregon Territory east and north of the Columbia and Snake. The new president, Franklin Pierce, appointed Isaac Ingalls Stevens its governor. Stevens was a first-in-his-class graduate of the U.S. Military Academy at West Point and, like Joe Lane, a veteran of the Mexican War and a Democrat. Just thirty-four years old, Stevens had ambitions for national political office. In addition to his commission as Washington Territorial Superintendent of Indian Affairs, Stevens also was assigned by the War Department to survey a possible northern route for a transcontinental railroad. Thus, when he came to the West, Stevens had three assignments—all aimed at opening the land to white settlement.[253]

A diminutive man at a height of five foot three inches, Stevens exuded confidence and ability. Described as a high-energy, intelligent individual who could be a masterful leader of men, he also struck some people as arrogant, insensitive, and rude. The name "Isaac Ingalls" was shortened to "I. I." by the press, which used it humorously, calling him "Two-Eyed Stevens" and writing phrases like, "Glory to II of Oregon."[254] The people who came in contact with Isaac Stevens either loved him or hated him. William Craig and Isaac Stevens were destined, during a tumultuous year, to work closely together.

While the first governor of Washington Territory was sailing to the West Coast, the Craig family added a new member. On June 12, 1853, daughter Anna was born.[255] They now had a rather large family in their comfortable house near Waha (later called Sweetwater) Creek and were quite unaware that the arrival of Isaac Stevens would change their lives considerably.

One of Stevens' first orders of business upon arrival in the muddy little settlement of Olympia was to seek, from white men, information about Indian tribes. He sent an express rider to William Craig, asking a number of specific questions about the Nez Perces, their country, and their wealth.[256]

Craig replied that he was so busy getting ready to "start below" (a trading trip to the Walla Walla Valley, HBC's Fort Walla Walla, the Columbia River villages, *siláylo·*, and/or the Willamette country) that he could not take time to write a very full explanation. He thought, however, there were about 2,000 Nez Perces divided into about ten bands living on the Snake, Salmon, and Clearwater rivers.[257] Stevens estimated 5,000 white inhabitants in all of Washington Territory at that time.[258] Craig noted that the Nez Perce people made a living by hunting, fishing, and farming, trading both at the Hudson's Bay Company post and at The Dalles. Craig stated that the Nez Perces owned "a great number of horses and some cattle." He described the country as "rough, but well adapted to stock raising," and he thought the best place for reservations to be the Snake River country. To Stevens' query about how the Nez Perces felt about making a treaty with the Americans, Craig said he had never asked the question nor heard them discuss such a matter (did Anson Dart's council slip his mind?), but Craig knew them "to be friendly disposed to the whites and especially to the American Government."[259]

In February 1854 the first Washington Territorial Legislature convened in Olympia. Sixteen counties were created—one of which, Walla Walla County, encompassed all the land now in eastern Washington, northern Idaho, and western Montana. Walla Walla County would be the predominant setting of the Craig family's activities for years to come.

In addition to the creation of Washington Territory, two pieces of legislation were passed in the United States Congress in the early 1850s that profoundly affected the Pacific Northwest. The first was the Oregon Donation Land Law of 1850 (9 Stat. 496), under which any white male adult U.S. citizen could claim 320 acres of public domain land in the Northwest; his wife could also claim 320 acres. In passing this law, Congress continued to recognize the validity of Indian "title" (an American—not American Indian—legal concept) to the land; but it had already violated its own laws by encouraging Americans to go to the Oregon Country and settle on lands before the government had acquired title to them.[260] Although the American government never set out to destroy the Indian people, it also never took its eye off their lands. Each year, more white people came to the Oregon Country for free land, and each year there were more confrontations between the Indians and the trespassing whites. To rectify the untenable situation it had created, Congress in 1854 authorized land treaties with Northwest Indians and Isaac Stevens was approved to conduct treaty councils with the tribes in Washington Territory.[261]

Since Oregon, California, and Texas had been annexed to the United States, it was no longer as feasible to remove Indians west of the Mississippi River, as it had been when the entire area west of the Mississippi was not part of the United States. Treaties were now being drafted calling for tribes to cede land to the United States and move their people onto small areas reserved for them, where they could be gradually assimilated into American culture while kept out of the way of American settlement.[262]

In addition to securing land for its constituents to settle on, Congress wanted to build a transcontinental railroad. Stevens had surveyed a possible route that went through Blackfeet Indian lands. For railroad construction to proceed, warfare between the Blackfeet and their neighbors must cease. It was to accomplish these goals—land cession, reservations, assimilation, and peace to enable railroad construction—that Stevens enlisted the support of William Craig and other white men living among the indigenous people in the Northwest.

Isabel and William, meanwhile, continued working on their home and farm and trading business, unaware that Stephens' letter signified Congressional machinations that would soon change their lives. The Craig home was on a main route between the Bitterroot and the Walla Walla valleys; in all seasons but winter there was a steady stream of travelers between those places. The majority of the travelers were Nez Perce or allied bands, and few of them traveled by the Craig establishment without stopping for food, animal care, sleep, or a visit. However, non-Indian people—although a minority—left the bulk of written records. One of the Craigs' visitors, George Hodges, had helped John Owen set up a trading post in the Bitterroot Valley. Hodges left The Dalles in November 1852, heading back to Fort Owen, and stopped at the Craig place. Hodges noted on December 14, 1852, that he was leaving the Craigs' ranch; he traveled as far as the deserted Spalding mission—which he noted was in a "Delapidated Condition." An elderly Nez Perce man warned him not to travel further in mid-winter: "[w]ith all the force of native eloquence & Life advised me to return & abandon the trip. I took his advice & returned to Mr. C." Hodges stayed with the Craig family until the end of January.[263] Also in the winter of 1853 Abiel W. Tinkham, following orders from Stevens, explored the Southern Nez Perce trail (between present Darby, Montana, and Elk City, Idaho). Traversing the trail from east to west through heavy snow, Tinkham reported on the hospitality of the Nez Perces with whom he stayed after descending the western slope and noted that William Craig had eight acres under tillage at his valley home.[264]

John Owen, who had purchased St. Mary's Mission in the Bitterroot Valley for his trading post, often transported goods and stock between the Walla Walla and Bitterroot valleys. In September 1854 Owen spent three days camped at the Craig farm and feasted "all the time on Melons Tomatoes Corn &c...which he [Craig] turned out to Myself & party with a liberal hand." Craig and a new neighbor, Henri M. Chase, rode with Owen as he left; they stopped at a creek, led the animals to the water and good grass, and then had "a parting glass" of whiskey Craig had brought for the occasion. The Craigs ran an inn, an operation where travelers could leave their horses and mules to graze. Owen "left at Mr Craigs two Mules and three horses..." and "Took from Mr Craig two Govt horses which I found fresh & fat."[265]

Shortly after Owen's visit, the Craigs welcomed another person who was to leave his imprint on the land and people. John Mullan, with an Indian guide and a small party of men from Stevens' railroad surveying team, traversed the Lolo Trail. They found it open, with little fallen timber cluttering the trail, and found no game larger than squirrels and grouse. After struggling for eleven days, they emerged onto the Weippe *qémes* (camas) prairie and then followed a wide road to the Clearwater River. On a warm, pleasant day in October 1854 they stopped at the Craig place, where they saw many pigs and chickens and obtained a large supply of vegetables.[266]

In Olympia, Stevens calculated how best to achieve the results Washington City expected of him. To extinguish the Indians' title to the land, Stevens planned to first make land treaties with the coastal people, next the tribes east of the Cascade mountain range, then those in the valley of the Bitterroot, ending with a Blackfeet peace council east of the Rocky Mountains. Some recent Nebraska treaties served as models for Stevens' drafts, the outcome of which would be to isolate Indians on tracts of land that would eventually be surrounded by American settlers.[267] In Stevens' view, the Indians had no choice but to sign treaties in much the same form as he wrote them. Once Indians had ceded the land, Stevens was to focus on building a vast new American empire in Washington Territory.

Before sailing back to the east coast, Governor Stevens in early 1854 assigned his staff responsibility for preparing the tribes to meet with him upon his return. After he conducted fieldwork with the coastal people, James Doty—a member of Stevens' railroad survey crew and the son of the former Wisconsin Territorial governor—went east of the Cascade Mountains to prepare for a treaty council with plateau tribes.

While Stevens and his men were laying groundwork for treaties, U.S. citizens in the Northwest were positioning themselves to claim the land expected to be purchased from the tribes—William Craig among them. The 1850 Donation Land Law required that land be cultivated for four years before it could be claimed; Craig had started farming near Waha Creek in mid-September 1846. On June 4, 1854, Craig filed paperwork at Washington Territory's newly established Land Office in Olympia, showing his intent to claim that land.[268]

In December 1854 Stevens returned to Olympia and before the end of January 1855 he had finalized four treaties with twenty-three different groups of coastal people, assigning each to a small reservation. A local newspaper published a list of surveyed reservations and informed its readers: "Information is given to the public, that settlers may take action accordingly in locating claims."[269] This announcement of treaty contents before Congressional ratification caused settlers to claim land prematurely—an action to be repeated (with violent results) after the upcoming treaty negotiations with the plateau tribes.

Isaac Stevens typified the belief among Americans that they were chosen to occupy and rule the North American continent from sea to sea, a movement dubbed "manifest destiny" in the mid-1840s by John O'Sullivan, a New York newspaper editor. It was from long accumulation of Indian-white history that Stevens and many Euro-Americans convinced themselves that the Indian civilization was inferior to that of Americans and that Indians deserved to be removed from the Americans' path. Less than one hundred years later, Adolph Hitler studied history and admired the efficiency with which United States government exterminated American Indian populations. Some historians believe that Hitler's concept of concentration camps, starvation, and uneven combat as means to annihilate the Jewish people was influenced by the United States' Indian policies.[270]

The idea of keeping Indians separate from whites had evolved after years of frontier violence as American settlement spread west; it appealed to humanitarians in America's East as a way to prevent Indians' destruction. A product of the process in America's South was a Supreme Court decision in 1831 holding that, once Indians signed treaties ceding land to the U.S. in return for protection, they were wards of the government (although somehow still sovereign).[271]

The indigenous coastal people dealt with, Stevens moved forward quickly to inform himself about conditions east of the Cascade Mountains and north of the Columbia River preparatory to setting up treaty talks. Among his contacts was HBC trader Andrew Dominique Pambrun, a son of Pierre. Stevens asked Pambrun for information on the Columbia Plateau people and Pambrun's response included the report of gold being found in the Colville area. Established in 1825 and named for Andrew W. Colvile, Fort Colvile was the Hudson's Bay Company fur-trading fort near Kettle Falls on the Columbia River.[272] The gold discovery had caused great excitement among white men and would likely bring more men to Colville in the spring.[273] Gold seekers trespassing on Indian lands usually led to trouble, another reason to hurry the plateau treaty process.

In February 1855 James Doty led a small party up the Columbia River from Portland to finalize arrangements for Stevens' council, and in early March William Craig rode into Doty's camp at The Dalles. Doty asked Craig if the reports circulating were true about the "Plots and Counterplots"—referring to rumor that many plateau tribes had gathered at the Grand Ronde, planning to join forces and drive away the white people. Craig assured Doty the Nez Perces were "perfectly quiet and as well disposed as formerly... All these Indians desire is payment for their lands and Reservations secured to them against the intrusion of the whites." After talking with Craig, Doty predicted that Stevens would have little trouble treating with the Nez Perces, Yakamas, and Wallawallas.[274]

However, a Cayuse faction continued to rally allies to fight the whites and get rid of them forever. When the railroad survey party came through the lands of the Yakama, Spokane, and neighboring tribes, messengers hurried between villages saying the whites had finally arrived to take away their lands. Many Palouse warriors, as well as some Nez Perces, joined the Cayuses who talked of defending their homelands.

Adding to the worries of the interior tribes was the continual buildup of United States soldiers: there were now military forts on the Columbia River at Vancouver, Cascades, and The Dalles. To police the situation as its citizens sought new homes in the fertile valleys of Oregon and Washington Territories, the U.S. Army was establishing its presence in the Northwest.

Qamáya'qin, one of the Yakama people's leaders, was also working to unite all Northwest tribes against the whites. Qamáya'qin was a politically powerful man who had an Asotin Nez Perce grandfather, a

Spokane grandmother, parents who were Snake River Palouse and Yakama, and a wife who was a daughter of a Yakama chief.[275] With blood and marriage ties to people across the Columbia River Basalts, as well as kinship with bands on the west side of the Cascades, Qamáya'qin was an influential man beyond his own tribe.

Father Charles Marie Pandosy, a Catholic missionary, had in 1853 warned settlers of the Indians' plans for a war against the Americans who were going to seize their lands.[276] The Indian strategy was for the people to meet with Stevens and hear what he had to say, but give up no land; each chief would instead insist on a reservation that encompassed the people's entire homeland. It was hoped they might buy time to rally a large enough war party to drive away the white people.[277]

Following protocol developed in its long history of treaty-making, the U.S. Congress had budgeted for tobacco, food, blankets, clothing, and tools to be given as gifts to Indians meeting Governor Stevens in treaty councils. Doty hired teamsters to transport the treaty goods from the coast to The Dalles, then ferried them by muletrain to the Walla Walla Valley council site. There were nine men in Doty's party, including agents Dr. Richard H. Lansdale and Anthony J. Bolon, Joel Palmer (who had been appointed commissioner), and a young man, A. H. Robie (who would one day marry one of the Craigs' daughters), who brought the wagons of supplies; William Craig, traveling back home from The Dalles, returned a strayed mule to Doty's packtrain and earned $15 for his trouble.[278] By late March, Doty's party was camped two-and-a-half miles east of Fort Walla Walla.

After meeting with the Yakama leaders, Doty and Dr. Lansdale made a three-day trip to meet with the Nez Perces. On April 15 they arrived at the Craig home, which Doty described as three "substantial log houses enclosed by a neat picket fence," on about thirty acres "well fenced and cultivated" with an "air of thrift and comfort."[279] Doty knew that Craig had lived among the Nez Perces for fourteen years and had earned their trust. He had already hired one interpreter who spoke all of the tribes' languages. He believed Craig would be "a good Nez Perce Interpreter & it may be politic to employ him as such."[280] Stevens agreed.

When Craig returned from a downriver trading trip the day after Doty arrived, he brought none of the instructions from Stevens that Doty had expected. Later in the day, however, William Pearson—a tough express rider from Pennsylvania who would share perilous times with Craig in the coming year—rode in with mail from Stevens, having made the journey from Vancouver in just six days.[281]

On April 17 Lawyer and ten other Nez Perce headmen, with 200 of their people, arrived.[282] Doty bought a beef from Craig and had it butchered and distributed to the people. The following day the Nez Perces trimmed the branches off a tall pine tree growing in the open, tied to the top of the bare trunk the American flag they had received in 1848 from Palmer, Lee, and Newell, and gathered around it for a council.[283]

After the pipe ceremony, Doty explained (with Craig interpreting) what commissioners Stevens and Palmer had in mind when asking for a council. It was much the same message that he had delivered to the Yakamas: the U.S. wanted to buy all of their land; "one or more" reservations would be set aside for the Nez Perces, who would have to live there. They could have houses, farms, and an agent, and no white person could come on their reservation without their permission. The government would build "a schoolhouse, blacksmith and carpenter shop, farm house and mills" and hire people to "manage them for the exclusive benefit of the Indians, and without charge." He spoke of the homestead provision of the U.S. government that allowed whites to claim land, and explained that Nez Perces could graze livestock on land that was not claimed. The people, Doty explained, would always be able to travel freely, to fish at the accustomed places and go to the mountains for berries and hunting. The Nez Perce children would be taught to read and write and be trained as carpenters, blacksmiths, millers, and farmers, so they could take their place among the whites.[284]

The Nez Perces received Doty's talk in silence. The headmen then briefly discussed his proposal among themselves before agreeing to meet with Gov. Stevens and General Palmer. They went along with Qamáya'qin's choice of the Walla Walla Valley as council grounds—rather than Craig's place, which they preferred—even though several of the bands lived more than a hundred miles away on the Salmon River and it was doubtful they could be induced to travel as far as the Walla Walla Valley.[285] Doty then asked William Craig to act as an official interpreter at the council, which was set for May 20.[286] After distributing presents, Doty left the council, believing that a "general good feeling seemed to prevail."[287]

The council site selected by Doty was six miles from Waiilatpu on Mill Creek.[288] The area had always been a good place to meet because there was some timber for fires, good water, plenty of grass for horse feed, and enough space for all the people to set up their tepees. The site held special significance for the Americans: Stevens and Palmer later pointed out to the Commissioner of Indian Affairs, the "Council Ground was in the Cayuse country near the place consecrated by the blood of the Missionary Dr. Whitman and his family who were killed in 1847 by the Indians of the Cayuse tribe."[289] It had not been eight years since that event.

People from many points on the plateau soon began traveling toward the council grounds. William Craig rode out ahead and informed Doty on May 17 that the Nez Perces were on their way; when he left them they were at the mouth of the Clearwater (now Lewiston, Idaho). On May 21, wet from riding in the rain, Isaac Stevens and Joel Palmer arrived. In the morning of Thursday, May 24, Nez Perce people arrived: about 900 had come—nearly half the tribe—and they made their usual grand entrance.[290] The colorful sight of painted warriors on decorated horses was noteworthy, and Gustavus Sohon, a soldier with artistic talent, captured the scene as quickly as he could sketch. In the sketch William Craig, taller than most and wearing a plumed hat, stands with the Nez Perce leaders facing the white men of the treaty team. They are gathered at a flagstaff.[291]

Only a portion of the Palouse people came, yet most tribes east of the Cascades were represented. Two days after the arrival of the Nez Perces, the Cayuse and Wallawalla leaders came with about 400 people. Their warriors whooped, sang, and rode around the Nez Perce camp but did not so honor the white men's camp. Although they shook hands with Stevens and the other officials, they refused the offers of the pipe and gifts. There were Yakamas from north of the Columbia – who also refused provisions and pipe—and headmen from the basin formed by the Columbia's bend.[292] In all 1,800 to 2,000 Indian people and just over 100 white men congregated in the Walla Walla Valley.[293]

In addition to Isaac I. Stevens, Commissioner for Washington Territory, and Joel Palmer, Commissioner for Oregon Territory, the officers included the two territorial secretaries, James Doty of Washington Territory, and William C. McKay of Oregon Territory. Agent R. F. Lansdale was "in charge of Washington Nes Perses, Cayuses and Walla Wallas," while Agent R. R. Thompson was "in charge of Oregon Nes Perses, Cayuses and Walla Wallas." William Craig was the interpreter from Washington Territory, Mr. Daupher and John Flette interpreters from Oregon Territory.[294] Also on the treaty grounds was Lt. Archibald Gracie, commanding a detachment of more than 40 regular army troops requisitioned by Stevens and Palmer from Major Gabriel J. Rains at The Dalles.[295]

Both sides in the "negotiations" recognized the importance of accurate interpretation. Yellow Bird had requested more than one interpreter at the council, "that we may know they translate truely."

After the opening day's pipe ceremony, Stevens began: "My Children," he said,

Before entering upon the council we must have good and faithful interpreters. We want men who will state truly and exactly all that is said; we want men that you know to be good men; men that you can trust. We want no others. We propose as interpreters for the Nes Perces, William Craig, this man, [pointing to Mr. Craig] who has longer lived with you, also McDouphin [Mr. Daupher] and Delaware Jim.[296]

Stevens then proposed two white men (A. D. Pambrun and Nathan Olney) as Cayuse interpreters and John Whitford for the Wallawallas. The headmen agreed to the choices, and an oath was administered to the interpreters:

You solemnly swear in the presence of Almighty God, that you will well and truly interpret to the best of your ability what may be said by the Commissioners for the United States holding this council on the one part; and the cheifs [sic] and head men of the tribes and bands of Indians here present on the other part. So help you God.[297]

The interpreter's job was to translate, sentence by sentence, the spoken words of delegates: a crier then repeated the translation to the Indian people; Indian-white translation involved no criers. In the case of the Nez Perce people, William Craig translated the commissioner's English sentences into Nez Perce or Chinook jargon to Timothy, who acted as crier for his nation during the council. Timothy would repeat in a loud voice to his people the sentence Craig had translated. Conversely, when a Nez Perce delegate spoke, Craig translated their Nez Perce into English for the commissioners and secretaries. Translating speeches was a slow and cumbersome process.

However, the meaning of some Nez Perce speeches as recorded in the official proceedings is impossible to determine, raising questions about the accuracy of the interpreting, the recording, or both. Chinook jargon, the ancient Northwest trade language, could have been spoken at times in council, for most Native Americans and those whites not new to the area were fluent in it.[298] Chinook jargon had been the language used when Stevens met the coastal people in treaty councils.[299] However, the jargon's simplistic vocabulary was not adequate to express complex ideas or subtleties. It would not be surprising that many native delegates believed the depth of their feelings or the logic of their words was not well translated if Chinook jargon was a part of the interpretation process.

Although the valley of the Walla Walla had long been a rendezvous site, it is doubtful the valley had ever witnessed such a meeting as the one held in late May 1855.[300] Near the flagpole was an "arbor" of upright poles with a platform of boughs. Stevens and Palmer sat on a bench under the arbor near Stevens' tent, with the Indians facing them in a semicircle. The chiefs sat in the first rows with their people ranged behind them—often as many as 1,000 people—with women and children at the back. At a makeshift table near Stevens and Palmer sat the secretaries, charged with taking minutes of the proceedings; also recording the proceedings were Timothy and Lawyer—who had earlier worked with Spalding and Asa Smith to, for the first time, put the Nez Perce language into writing—and perhaps one or two other men. There was a table from which the agents distributed to headmen goods such as clothing, blankets, sugar, and coffee. The bulk of the merchandise was stored in a nearby log structure Doty had built for that purpose. The forty-seven-man military force under Lt. Gracie bivouacked in huts made of boughs and pack covers near the commissioners' tents, and about a half-mile or more away, around the periphery of the council site, were the tepees of each tribe.[301] Stevens' little black pony, brought by Doty to the council for the governor's use, was one of thousands of horses.[302] A herd of cattle purchased from Brooke, Bomford, and Noble's cattle ranch at Waiilatpu provided meat for the people.[303] As far as the eye could see were people, horses, mules, cattle, tepees, and cooking fires: it was a meeting of large scale.

The first few days of formal council heard only the words of Stevens, Palmer, their interpreters, and tribal criers. Based on Stevens' perception that his government was soon to be the father and the Indians its wards, he continued to address the leaders as "my children." For long hours Stevens and Palmer talked of all the goods and services the tribes would be paid for land they "didn't need."

Most evenings the Nez Perce camp—and it seemed to be the Nez Perce camp only—was the site of horse races, foot races, gambling, dancing and drumming. Some of the bets on the winner of a footrace were as high as 16 or 18 blankets. The sounds of singing and drumming would go on into the night, with shadows of dancers silhouetted around the fire.[304]

After three days of speeches by Palmer and Stevens, the commissioners wanted to conduct no business the next day, a Sunday. Yellow Bird disagreed. Indian leaders were waiting for their turn to speak and Sunday would be as good a day as any, even though it seemed to the other tribal leaders that the Nez Perces had already made agreements with the white men through their interpreter, William Craig:

It appears that Craig knows the hearts of his [white] people, that the whole has been prearranged in the hearts of the [Nez Perce] Indians; that he [Craig] wants an answer [from other tribal leaders] immediately without giving them time to think.[305]

Although he was ready for an opportunity to speak what was in his heart and on his mind, Yellow Bird's distrust of the white men overcame his impatience. He had spent time in California; he had watched white men and Indians do business. After hearing Stevens and Palmer talk for three days, he still disbelieved them. He urged Stevens and Palmer to tell the truth: "Speak straight...you have spoken in a manner tending to Evil."[306]

Deferring to the Christian Nez Perces and explaining that, "We do not wish to speak on Sunday because our Great Chief does not want us to do business on that day," Stevens adjourned council until Monday.[307] When it reconvened Monday, June 4, the Indian leaders finally spoke in turn. Toward the end of the day, Stevens presented what the Indians had been waiting to hear: which lands the commissioners called "reservations." Stevens proposed one reservation in Nez Perce country for the Cayuses, Umatillas, Wallawallas, Spokanes, and Nez Perces and one in Yakama country for the Yakamas, Colvilles, Okanagans, Palouses, Klickitats, and some other plateau people.

The Indian leaders were thunderstruck.

That night, desolation and anger hung over the camps of the Cayuses, Wallawallas, Umatillas, and Yakamas. Dancing, singing, and drumming went on until late in the Nez Perce camp, but the other camps were quiet. Cayuse, Wallawalla, and Umatilla leaders could not entertain the possibility of being moved from their homelands to lands

of the Nez Perces. According to their descendants, they were not just
hostile to the two-reservation plan, but flatly refused to leave their
homelands.[308] Men met and discussed the plan for the warriors to unite,
kill the soldier escort and the other white people at the council, and
then attack the fort at The Dalles before wiping out the white settlers.[309]
But the majority of Nez Perces refused to join the attack and it did not
go forward without them. During the night Lawyer had his family's
lodge moved from the Nez Perce camp to Stevens' camp, perhaps
seeking safety from those angry at his friendship with the whites.[310]

Meanwhile, alternative approaches to overcome that hostility were
being explored by Isaac Stevens and the Nez Perces. By the time the
formal council reconvened the next day, a strategy was in place to
move the process forward toward signed treaties.

Council minutes for June 5 contain Stevens' words trying to
convince each tribe they were better off together on one or two
reservations than on separate reservations surrounded by whites.
Palmer explained the railroad and telegraph lines and roads soon to
come through their countries. In response, Stickas tried to make the
commissioners understand that what they proposed would take their
mother, the earth that nurtured them all and held the graves of their
ancestors, from the Cayuses, Umatillas, and Wallawallas. Five Crows
said he needed time to think. Council was set again for the next day.

No council was held the following day, however, and it was not
until Thursday, June 7 that council reconvened. Stevens called
immediately for the Indians' thoughts on the proposals. Lawyer, as
Nez Perce "head chief," was first to speak. Although he rambled, his
message was clearly in favor of a treaty with the United States.
Thinking ahead to implementing the United States' offer of teachers,
mills, gunsmiths, blacksmiths and carpenters, Lawyer thought the
"stream just below where Mr. Craig lives will be a good place for one
mechanic."[311]

Then, on June 8, Commissioner Palmer offered the Cayuses,
Umatillas, and Wallawallas a separate reservation on the Umatilla
River. It appears that the offer may have been made after Stevens,
Craig and some Nez Perce leaders came up with a plan to sway
recalcitrant leaders toward signing treaties. It is speculated that the
plan was as follows: the Wallawallas, Cayuses and Umatillas could
share a small reservation on the Umatilla River; no other tribes would
be placed with the Nez Perces (Stevens would deal with the Spokanes
later); as a trade-off for working to keep the Nez Perce leaders allied to

the United States William Craig would not have to leave his Lapwai Valley ranch when that land became part of the Nez Perce reservation. With the Nez Perces offered a large reservation in their own lands, having to share it with no other tribes—and with Craig as his go-between—Stevens could keep some strong Nez Perce leaders loyal to the United States. Without the support of the Nez Perces, those hostile to the United States would be unable to raise enough of an Indian coalition to attack the whites at the treaty grounds. And the treaties would be signed.[312]

There is no written record that such a deal was struck, but the likelihood is compelling. The paperwork for Craig's land claim was prepared at the treaty grounds, after council hours; the process was not reflected in council minutes. Further evidence that such a deal was cut appears in a letter from Stevens to Secretary of War Jefferson Davis stating that the Nez Perces were in his hands, that he had managed them, and did so without force.[313]

The commissioners proposed a reservation on Yakama lands to be occupied by Yakamas, Klickitats, Palouses, and other people whose homelands were East of the Cascades within the big bend of the Columbia River.[314] (The Sinkiuses, Wenatchees, Rock Islands, and others would be placed on the Yakama reservation even though they were not represented at the council.)

If the treaties about to be consummated resulted from an after-hours agreement, Craig was the linchpin holding together the agreement between the Nez Perces and Stevens. Somewhere in camp on June 4— probably after council adjourned at 6:00 p.m.—papers were prepared pursuant to the Donation Land Claim Act for the 640-acre tract Craig had been preparing to claim in the Lapwai Valley. Two men, Henri Chase and William C. (Billy, "Sleep Eyes") McKay, had sworn before Henry R. Crosbie, clerk of the federal district court in Clark County and commissary to the treaty council, that Craig had lived on the tract since they had known him.[315] Craig met the four-year cultivation requirement of the law, as Chase had known him since mid-October 1849, McKay since early June 1847. Because a married couple could each claim 320 acres of land, Louis (The Mosquito) Raboin signed an affidavit that William and Isabel had lived together as man and wife from the 6th day of July 1838 until the present and that "they are and were reputed by their neighbors as such during said period."[316] Thus was the stage set for William and Isabel Craig to acquire legal title to 640 acres of land within the boundaries of a reservation to be set aside for the exclusive use of the Nez Perce people.[317]

The American proposal treated the Nez Perce nation more favorably than it did the other tribes. Although Yellow Bird (who had a Nez Perce wife and offspring living on the Potlatch River in Clearwater country) pleaded for the Indians to remain friends and brothers, resentment was strong. Five Crows put it straight: "Listen to me you Chiefs. We have been as one people with the Nez Perces theretofore; this day we are divided."[318] The wedge that white settlers first drove between the plateau tribes after the Whitman massacre was being forced deeper.

As long as they did not have to leave the country where their families were buried and move to the Nez Perce land, Cayuse leaders concluded that they had no choice but to agree to the treaty and provide a safe place for their people; Umatilla and Wallawalla leaders also agreed to move onto the shrunken lands. The paper to which they were about to put their marks promised they would have a year to move onto their reservations after Congress ratified their treaty and Stevens said that they would not have to move for two or three years.[319] The treaties with Americans would keep their families safe until they could consider, without rush, what next to do.

By June 8 the chiefs and head men of the Yakamas, Palouses, Klickitats, Wallawallas, Cayuses, Umatillas, Nez Perces, and smaller tribes and bands were prepared to sign the three treaties prepared for them. Qamáya'qin, who had refused to consider such a thing, was pressured by other Yakama chiefs to accede to the treaty—but he and his brothers believed they were misled as to the type of document they were asked to sign: they thought that it pledged friendship only.[320]

Wallawalla chief Yellow Bird seemed resigned, as did Young Chief of the Cayuses. Descendants of the Wallawalla, Cayuse and Umatilla treaty-signers are today united as the Confederated Tribes of the Umatilla Indian Reservation, through which the Umatilla River runs—and Young Chief is credited with not having bargained away the land of the Cayuse nation.[321]

Following the statement of Old Joseph of the Wallowa Nez Perces that the reservation would be a safe place for his children, "a place to live, a place for our good...," Red Wolf stood and made the following request:

I want Mr. Craig to stay there in the Nez Perce country, and not go away. The reason why I wish Mr. Craig to stay there is because he understands us. He speaks our language well. When there is any news

*that comes into the country we can go to him and hear it straight. The
same for us when anybody comes to speak to us he will set down with
us and we understand them. It is good for him to stay there to interpret
on both sides so that each can understand the other.*[322]

A clause was inserted in the treaty between the United States and
the Nez Perce Nation:

*Article 10. The Nez Perce Indians having expressed in council a
desire that William Craig should continue to live with them, he having
uniformly shown himself their friend, it is further agreed that the tract
of land now occupied by him, and described in his notice to the register
and receiver of the land-office of the Territory of Washington, on the
fourth day of June last, shall not be considered a part of the reservation
provided for in this treaty, except that it shall be subject in common
with the lands of the reservation to the operations of the intercourse
act.*[323]

The delegates were preparing to sign the treaty documents when Old
Looking Glass unexpectedly joined the council. He and his
companions had ridden hard, coming from the Bitterroot Valley in just
seven days, and he immediately reversed the direction of the
negotiations: "My people, what have you done? While I was gone you
have sold my country."[324]

The majority of the Nez Perces at the Walla Walla council was of
pro-*so·yá·po·* persuasion; and now Old Looking Glass interjected his
point of view. He did not trust the Americans and usually advocated
clearing the country of them. On this matter long-time companions Old
Looking Glass and Thunder's Eye disagreed. Eagle from the Light was
another leader who steadfastly repelled friendship with Americans: his
wife was a Shoshone, they lived with their family at the mouth of Slate
Creek on the Salmon River, and he was to eventually seek alliances
with the Shoshones and Salt Lake Mormons to drive out the
Americans.[325] Whatever their reaction was to the proposals, however,
most leaders recognized the futility of war.

On Sunday the Nez Perces held their own council, evidently
considering a proposal to appoint Old Looking Glass "head chief"
instead of Lawyer. A white observer commented: "Should this
proposition be carried into effect it would give a quietus to the
treaty."[326] Lawyer rallied enough support to remain "head chief" of

the Nez Perces—but even so Old Looking Glass remained a strong leader.

Stevens was anxious to be done with the treaties and move on, and between June 9 and June 11 three treaties were signed. [327] The first was with the Wallawalla, Cayuse, and Umatilla tribes, the second with the Yakama, Palouse, Klickitat, Wenatchee, and allied people, and the third with the Nez Perce tribe. Stevens announced that the treaties and speeches would be sent to the president for approval, that he expected to hear back from the president the following year, and that he expected the treaties to be approved. (An oversimplification: the treaties had to be ratified by the U.S. Congress, a process that was not accomplished until 1859.) As Red Wolf had asked, William Craig was designated the interpreter for the Nez Perces. William H. Tappan was to be their agent. The Umatillas, Cayuses and Wallawallas would come under the authority of Joel Palmer of Oregon Territory.

Stevens, in just over one year, had finalized fifteen treaties, the ratification of which would clear much of the Northwest of native title. [328] Stevens announced his next stop on the treaty-making trip was to be a council for peace with the Blackfeet in the buffalo country. To the Nez Perces he said:

> ...*nearly one fourth of your people live there. ... I want some chiefs of courage and character, and one hundred of your braves to go to that council. I say to Lawyer, the head cheif, of the Nez Perce's, I would be glad to have him go, I would be glad to have Looking Glass go. Arrange this among yourselfs. I hope and trust that Mr. Craig will go with you.* [329]

Stevens also wanted some Cayuse, Wallawalla, Umatilla and Yakama leaders to go to Blackfeet council with him, as well as Flatheads, Coeur d'Alenes, Kootenais, and possibly Spokanes. (If any went, their presence was not reflected in the signed Blackfeet treaty.) He promised to visit the Nez Perces and the Yakamas after he returned from the Blackfeet council.

Among the closing speeches were two from people closely associated with the Craig family. Theentheenmeetsa of the Catholic Cayuses, who would one day be their chief, pointed out that the U.S. government had trouble controlling its citizens but that Indians were in no position to insist on parity. "We are never the beginners in doing wrong to the whites. All Indians here understood well what has been said. When your white children come into this country they do things at random."[330]

Thunder's Eye had said nothing on the record during the long days of negotiations, but he (as "James") was the fourth signer of the treaty. He now explained the influence both Henry Lee and his own son-in-law, William Craig, had on him and the service William provided in the changing world of the Nez Perces:

It is not from anything bad that I have not spoken. It [is] as though the man I speak of is not of the party. When the white people came to my country Mr. Lee told me when he came there he was coming for good and not for bad. When the white people come and they would come in great numbers do not do anything bad to them. I have never done bad to them. I wish Mr. Craig to stay with us and hear the Indians speak for he could speak to our people and they could understand him—therefore I wish him to stay.[331]

The Council officially closed on June 11, 1855. James Doty believed that the council and resultant treaties would avoid bloodshed and expensive wars by accomplishing the "almost absolute necessity of opening this land... to occupation by the Whites."[332]

There was pronounced relief on the part of the white men. Agents distributed gifts of coffee, sugar, beef, and flour to the headmen and chiefs, who then divided them among their people. Stevens' clerks and secretaries "were busily employed in preparing the correspondence for the Department at Washington and notices for the newspapers in Oregon and Washington Territories."[333] The military struck camp and left to join Major Granville O. Haller's command near the Umatilla River.

To honor the occasion, the Nez Perces put on a scalp dance, using a fresh scalp brought by Old Looking Glass from the buffalo country, before preparing to move. If usual practice prevailed, by the day following the council's end the Nez Perce women would have packed in parfleches their family's fancy clothes and household goods, struck their tepees and loaded their horses.

William Pearson was sent to Olympia with, among other things, a packet containing the three treaties. Transport between east and west coasts was usually done by ship. The packet would have arrived in New York in about three months and by early September it was likely on the desk of the Commissioner of Indian Affairs in Washington D.C.

Less than two weeks after the council ended, the notices that had been prepared for the newspapers were in print. One, published in the *Oregon Weekly Times* over the signatures of Stevens and Palmer, read in part:

By an express provision of the treaty the country embraced in these cessions and not included in the reservation is open to settlement, excepting that the Indians are secured in the possession of their buildings and implements till removal to the reservation. This notice is published for the benefit of the public...Oregon and Washington papers please copy.[334]

Stevens deployed his staff strategically in order to be ready to hold at least four more treaty councils before winter. Traveling toward the Flathead country, he and his party stopped in Red Wolf's and Timothy's village on the Snake River and again at the Catholic's Coeur d'Alene mission of the Sacred Heart and arrived in the Bitterroot Valley in early July.[335] Rather than treat with the Spokane and Coeur d'Alene people on his trip east, Stevens had left Andrew Bolon to arrange a council with those tribes on the return trip. Bolon was also to reconnoiter the new Yakama reservation to be sure there was enough room for additional people.

William Tappan, the new Nez Perce Indian agent, was told to travel through the Nez Perce country, learn all he could about the different bands of people and the "character of reservation," and collect a "proper delegation to attend the Blackfeet Council."[336] Craig's duties were to help Tappan and then to meet Stevens' party in the Bitterroot Valley.

The Nez Perce men agreeing to come to the Blackfeet peace council included leaders of bands that regularly crossed the mountains to hunt buffalo and who just as regularly fought the Blackfeet. Craig and Tappan joined men who had great interest in making peace with the Blackfeet: Old Looking Glass, Three Feathers of the lower Clearwater, Eagle from the Light from the Salmon, Plenty Bears from the Snake River country, White Bird from Lamata on the Salmon, Jason from Asotin, Spotted Eagle from Kamiah, and Stabbing Man from Lapwai.[337] Thunder's Eye did not go to the Blackfeet council so he could keep an eye on the young men at home.[338] The Nez Perce delegates met at the South Fork of the Clearwater River and traveled together over the South Nez Perce trail.

Stevens was midway through the treaty council with the Flathead, Kootenai, and Pend d'Oreille leaders when Craig and his party arrived. The council lasted from July 9 until July 16, when the chiefs and leaders placed their marks on a treaty much like those signed at the Walla Walla council. William Craig was among the white men who, besides interpreting for the Nez Perces, signed as a witness to the treaty.[339] The Flatheads/Kootenais/Pend d'Orielles treaty resulted in some 25,000 square miles of land being ceded to the United States; as Stevens left the council grounds, "he boasted that 11,300 of 15,000 Indians in his jurisdiction were under treaties."[340]

All of the Stevens' treaties up to this point had been for land, but the next treaty was to be different: Stevens planned to treat with the Blackfeet bands for peace. In return for promises of peace between the Blackfeet and their perennial enemies, Stevens was to offer them land north of the Missouri River and annuities from the U.S. government. With peace on the plains, he believed, he could convince Congress to fund the transcontinental railroad line by the northern route.

One of the men in Stevens' treaty party, A. H. Robie, had come west as a "cook boy" with the railroad survey crew.[341] Both Craig and Robie were part of the team supporting Stevens' treaty-making plans, and Craig could hardly have guessed that Robie would someday play a role not only in the Craig family but in the future of Boise City, Idaho Territory. For now, however, Robie served as a laborer on Governor Stevens' pack train while his future bride, Martha Craig, was a thirteen-year-old in a comfortable house in the Lapwai Valley.

On July 30, Craig, William Tappan, Thomas Adams, John Owen, and Benjamin Kiser left the Bitterroot Valley, heading across the Continental Divide to join the Stevens party for the Blackfeet council.[342] Soon the Nez Perce and Flathead delegations joined Craig's group, and for the next week they all traveled together. After they received word from Stevens that supplies from St. Louis for the council had not yet arrived (the American Fur Company boat had offloaded the goods at Fort Union rather than 300 miles closer at Fort Benton) it became critical that food be provided for all the people gathering for the council.[343] The Nez Perces and Flatheads and Tappan left to hunt buffalo, while Craig and the others continued toward Fort Benton.

After days of travel, Craig and his companions reached Stevens' camp on the Teton River above Fort Benton. The camp was near where Craig had jumped from the bateau years earlier, as a young man just entering the fur trade. He had been in the area many times during his fur-trade days, but it was no doubt a pleasure to once again see the familiar bluffs and serpentine path of the Missouri River.

When Stevens found no supplies and no co-commissioner (Alfred Cumming had been appointed) waiting for him, he angrily started down the Missouri to meet them. The Indians scattered in search of food and Stevens sent his staff out to hunt buffalo, for the people gathered near Fort Benton for the big council were getting hungry.

When the supplies finally arrived at Fort Benton, Stevens doled out the liquor to his men, and for days the fort was the scene of "fighting, cursing, and general uproar." Cumming accused Stevens of irresponsible behavior, but Stevens said that his men had been "engaged in continuous, arduous duty since April and deserved an opportunity to let off steam"[344]

While John Owen had traveled with Craig and his party to Fort Benton for the Blackfeet council, when the start date was delayed he (along with many others) found it necessary to return home. The same day that Owen headed back to his trading post in the Bitterroot Valley, William Pearson rode into Stevens' camp with the packet of mail.[345]

Pearson had ridden from Olympia (a distance of more than 550 miles) in just twenty days, and would return after a short rest. Among the letters was one for William Craig from acting governor Charles Mason. Mason's letter informed Craig that the voters of Walla Walla County had elected him to Washington Territory's Legislative Assembly. On his return trip, Pearson carried Craig's letter back to Olympia:

> *Camp on the Missouri near Fort Benton*
> *Nebraska Territory*
> *Aug 27 1855*
>
> *Sir:*
>
> *Understanding that I have been elected at the last General Election to represent the County of Walla Walla in the Legislative Assembly of the Territory of Washington. I herewith tender you my resignation, circumstances being such as to prevent my accepting the honor conferred upon me.*
>
> *Respectfully*
> *Yr obt Svt*
> *William Craig*[346]

Craig was now Isaac Stevens' conduit to the Nez Perce nation: he could hardly accept a job that would distance him from the tribe. Moreover, holding public office was probably not wise for a man with a secret or felonious past. Perhaps Craig felt torn by his dilemma, but his quick response did not suggest that the decision was a difficult one.

The shorter days of September and early October were spent waiting for the boats to arrive and trying to keep the tribes near enough to Fort Benton to attend the council when it was convened. Wrestling the boats upriver was taking longer than anyone had imagined, but finally they were reportedly nearby and the date of October 3 was set for the council to begin.

Craig was among Stevens' staff that rode out to notify tribal encampments to head for Fort Benton. The Crows could not be found, although they had been on the Big Horn River. But disease had come upon them: many had died of the measles and the rest had fled. Craig, Tappan, pack master Christopher P. Higgins, Delaware Jim, and a voyageur named Légaré, rode hard up the Yellowstone River, "making fifty miles a day," and on October 6 Craig accompanied a large delegation of Nez Perce chiefs to the council grounds. The Nez Perce delegation did not bring their families, for theirs was a large camp and they were afraid there would be insufficient game to feed them. The Snakes could not be found, the Blackfeet were en route, the Gros Ventres were on the Milk River, the Piegans on the Honkee, and the Pend d'Oreilles on the Highwood. There were huge herds of buffalo between the Marias and Milk Rivers, coming within twenty miles of Fort Benton. The tribes were now together at the council grounds for what the Nez Perces referred to as the "hunting treaty."[347]

But the supply boats still did not come, so Stevens moved the council from Fort Benton to the place the boats had reached. The new council grounds were on a wide, level plain on the left bank of the Missouri River just below the mouth of the Judith River, some hundred miles to the east of Fort Benton.[348] On the sagebrush plain were now camped 3,500 representatives of the Blackfeet nation: Gros Ventres, Piegans, Bloods and Blackfeet—along with Nez Perces, Pend d'Oreilles, Kootenais and Flatheads—in fifteen large camps.[349]

Governor Stevens' camp was under big cottonwood trees. Just downriver was the camp of about one hundred German boatmen who had dragged the supplies up the river; "having many fine voices among them [they] were fond of spending the evenings in singing." The "office tent" used by Governor Stevens was a large lodge, a "great cone of poles covered with dressed and smoke-stained buffalo skins." Late every night, after the work was done, Stevens would host a "feast of buffalo ribs, flapjacks with melted sugar, and hot coffee." He would invite some of the tribal delegates, some interpreters and other staff; they would pass around whole sides of ribs and each man would "cut off a rib for himself with his hunting knife and sit there...tearing off the juicy and delicious meat with teeth and knife, principally the former." Everyone had a good appetite and enjoyed listening as "Craig, Delaware Jim, or Ben Kiser related some thrilling tale of trapper days, or desperate fight with Indian or grizzly bear."[350]

The peace talks that would forever change inter-tribal relations in the Rocky Mountain region opened the morning of October 16. The Blackfeet leaders came ready to do business, for Stevens' staff had been working with them for two years to make peace with their neighbors. William Craig and Delaware Jim were sworn in as official interpreters for the Nez Perces, who were there as observers. Stevens came to the council with a map on buffalo hide and a treaty containing sixteen articles ready for signature, but first he put to rest the rumors that land was to be taken from the tribes. "We want you to have cattle and raise crops.... This country is your home. It will remain your home..."[351] Diplomacy was the watchword, and there was little opposition to the proposals. "Peace, friendship, and amity" was to exist henceforth between the United States and all the parties to the treaty.[352] Clauses similar to those in the Walla Walla treaties prohibited liquor, promised annuities, teachers, goods and services designed to help the Blackfeet Nation stop hunting buffalo ("the Great Father does not want you to starve when the Buffalo passes away") and become farmers.[353] When the council closed on October 17, every important chief, headman, and delegate representing the Piegans, Bloods, Gros Ventres, and Blackfeet had made his mark after the signatures of Cumming and Stevens. Twelve Nez Perce leaders made their mark on the treaty; William Craig and Delaware Jim signed as Nez Perce Interpreters.[354] The treaty council that had taken two years of preparation was finished in two days.

With the hunting treaty finished, the Nez Perce headmen who had come with Craig from their camp on the Yellowstone River collected their share of the goods and rode back to their families. Commissioner Cumming started for St. Louis.[355] The Nez Perce delegation from west of the mountains, along with William Craig, started toward the South Nez Perce trail. Isaac Stevens, James Doty and twenty-three other men pulled out of the Judith country heading toward Fort Benton, planning to treat next with the Coeur d'Alenes.

Down in the Bitterroot Valley, more than 200 miles away, John Owen noted in his journal that William Pearson had spent the night with him and left the following morning with "Mch Mail for Gov Stevens Camp at Fort Benton."[356] When, three days later, an exhausted Pearson rode into camp carrying mail, Isaac Stevens' forward momentum came to an abrupt halt. Pearson brought a letter from Mason containing:

> ...the startling intelligence that the Yakima Indians had broken out into open war. Murdered their Agent A. J. Bolon, and several other White men on their way to the mines near Fort Colville, and declared a war of extermination upon the Whites. [It was believed] that other Tribes would join them.[357]

As Stevens would later discover, events had been unfolding in relatively undramatic fashion since they left the Walla Walla Valley. News of the gold strike in the Colville region had triggered the expected spate of gold seekers.[358] And as soon as the newspaper stories prematurely opened the plateau to white settlement, people from Puget Sound headed east. A young Yakama warrior, Qualchan (son of Owhi), was the leader of a band of warriors who attacked and killed miner Henry Matisse and two companions after they crossed Snoqualmie Pass in the summer, and shortly thereafter a group of five miners was killed on the Yakima River.[359] These murders were not the result of policy by Qamáya'qin or other Yakama chiefs, but rather the work of young men acting independently to avenge the rape of one of their women by miners.[360] The gold strike at Colville was not particularly rich, and the number of miners decreased with the approach of winter, but then several young Yakama men committed a deed that started a war.

After spending the summer with the Yakamas, Agent Andrew J. Bolon in September rode to The Dalles to organize supplies for Stevens' treaty council with the Spokanes.[361] After he arranged for teamsters to deliver supplies to the Spokane council grounds, he rode to the Yakama country to investigate the attacks on passing miners. But he was warned away by a friend of his, Shumaway (Qamáya'qin's brother), who told Bolon that some young Yakama warriors were on the warpath and he had better leave. Bolon turned around; but on the trail back to The Dalles, Mosheel (the son of Shumaway) and his companions killed him.[362] Yakama warriors prepared to defend themselves from what they knew was coming: an army of American soldiers out to avenge Bolon's death. The white communities called for punishment of the Yakamas, and their anger was directed at Yakama chief Qamáya'qin.

Meanwhile, Stevens had carried on his agenda in ignorance of events unfolding west of the Rockies. Bolon had been killed while Stevens was waiting for the treaty supply boats to arrive.

On October 3, when Craig and others were gathering tribes to meet on the Judith River, Brevet Major Granville O. Haller, with 102 men, marched into Yakama country to punish the Yakamas. But Haller's forces were defeated and forced to retreat. News of the retreat emboldened more bands to join the Yakamas against the whites. Settlers on Puget Sound called for retaliation against the Yakamas, with a newspaper (reminiscent of the cry aimed earlier at the Cayuses) declaring: "We trust they will be rubbed out—blotted from existence as a tribe."[363]

A call had gone out in both Oregon and Washington territories for volunteers, and West Point graduate Gabriel J. Rains was made Brigadier General in command of the Washington Territory Volunteers. Brevet Major General John Ellis Wool, the 71-year-old commander of the U.S. Army's Department of the Pacific in Benecia, California, responded to requests for troops by requisitioning a regiment from the East Coast. Oregon Territory raised a volunteer militia of five companies totaling 800 men under Colonel James W. Nesmith. By the time Pearson brought the news of Bolon's murder to Stevens, volunteer and regular army troops had marched into the Indians' country west of the Rockies, warriors had rallied to protect their people and livestock, and it was doubtful any white person could safely travel across the plateau.

1855 Sohon sketch: Nez Perce arrival at Walla Walla treaty council
(Washington State Historical Society)

5
War (1855-1856)

Craig and the Nez Perce warriors were riding towards home when Stevens learned that a general Indian war was expected.[364] It was late October of 1855, and the delegation had been planning to snowshoe over the Bitterroots on the South Nez Perce trail; but Stevens caught up with them at Hell Gate (present Missoula, Montana).[365] Acting Governor Mason's letter had warned Stevens that hostile warriors were waiting to kill him and recommended the governor return to Olympia by traveling East to New York and booking passage on a ship (a suggestion Stevens later attributed to Gen. John E. Wool, who would become his antagonist).[366]

Craig once more acted as interpreter between Stevens and the Nez Perce leaders, but this time Stevens asked his allies for their help. True to their vow of friendship to the Americans, they agreed. They pledged a bodyguard of warriors once they reached Nez Perce country; warriors who would travel with Stevens on the now-dangerous road to The Dalles and protect him from his enemies.[367]

Stevens, Craig, Pearson and the warriors, never ones to run from danger, once more headed west. It was now mid-November, and the mountain passes were deep in snow. Nonetheless, Stevens insisted they try to cross to the Coeur d'Alene tribe, for he had yet to make a treaty with both them and the Spokanes.

On November 14 the party headed out from the Bitterroot Valley and up the mountains toward the "Coeur d'Alene Pass" (general route of today's Highway 90). Stevens later told Jefferson Davis that they went through upwards of three feet of snow at the summit, but he neglected to add that the going was made possible because, as luck would have it, a large group of Coeur d'Alene people had crossed from buffalo country a couple of weeks earlier, trampling a good path, and it had not snowed much since.[368] Doty led the pack train and Isaac Stevens' 13-year-old son, Hazard, was a member of the party.[369] Heading downhill at last, early in the morning of November 25, Stevens chose a few companions to leave the train and ride ahead with him to Sacred Heart.

The men he picked to accompany him on a daring charge into the

Coeur d'Alene village were four Nez Perce warriors—Old Looking Glass, Spotted Eagle, Three Feathers, and Captain John—as well as William Pearson and William Craig. By sundown they had the lodges and buildings of the Catholic mission in sight.[370] Stevens gave orders, according to young Hazard Stevens: They were to ride fast into the village with guns drawn and, at the first sign of hostility from the Coeur d'Alenes, were to shoot and kill as many of them as possible, then run for the church, barricade themselves and hold out until the rest of their men came the next day. They kicked their horses into a gallop and rode into the Coeur d'Alene camp, guns leveled at the people who came out of their lodges to see what was going on. Stevens yelled out, "Are you friends or enemies? Do you want peace or war?"[371] Taken by surprise and faced with questions barked from behind loaded guns, the Coeur d'Alene men answered (not surprisingly) that they were friends. There was no overt hostility. The Coeur d'Alene people gathered around the audacious interlopers and made them welcome.

They held a council the following day, passing the pipe to clear their minds and soothe their hearts before getting down to business. Stevens had asked the Nez Perces to tell the Coeur d'Alenes of the wonderful treaty just made with the Blackfeet, that from now on they could hunt buffalo without attack from their traditional enemies. Doty noted that the Coeur d'Alenes were in an agitated state, some men ready to fight the Americans, others counseling not to fight. "They were much excited, on a balance for Peace, or for war and a chance word might turn them either way."[372] In council Stevens urged the Coeur d'Alenes to keep their young men from joining the warring Yakamas. The Coeur d'Alenes allowed the Stevens party to leave in peace.

The four men hired by Bolon to bring treaty supplies to the Spokane prairie were now stranded at Antoine Plante's place, where the council was to have been held. Stevens and Plante, a mixed-blood Indian, were no strangers to one another: Plante had worked for Stevens in the summer of 1853 as a scout for the railroad survey crew led by Lt. Rufus Saxon.[373] Also at Plante's establishment were fifteen or so miners, who had been on their way from the Colville gold fields to the settlements and were now trying to avoid the fighting to the south. Stevens decided to retrieve the government property, beef up his armed guard with the white men, and have a talk with the Spokanes and Colvilles before going to Craig's place in the Nez Perce country.

Craig and the remainder of the Nez Perce delegation were sent ahead to ascertain where the Nez Perces stood on war against the whites, while Stevens and a few warriors visited the Spokanes.[374] If the

Nez Perces were still peaceful, Craig was told, he should call the people together for a council with Stevens. After an absence of over six months, he arrived safely home in the Lapwai Valley in December.

Two months earlier, in October 1855, a U.S. Army unit led by Maj. Haller had marched into the Yakamas' country and was met by about five hundred warriors who defeated them in battle near Toppenish Creek in the valley of the Yakama. At about the same time, warriors at Rogue River (to the south) and Puget Sound (to the west) had attacked nearby white people. In near panic, the settlers put out a call to arms for volunteer soldiers to help the regular army.[375]

Among the Willamette Valley volunteers were Robert Newell and Joseph Meek. Newell was now a prosperous resident of Oregon City with a new young wife. (Kitty had died in late 1845, leaving Newell with five little boys; within six months he had married 14-year-old Rebecca Newman, a neighbor at Champoeg.)[376] When the call went out for volunteers, Newell raised a group of men to serve as scouts for Gabriel J. Rains, now a general with the Washington Territorial Volunteers.[377] Joe Meek, after he returned from leading a lackluster gold hunting expedition to the Pend d'Oreille River, enlisted as a private in Captain Alfred V. Wilson's Company A of Oregon's First Regiment of Mounted Volunteers.[378] Another member of Wilson's company was a Pennsylvanian named Samuel Phinney, who would later become the husband of young Adeline Craig and carry on the Craig family legacy for many years in the Lapwai Valley.[379] Another future Craig son-in-law, A. H. Robie, was soon to be appointed quartermaster and "Commissary of subsistence" of the Washington Territorial volunteers at The Dalles and given the rank of captain.[380] When war broke out in 1855, Craig's former companions from fur trapping days, as well as future sons-in-law Robie and Phinney, served on the side of the Americans.

Meanwhile, far to the northeast, Stevens reached Antoine Plante's place and, backed up by Old Looking Glass, Three Feathers, Jason, and Captain John, learned the Spokanes were not involved in the war against the whites.[381] With the stroke of his pen, Governor Stevens turned his companions into militia to guard him the rest of his journey. He created two military units on December 2 (both of which, upon later scrutiny, were found to have no legal standing). The party of miners he called the "Spokane Invincibles"; and Stevens' own twenty-six men (including his son, Hazard, and Nez Perce warrior Captain John) he named "Stevens' Guards."[382] Additionally, Stevens appointed James Doty "Aid de Camp and Adjutant with the rank of Lieut Colonel" and

William Tappan as "Commissary and Quartermaster with the Rank of Captain."[383] Military men now protected Stevens and he spent several days talking with the Spokane tribal leaders.

It would later become known that on the day Stevens departed the Spokane camp heading for the Craig place, another sequence of events was occurring in the Walla Walla Valley. On December 6, 1855, Oregon volunteers under command of Lt. Col. James K. Kelly killed the Wallawalla chief, Yellow Bird.[384] The Wallawalla Indians had not been at war with the whites but had come to protect their stock from the army of volunteers who marched into their land. Yellow Bird and about forty warriors had come to the volunteers' camp to have council with the leaders. The truth may never be known about the circumstances leading to the death of Yellow Bird and five of his men, but they were evidently in the volunteers' camp either under a flag of truce or as hostages when they were killed. Some of the white volunteers scalped and skinned Yellow Bird's body, cut off his ears, buried his corpse, then exhumed it for further mutilation.[385] Later historians identified B. F. Shaw as the person responsible for disinterment of Yellow Bird's corpse.[386]

As yet unaware of Yellow Bird's death, Governor Stevens and his new militia traveled to the Craig place. At Camas Creek they talked with two Frenchmen on their way to Spokane country, and their news was not good. The Walla Walla Valley was overrun with hostile warriors, all the white settlers had fled, their houses had been burned and stock driven off. But the only excitement the Stevens party experienced, according to young Hazard Stevens, was when two riding horses drowned, their riders barely surviving, while fording the Clearwater at a dangerous place just upstream from the mouth of Lapwai Creek. With great relief, Stevens and his men moved "seven miles up the Lapwai, [to] Craig's hospitable house" and the end of one leg of their journey.

They made camp near the Craig home, around which were "208 Nez Perce Lodges, containing not less than 2000 men, women, and children, and able to muster 800 warriors." More than twice as many Nez Perce people were gathered at the Craig place to hear what Stevens had to say as had attended the Walla Walla treaty council.[387] A large lodge was erected, about "100 feet in length constructed in the usual manner of poles, mats, and skins, in which were assembled some 200 Nez Perce including all the principal Chiefs; Lawyer presiding."[388]

On the evening of December 10, the day before the council was to begin, Old Looking Glass, Lawyer, and several principal chiefs came to Isabel and William's home to catch up on the news. Craig interpreted a letter from Oregon Agent Nathan Olney, which seemed to leave no doubt about the fighting.[389] Stevens' concern was making it back to Olympia, for the route ran through the Walla Walla Valley to The Dalles; he thought all the Nez Perce warriors who had rifles and ammunition should accompany him. Old Looking Glass believed fighting and "bodies lying on the Prairies on both sides" blocked the road to The Dalles.[390] He told Stevens that the old chiefs (Thunder's Eye was one) had been waiting for the delegation to come back from the Blackfeet treaty to help control the young men, for many young Nez Perce men had gone off to fight the whites.

An ox had been killed the first morning and a feast prepared for the men in the meeting. Young men served as the cooks: they roasted the beef over fires in the lodge then they cut the meat up into small square pieces. The bite-size steak was piled in "large pans, placed so that from four to six persons could help themselves from each pan..."[391]

While they were eating, Red Wolf, Timothy, and others arrived with news from downriver: a big group of volunteers had whipped the Indians in battle near Whitman's old mission, killing a great number and sending the rest running. (As was the custom, Yellow Bird's name was not spoken now that he was dead.) They reported that Five Crows had fled alone down the Tucannon. Old Looking Glass, Lawyer, Old Joseph, and Spotted Eagle spoke in turn, all sad and sorry that their relatives and friends among the Cayuses, Wallawallas, Yakamas, and Umatillas had danced the war dance and were fighting the whites. Thunder's Eye spoke, and it was clear that he had tried to keep his young men from entering the fight. He said that when he got word that:

...beyond the Columbia they were fighting, I spoke to my children to be still. When Pearson was passing here, carrying you news of the war, I told him my people were not going to fight.[392]

Thunder's Eye said he did not think it would have done any good for him to speak to the Cayuses—that his heart had been with Old Looking Glass and Spotted Eagle in the country where they were making peace with the Blackfeet. He was ashamed of the fighting, because he knew the governor was spreading the news that the people on this side of the mountains were friendly and had made treaties. He said it seemed like only yesterday that Governor Stevens had spoken to them at the council, and he thought Stevens':

...heart will be glad to find we have listened...It is long since we had the laws sent among us. The Law [treaty] was, to love the White people. If my children go into the lower country to war, and their bodies are left there—I cannot look toward them, it will be their own faults. It is those people below who will not listen that are making us tired.[393]

"Laws," as used by Thunder's Eye and Lawyer, refers to treaties.[394] The reference may be to those of Elijah White but it is more likely that Thunder's Eye spoke of the vows of friendship Nez Perce leaders made with Meriwether Lewis and William Clark. Thunder's Eye's words were those of a man solidly for peace with the whites, doing his best to uphold the Nez Perce-American alliances of many years standing.[395] It seems to be the last time Thunder's Eye's words were recorded in Nez Perce country.

Red Wolf was concerned about Stevens and his party "and for William, who has a house here."[396] Other speakers reiterated that the Yakamas and Cayuses had sent word to them to join up and fight the whites—had offered horses to tempt them—but that they would keep the treaty and not fight Americans. Leader after leader spoke of their commitment to follow the treaty, to stay at peace, and to protect their white friends now among them.

With all the leaders offering support and the services of their warriors to escort him to The Dalles, Stevens promised he would make special effort to see that the white volunteers did not harm the "friendly" Cayuses and Walla Wallas. (It would not be a month, however, before he would deny a request from them to come to the safety of the Nez Perce country.) Stevens also promised the Nez Perce men that they would be paid for their military service "like the White volunteers" after he could write to the president.[397]

Stevens left the Craig establishment prepared to fight his way west. Riding with him were seventy Nez Perce warriors, William Craig, miners, teamsters, and his own seasoned crew. They made a colorful picture: miners and packers wearing heavy cloth overcoats and black felt hats; mountain men fur caps, buckskin shirts and leggings; Nez Perce men painted for battle, some with eagle feathers in their hair. Most warriors brought three horses to be ridden using wooden saddles covered with bear, buffalo, or mountain goat skin.[398] Setting out in the early morning of December 15, the men overtook the supply train that had departed the evening before. The caravan included 22 miners from the Spokane Valley, 25 packers and expressmen and 12 chiefs among the 70 Nez Perce warriors.[399]

They spent the next night at the *simí·nekem* (confluence of the Snake and Clearwater rivers now Lewiston, Idaho). Eagle Shirt was the headman of the band that kept canoes beached on the Snake River shores.[400] The following morning, "Indians with their canoes ferried" Stevens' party across the Snake River. The ancient trail took them through Red Wolf's ground to the usual camping place four miles west on the Alpowa.[401] Doty later wrote that the Nez Perce people who usually lived on the left (west) side of the Snake (now Clarkston, Washington) had rounded up their horses and cattle, struck their tepees, and moved to the opposite side of the river, leaving no canoes behind; the travelers deduced that this move had been made to keep the hostile warriors out of Nez Perce country as well as to safeguard Nez Perce herds.[402]

One of the Nez Perce warriors brought the son of the Cayuse war chief into the Alpowa camp. Umehowlish had sent his son to Stevens' camp to arrange a meeting, saying he had "fled from Walla Walla on the last day of the battle; that he had not been engaged in it," and had come this way hoping to talk with Stevens. Stevens' intelligence was however, that Umehowlish had been involved in the fighting, so a plan was made to capture him. Stevens sent a message off with the son, saying if Umehowlish would turn himself in to the governor as an "unconditional prisoner," he would get a trial at the settlements under white man's law and could there prove whether or not he had been involved in the war. The following evening, as Stevens' caravan camped near the crossing on the Tucannon River (between the current towns of Pomeroy and Dayton, Washington, where "Marengo"—the settlement named for Louis (Mosquito) Raboin—once stood), Umehowlish came into camp and surrendered, trusting his life to the Americans' justice.[403] He was made a prisoner and was to cause Craig trouble in the months to come.

As the caravan moved west and encountered no hostilities, the men relaxed and began enjoying themselves. The warriors told stories, cracked jokes, laughed, and shouted; Craig translated their jokes and stories so the white men could also enjoy them. While riding across a broad flat plain covered with tall rye grass, Craig told a story on Lawyer that was appreciated by the young warriors:

When yet an obscure young warrior, Lawyer was traveling over this ground with a party of the tribe, including several of the principal chiefs. It was a cold winter day, and a biting gale swept up the river,

*penetrating their clothing and chilling them to the bone. The chiefs sat
down in the shelter of the tall rye grass, and were indulging in a cosy
[sic] smoke, when Lawyer fired the prairie far to windward, and in an
instant the fiery element, in a long, crackling, blazing line, came
sweeping down on the wings of the wind upon the comfort-taking
chiefs, and drove them to rush helter-skelter into the river for safety,
dropping robes, pipes, and everything that might impede their flight.*

*For this audacious prank Lawyer barely escaped a public
whipping.*[404]

The men got along well, albeit young and old, native and
newcomer. There was good-natured ribbing between the generations of
Nez Perces. Stevens had assigned the warriors the job of guarding the
horses and the Americans the job of guarding the camp. The horses
had to range far and wide to find enough grass to eat, as much had been
burned off. Every evening the young warriors would stay around the
campfires as long as possible, not looking forward to spending a
horseback night on the cold prairie. Young men lingering by the
campfire would cause the older warriors to point out the laziness of
youth and boast that when they were young, men were braver and
stronger. Nevertheless, the young warriors lost no horses on the trip.
Nor did the party meet any resistance.[405]

When Stevens' caravan reached the Walla Walla Valley on
December 20, Oregon volunteers greeted them like returning heroes.
Officers rode out to meet them, and in camp the men lined up to
welcome them back from Blackfeet country. Riding past the parading
volunteers were "fifty sturdy, travel-stained whites…followed by
the…proud and flaunting braves, curveting their horses and
uttering…war-whoops." Governor Stevens gave a brief speech in
which he complimented the volunteers for coming out to do battle in
the winter, proving they were not just "summer soldiers," and for their
"gallantry in engaging and routing a superior force of the enemy," and
thanked them for opening the road.[406]

Stevens planned to mount a winter campaign to fight the hostiles,
but sub-zero temperatures cancelled it. A little ice age was finally
losing its grip on the Columbia Plateau.[407] It was so cold in the latter
part of December 1855 that horses and cattle froze to death in the fields
and men suffered mightily in their shelters. Just before Christmas the
thermometer registered 27 degrees below zero at midnight and there
was a foot of snow on the ground.[408] One volunteer wrote—using
some Chinook jargon—that food was scarce and there was a lot of

grumbling: "*Muck-a-muck* [food] scarce. *Hi-yu* [plenty] grumbling."[409]
Stevens moved into an abandoned house and stayed relatively
comfortable.[410]

The cold weather did not let up and the Americans could not feed
the militia in camp, much less outfit them for movement. Ice on the
Columbia River cut off food and supplies coming from the Willamette
Valley, and the volunteers at Waiilatpu were running out of provisions.
They helped themselves to the cattle and horses owned by local Indian
people. By year's end the volunteers had no flour, no salt, and nothing
to eat but other people's beef.[411]

Meanwhile, Eugene Casimir Chirouse, a Catholic Priest and
missionary to the Cayuses, in a postscript to a letter kept very private,
listed by name those Indian leaders he believed to have started fighting
the Americans.[412] He was familiar with many of the people in the
conflict, having been ordained at Fort Walla Walla in 1848 and
subsequently served on the Umatilla as the resident priest at Mission St.
Rose.[413] His list contained, among others, the name of (now dead)
Yellow Bird leading some Wallawalla warriors; Qamáya'qin, Owhi and
Skloom leading the Yakamas; Five Crows and Big Belly (Qemespelu)
leading the hostile Cayuses; a number of Palouses; and an American,
"Al Tallman…who was now at the Dalles." The letter was written to
John F. Noble, one of the operators of the cattle ranch at the old
mission site, who passed it on with the following note:

> *The above is a P.S. to a letter from Father Cherouze [sic] of the
> Whitman valley that I have just recvd. His letter is filled with
> interesting news but I do not feel at liberty to make public any more
> than the above—which may be of some importance to you, For his
> letter is strictly private. – J. F. Noble*[414]

The intelligence from Father Chirouse marked many men
for death: Yellow Bird and his group had been among the first.

Chirouse also listed names of those who, he believed, "remain good,
viz.—Owlishwampum who fought to defend your [Noble's] house and
goods" and six others, among them Theentheenmeetsa, who "neglected
nothing in the care of your property, but could not resist superior
force."[415] Theentheenmeetsa remained a Catholic the rest of his life.

Trapped by frigid temperatures, Stevens set up, on paper,
the human mechanism to fight a war in the spring. On
December 27 he issued a proclamation that created a "military

district" of the land from the Cascades to the Bitterroots and placed Lt. Col. Benjamin F. Shaw in charge.[416] He released the Nez Perce warriors to return home with Craig and gave them their orders: They were to help Craig by being messengers to the Spokanes to keep them peaceful, by not joining warring parties, and by keeping hostiles out of their country.[417] He had, at the Lapwai Valley council, offered them pay. Stevens reasoned that there was less likelihood of the Nez Perces joining their hostile neighbors if they were kept employed and flattered and had a promise of pay in the future. The Nez Perce warriors, pleased with the offer of pay, promised to provide all the fresh horses the Oregon volunteers might need to continue their campaign.[418]

William Craig, Stevens decided, would become his agent to the Nez Perces. Craig could be extremely useful to the Americans now that there would be open hostilities. He told the Nez Perce headmen:

If any of those [hostile] Indians come to kill you tell Mr. Craig and he will send word below and we shall try and send troops to assist you…I will leave your friend Mr. Craig to take care of you… I want you now to understand from me that Mr. Craig is your Agent…[and he] will do the best he can for you.[419]

Finally, Stevens issued General Orders B, appointing Craig Aide to Commander in Chief with the rank of Lieutenant Colonel.[420] He wrote Craig the following letter:2

December 31, 1855, Headquarters Camp

You will on your return to the Nez Perce Country, communicate with the settlers and Indians on the Spokane from time to time to procure reliable information in reference to their disposition and with the view of guarding against the many false reports which are constantly in circulation in the Indian Country.

By the passing to and fro of such reports both Whites and Indians are misled, and mischievous results follow.

Col. B. F. Shaw will remain in this Valley as Special Agent of the Remaining Tribes of Washington between the Cascades and Bitter Root

Mountains. You are directed to communicate fully with him, and your letters to the office will be sent to his care.

You are authorized to employ in addition to your Interpreter one laborer as a herder.

I shall at the earliest possible moment send you funds, Indian Goods and supplies. But should you be of opinion that no injury will result to the public service, you are authorized to visit the Dalles, should you desire it, making the best arrangements in your power for the charge of your Indians...[421]

Stickus, the Cayuse leader friendly to Americans, had asked that he and his lodge be allowed to move into Nez Perce country, pointing out what had happened to Yellow Bird at the hands of the Oregon volunteers. But Stevens refused—basing his decision on the wisdom of keeping all Cayuse people away from his Nez Perce allies, lest they be lured away from him.[422]

Stevens and Craig left the Walla Walla Valley the first day of 1856, heading in opposite directions but with common purpose. The cold winds at his back, Craig was riding alongside the same warriors he had come down with, but it must have seemed to him that everything else had changed. Tucked into his saddlebags were a copy of Stevens' General Order B and his letter of instructions addressed to "Lieut. Col. Wm. Craig, Spec. Agent." Although he wore no uniform, he was now a military man, and still responsible for keeping the Nez Perces allied to America.[423]

Meanwhile, as Craig was riding east, Isaac Stevens was heading into the wind and toward The Dalles, accompanied by Hazard, William Pearson, Robie, Captain John, and their Cayuse prisoner, Umehowlish, who would there be turned over to Oregon authorities.[424] At the end of January, after an absence of almost nine months on his treaty tour, Governor Stevens arrived in Olympia and found business at a standstill. White settlers were living in blockhouses for protection from warriors on Puget Sound who had also rallied to fight for their land.[425] Although separated by the Cascade Range, the tribes to the west were connected by kinship to the tribes on the east. The Nisqually chief, Leschi, was a cousin of Qamáya'qin.[426] A 38-gun salute and hero's welcome greeted Stevens and he declared that "[t]he war shall be prosecuted until the last hostile Indian is exterminated."[427]

Meanwhile, back in Clearwater country and reunited with Isabel and the children, William wrote letters to the few white men up north in the Spokane and Coeur d'Alene country. He hired William Simpson as a herder, to be responsible for the horses and cattle belonging to the Indian agency, and did the paperwork to muster the Nez Perce warriors out of the service.[428]

In Craig's report for January 1856 he spoke of the difficulties inherent in separating and isolating people based on their current allegiance to Americans. Four warriors in the war party had come to his house that month, wanting to be at peace. He had sent them to see Col. Thomas Cornelius (commanding the Oregon volunteers) to give themselves up, telling them that Cornelius:

...had not come to punish good people but it was bad Indians he wished to punish. Some of them took my advice while others returned to the War party, which was at that time on Snake River some forty miles from my place.[429]

It was about this time that the settlement of Seattle was attacked. Yakama warriors from east of the Cascades joined Nisqually warriors and coordinated an attack on the town, the primary object being to seize ammunition and powder aboard the beached ship *Decatur*. But the vessel had guns and 150 sailors and marines, and an Indian spy had tipped off the captain, so the attack failed.[430]

The hostility of the Puget Sound bands galvanized Stevens to organize volunteer militia, request U.S. regular troops and make public his disagreements with Major General John Wool.[431] As commander of the U. S. Army's Department of the Pacific, Wool brooked no interference from civil authorities; he preferred negotiation to armed conflict with Indians and abhorred the indiscriminate killing and theft of stock that had marked the volunteer militia's path in the Northwest. He maintained that regular army troops could end the war in a few months if the volunteers were sent home and the whites stopped the policy of extermination. A veteran of the Cherokee removal efforts, Wool was sympathetic to the Indians' situation. He refused the Oregon and Washington Territorial Governors' pressure to annihilate the hostile tribes and thought Isaac Stevens' treaties niggardly and needlessly harsh. Stevens reported to Jefferson Davis that, without use of force, he had control of the Nez Perces and he wanted General Wool to quit interfering.[432]

Stevens was proud that he had the Nez Perces on his side and Craig worked diligently to keep up his end of the bargain. On the last day of January 1856, Craig wrote to Col. Shaw, informing him that the Nez Perce leaders were still allied to the United States, "that they had sent the Cayuses out of their country and intended keeping them out," and that Old Looking Glass had backed up Craig's advice to the homeless Cayuse contingent who came seeking sanctuary by advising them "to go and stand their trial."[433]

General Wool's counsel was scorned not only by Stevens but also by the settlers. The settlers were outraged when Wool suggested a moratorium on further settlement of the interior, for he believed the wars were the result of settler intrusion.[434] Wool may have had trouble with the Oregon settlers even without the Indian policy differences, for he was reportedly "somewhat of a prig."[435] Even so, he held fast to his principles until he believed peace had been attained—then asked to be relieved of his command.[436] In the long term, however, it was not Wool's policy that prevailed.

As winter wore on, Stevens agitated in Olympia to strike hostiles both east and west of the Cascades. In February he called for more volunteers and ordered Shaw to march with one battalion to the Walla Walla Valley. Robie was appointed "Quartermaster and Commissary of subsistence" at The Dalles, a position that would bring him again in contact with the Craig family.[437] But after Stevens declared martial law in the Puget Sound area, he was embroiled in a maelstrom of public outcry and had little time to devote to events east of the mountains. It was August 1856 before he announced that the Puget Sound war (if indeed it was a war) had ended.[438] Meanwhile, his staff east of the Cascades continued on the path he had set them.

Craig was running short of supplies, for the hostilities had interrupted food gathering, trade, and transportation of goods. Fort Walla Walla, the HBC trading post on the Columbia River, had been looted and burned by agitated warriors late in 1855, ending its thirty-seven year presence in their territory; the nearest trading center for Craig was now The Dalles.[439] When Craig left the Walla Walla Valley in December 1855, Stevens had promised him funds, Indian goods, and supplies; every day Craig expected the arrival of a pack train. But every day he was disappointed. He sent some men to the Tucannon area to round up some of Brooks's cattle and drive them to the Lapwai Valley, where they provided about 3,000 pounds of beef for the hungry families. It had been an appallingly hard winter. Not only were the Nez Perces running low on food, but also the agency was almost out of supplies such as stationery and Craig was out of whiskey, having "not even a d--- of the comforts of life."[440]

Although Craig signed his name over the title of Special Agent for Nez Perces, it was many months before the appointment was official.

Stevens suspended William H. Tappan on February 23 1856, because of "incapacity," and appointed William Craig as Special Agent.[441] Tappan, upon learning of his suspension, had an urge to visit the east coast and immediately resigned.[442] Eventually Stevens was notified that the Interior Department, which had taken responsibility for Indian affairs on its creation in 1849, had approved Craig's appointment.[443]

The Oregon volunteers had stolen horses from whatever territory they were passing through. The Nez Perces had "collected some horses which the Cayuses have been unable to get across the river and some which they had driven into the country for safety, which they have divided among themselves according to [Stevens'] orders."[444] The war party needed horses and knew where to find them. As the weather warmed, Nez Perce country was threatened by raiders reclaiming horses to replenish their herds.[445]

When Craig sent a messenger warning Col. Cornelius that the Indians were planning a horse-stealing raid, the messenger returned with news that Nathan Olney, the agent in Oregon Territory, was sending Stickus and his lodge of Cayuses to live in Nez Perce country.[446] Since Stevens had earlier denied Stickus' request for asylum, Craig had a new development to handle. It would be handled on his own, without orders from his commanding officer. And, despite Craig's warning, Cornelius' volunteers had many of their horses taken by the war party. Upon learning that many volunteers were now afoot, Lawyer and other allied Nez Perces furnished more than forty of their own horses to the Oregon men so they could continue their fight.[447]

The same day that Olney accompanied Stickus and his family to Nez Perce country, a messenger arrived from Colonel George Wright of the U.S. Army calling for the Cayuses to come out of hiding and meet him in council.[448] Col. Wright was following Gen. Wool's orders to negotiate peace with the hostiles. Yet while Wright was attempting to talk peace with hostile Indian leaders, Cornelius's Oregon volunteers were out of bounds in Washington Territory looking for Indians to attack. William Craig and the allied Nez Perce leaders were following orders to keep anyone hostile to the U.S. government out of Nez Perce country. It was obvious that the Americans were working at cross-purposes to one another; it was also clear that Craig and some Nez Perces were more closely aligned with the Oregon militia than with the U.S. Army. At the Coeur d'Alene mission, Father Ravalli, whose informants kept him apprised of the drama unfolding to the south, suggested that the Americans not tear down with one hand what they had built up with the other, but his advice was lost in the bizarre milieu.[449]

The spy network kept the war parties well posted on every movement of both white armies in the interior. Craig stated that even though he had done what he could to stop the flow of intelligence, there was such a high degree of surveillance being performed that it was not surprising that the Oregon militia couldn't find the hostile bands. He was, as always, trying to keep spies out of the Nez Perces' country.[450]

The mixed messages being sent out by the Americans put their allies in a tight spot. From a council on the Palouse prairie attended by the hostile Indians came the information that Col. Wright and his soldiers all wanted peace and it was only William Craig and the Nez Perces who did not want it.[451]

More Indians joined the war party, increasing the threat to the Nez Perces still allied to the Americans; Craig believed that an attack on the Lapwai agency was imminent and mustered in a squad of men for protection. Neighbor Henri Chase, Oregon Sub-Agent Al Tallman (who had accompanied the friendly Cayuses to Nez Perce country and was the same Al Tallman listed by Father Chirouse as among those starting the war), as well as Timothy, Spotted Eagle, and Louis Raboin, were some of the men Craig recruited, along with his now 16-year-old son, Joe. Absent from the company were Thunder's Eye, Old Looking Glass and Old Joseph, some of whom were east of the Bitterroots hunting buffalo. At least nine of the Nez Perce warrior volunteers had earlier escorted Stevens to The Dalles. There were fifty-two men in all, the majority of whom were Nez Perce warriors. They organized, elected non-Indian officers, and were ready for action on March 11, 1856.[452] Craig ordered the men to remain at the Lapwai agency to protect it, as well as prevent hostile Indians from coming into Nez Perce country.[453]

There was a compelling reason for the company to be pulled together at that time, for Craig had learned that a Palouse man named Umelaquitat, probably a spy, was in the Nez Perce camp at *simí·nekem*. As ordered, Craig intended to impede the flow of information to the hostile Indians: he sent Chase and Company M to find the enemy who had breached the Nez Perce borders. Craig later reported to Governor Stevens:

...the Chiefs had trouble in keeping the War party out of this country...When the Red Wolf came back from below, he said he had orders from Supt. Palmer and Agent Olney to move the friendly Cayuses into this country, which he done; and from that time there has

*been a regular communication express between their camp and that of
the war party. On the 11th March I heard that a Pelouse Indian by
name Ume-laquitat had come into the Nez Perce camp at the forks…I
immediately ordered Capt. Chase to the place for the purpose of giving
him a trial. After examining said Pelouse indian Ume-laquitat,
according to his own confession and the testimony of several witnesses,
he was found guilty of murder and also as acting as a spy for the war
party. As the penalty in both cases is death, he was condemned to be
hung by the neck until dead, which sentence was approved by me, and
executed on the prisoner Ume-laquitat at the hour of 4 p.m. March 12,
1856.*[454]

Craig, following orders from the Governor of Washington Territory,
had authorized the first known hanging in the place later to become
Lewiston, Idaho.[455]

Henri Chase later summed up the days' work to the Adjutant
General of Washington Territorial Volunteers by stating that:

*[On] the 12th of March, I took prisoner a Pelouse Indian from the
war party who came into the country to spy. On examining him he
confessed to having murdered two Americans. I hung him on the
afternoon of the day he was taken prisoner.*[456]

What had happened to Stevens' prisoner, Umehowlish, at The
Dalles? Umehowlish's name appeared on Father Chirouse's bounty list
as having done "good." General Wright had released him. He had
been allowed to return to his people in order to deliver a message to the
hostiles from the U.S. Army officers. Stickus and his band—
Umehowlish's people—were now living in Nez Perce country (about
four or five miles west of what is now Clarkston, Washington). Craig's
spies reported that Umehowlish had, upon his release, gone directly to
the friendly Cayuse camp on the Alpowa and sent for some of the war
party.

Craig sent Chase to the same place to intercept the war party leaders
and to arrest, "hold…a trial and punish them according to the nature of
their offences." Chase and his squad found a camp of five lodges
(about 30 to 35 people) on the "Snake River a few miles below the
mouth of Red Wolf creek," but the inhabitants, warned of their coming,
had escaped. Chase took four men, many women, and a herd of horses
into custody. Henri Chase said he had barely missed the "head chief of

the Cayuses" and that some Nez Perces had helped him evade capture. Chase brought his Cayuse prisoners and stock to the Lapwai Valley (where they were undoubtedly welcomed by their relatives) and, according to Craig, would have a "hearing."[457] The outcome of that hearing is unknown.

Three days later, Klickitat warriors attacked the white settlement at the Cascades on the Columbia. Col. Wright and Lt. Phillip Sheridan's forces rescued some settlers, but 16 white people and an unknown number of Indians died. Col. Wright had 10 Indian men hung as examples: "I have given them a lesson which they will long remember."[458] The frequency of hangings was, indeed, to be long remembered. Col. Wright was embarrassed by the Oregon volunteers attacking friendly Indians and believed if he was to provide the protection the Indians needed from the white men, he wouldn't be able to even put an army in the field.[459] The Oregon volunteers would soon be withdrawn from service.

When Stevens finally turned his attention to the situation east of the Cascades, he wrote to Craig that he was beholden to him "both officially and personally" for acting to stop the flow of information between his Nez Perce allies and hostile Indians. He instructed Craig to hang Umehowlish if he could "get hold" of him.[460] He could not.[461] Stevens also directed Craig to act as the Indian agent of all the "friendly" Indians on the plateau, as B. F. Shaw was busy commanding volunteer troops.[462] The governor approved, after the fact, Craig mustering in volunteers and hanging the Palouse spy and instructed Craig to "hang in like manner all hostiles who visit the Nez Perces to incite them to hostility."[463]

The intrigues were unraveling the alliance. When Craig had a chance to talk with some of the war party—who had begun threatening his place almost every day—he could see that they believed he was standing in the way of a negotiated peace with the U.S. Army. Craig reported that they believed that "Col. Wright wishes peace and that if I was out of the Country they would have peace that if they were to kill me the trouble would end."[464]

The vast herds of horses owned by the plateau people continued to change hands. "Strays" were rounded up and added to the herds of entrepreneurs on both sides of the war. At one time, William Craig bought from Indians two horses that had been "taken up as strays," paid $20 each for them, and sold them to the U.S. government for $125.[465] Craig's transaction was typical of those fueling General Wool's assessment that the Oregon settlers started the war for speculation.

Stevens had planned to send his volunteer militia east of the Cascades in the spring, as soon as there was grass enough to support the army's livestock; because of Wright's efforts to negotiate a peace, however, the Washington territorial volunteers were not deployed until late in the summer. The delay frustrated Stevens, who did not accept the wisdom of trying to avoid war and thought the Indians were stalling until they could rally a larger war party. Relying on Craig to forward intelligence from the Nez Perce tribe, Stevens thought Wright's information about the Indians' peaceful intentions was not true. He warned Wright about being thrown off his guard.[466]

Some Nez Perce headmen were questioning Stevens' orders to keep the Cayuses out of Nez Perce country. They knew Col. Wright was trying to make peace: could they be offending the federal government by keeping the Cayuses out of their country? To Craig's explanation that it was Governor Stevens' instructions and that they must obey him, the chiefs disagreed; being separated from the Cayuses, Craig judged, "caused considerable confusion and hard feelings among the Nez Perces."[467]

Following Stevens' orders, Craig sent letters to Hudson's Bay Company factor Angus McDonald at Ft. Colville, George Montour among the Spokanes, and Father Antony Ravalli among the Coeur d'Alenes, asking about the mood of the Indians with whom they lived. An indignant McDonald replied that the people in the vicinity of Ft. Colville were grumbling about not being sold ammunition—to which he told them to go back to using arrows—and took offense at Craig's asking if McDonald had invited the leader of the Cayuses to come talk with him. He noted that the hostile Indians were trying to turn the British whites against the American whites, but "I am too smart of an old horse not to see this."[468] George Montour reported that the tribes were peaceable, though the Okanagans had considered war until wiser counsel prevailed. Montour wrote that when Umehowlish came back from The Dalles he brought orders for the peaceful Cayuses to move north of the Snake River and that about two-thirds of them had done that, including Five Crows and Old Man Chief.[469] Father Ravalli answered that he detected no preparations for war among the Coeur d'Alenes and he tried to stay neutral, but believed peace now depended less on the Indians than on the behavior of the white people.[470]

Meanwhile, Qamáya'qin called a council in Palouse country at the qémes grounds and sent his two brothers to hear the Nez Perces' reaction to Col. Wright's peace proposal. Craig also sent someone to hear what was said, and the report was not good. From friends in Col.

Wright's camp came intelligence that the whites wanted to keep the Indians separated so it would be easier to kill them. It was said that it was "a certain fact they all had to die, and they had better take up their guns and all go to war together." Word came that the buffalo-hunting Nez Perce bands were on their way home and Craig was dreading their reaction to the "great number of curious & exciting rumors."[471]

In May, Craig and some warriors rode to intercept a war party, about seventy strong, at *simínekem*. The war party was made up of Cayuses, Wallawallas and Spokanes and they told Craig they had come for his horse herd. Old Looking Glass stopped them.

Looking Glass told them if they were after my [Craig's] goods they had better return immediately, but if they were in friendship he would accompany them to my place. They answered that their hearts were not good; they did not wish friendship from the Whites.[472]

The war party warned of a large coalition of warriors made up of Spokanes, Cayuses, Pelouses, Okanagons, Coeur d'Alenes, Colvilles, and Snakes who "would soon rub out the few whites and Nez Perces that is here." They said that Spokane Garry was going to lead them to the Nez Perce country and learn who their friends were and who was keeping the Cayuses away from the Nez Perces. Craig relayed word to Stevens that the Nez Perce leaders "beg and pray their big chief to send them some help; they are here in the middle of their enemies, without ammunition and they ask for their white friends to come & help them."[473] No one seemed to know where the volunteer army was, the U.S. Army had not been heard from; and since the upper Columbia country warriors had already received their horses as pay for fighting, they must have already joined the war party. Craig put it to Stevens straight:

Now Sir you can see how I am situated at this place: you said when we parted in Walla Walla Valley that you would send me some supplies early in the spring, and I have been expecting them since that time, but have received none. ...I am entirely out of everything I have not even salt for my bread, and I cannot remain in this country entirely destitute of everything. I want powder, ball, caps, flints, sugar, Coffee, Salt, Tobacco, Clothing for men & families if we do not get supplies we will...move to where we can get them. It is necessary for two companies to be sent into this country immediately for the safety of the people & property in it...[474]

Craig's letter had its desired effect. Stevens forwarded it to Jefferson Davis, adding that unless the Americans mounted a strong show of force, all the plateau tribes would be at war. Stevens believed the "long delay of Colonel Wright" trying to negotiate peace and the withdrawal of the Oregon volunteers had emboldened the hostiles and given them time to put together a consortium to fight the whites.[475] He told the Secretary of War that he was leaving immediately for The Dalles.

Just two days later (May 29, 1856) Craig again wrote to Stevens, reporting that the danger of attack by hostile Indians was not as imminent as first thought. But this information, along with another letter of Craig's dated June 8, was not forwarded to the Secretary of War nor brought up by Stevens until July 7, when Stevens at last informed Davis that letters had been received from Craig "speaking more favorably of the conditions in the interior."[476] Craig's desperate call for help was used by Stevens to continue his arguments against Gen. Wool's policies and to move more than four hundred volunteers against the plateau Indians, while Craig's quick reassessment of the urgency and danger was withheld until the volunteer troops were in the field.

By June 1856, B. F. Shaw and 200 volunteers were marching eastward with orders from Stevens that, once they were in the Walla Walla Valley, they were to "spare no exertion to reduce to unconditional submission any hostiles within reach." The supply train escorted by another 200 men was to leave The Dalles and join Shaw at the old Fort Walla Walla site. The Spokanes had not yet joined the fight (even though Qamáya'qin had tried to convince them it was in their best interest to do so) and the Nez Perces and agency at Craig's place had not yet been attacked, but the help Craig called for in the form of ammunition, food, and fighting men was on its way.[477]

6
America's Allies No More (1856)

B. F. Shaw and his Puget Sound volunteers arrived at the site of old Fort Walla Walla in late June of 1856; Craig sent him an express saying that everything was quiet in Nez Perce country and that he would be down shortly with some Nez Perce people to meet Shaw.[478] Joined by their supply wagons, Shaw's forces moved east to the valley of the Walla Walla and camped at Whitman's old mission site, passing deserted settlers' houses and unharvested wheat fields on their journey. A messenger rode into camp with information that Captain Robie's train was within six miles of them; then two Nez Perce men announced that Col. Craig was in the valley with about 120 Nez Perces. Stevens' Washington Territorial volunteer army and their Nez Perce allies were about to meet.

The Nez Perce delegation prepared to salute the Puget Sound militia and Craig, as vanguard, explained the drill. He rode to the volunteer camp and, according to one soldier, "informed us that the Nez Perces would give us a salute as we passed according to custom. We accordingly packed up, and commenced our march along Mill Creek." As the volunteers approached the Nez Perce camp, they saw about a hundred warriors coming toward them, "singing, dressed in their gayest attire, splendidly mounted and bearing aloft a large American flag." Still chanting, the warriors formed a line; as the volunteers rode past, the Nez Perces fired a salute. The volunteers gave three cheers for the flag, drew their revolvers, and without halting returned the salute. The ceremonial was so gratifying that the volunteers repeated their "three cheers and a volley" after the Nez Perces broke their old encampment and moved up to camp alongside the volunteer forces.

Robie arrived from The Dalles with the pack train of Indian goods and quartermaster supplies authorized by Stevens; it was a large outfit consisting of seventy-five packhorses, fifty wagons and a full crew of teamsters and herders. Once again, barely a year after the treaty council with Stevens and Palmer, people gathered in the Walla Walla Valley—but this time the white men far outnumbered the Indian people, and the intent was not to keep the peace but to make war.

Craig interpreted during a meeting between Shaw and the Nez Perce leaders. Shaw explained the reasons Governor Stevens had not visited as promised and assured them that Stevens appreciated their good conduct and excellent service. When Spotted Eagle told Shaw that some of the Nez Perces "looked down upon him because he had become a volunteer, and said that he was no longer a Chief," Shaw assured Spotted Eagle he was still a chief and would always be a chief in the eyes of Stevens and all whites.[479] But the Americans were concerned, for the number of Nez Perces loyal to them was no longer in the majority and, thanks to the hostilities and the Stevens-Wool dispute the treaty ratification process was stalled in Congress.

Craig planned to leave the following day for the Lapwai Valley but was in a quandary as to how to distribute the long awaited goods. The food, clothing, and supplies were meant for the Nez Perces and other American allies, yet his volunteer company also included a number of white men. He was desperate for distribution instructions, writing to Stevens that even though Pearson had delivered two letters from him and Captain John had delivered one, they included no directions for allocating the supplies.[480] Ultimately Craig made the decision himself: he decided the food should be distributed to the Nez Perce people, himself (as agent) and his government employees, but not to the white men serving in his volunteer guard. He authorized only a small amount of blankets, boots and tobacco be issued to Chase, LaFontaine, Raboin, Tallman, Leonard, Hilly, McGinnes, Stratton, Hale and Joe Craig.[481]

Not surprisingly, Craig's decision was unpopular among the white men. Henri Chase believed the white men's sacrifice in the remote Lapwai Valley should be partially repaid with items it was impossible for them to buy. He argued that while serving in Craig's company, they had almost no food or clothing and no way of getting any. "Beef was our only fare while it lasted, and after that was gone, roots."[482]

Craig's decision proved to be correct. Indian Service employees were, as part of their pay, furnished food; volunteer militia was not. "It is utterly impracticable to supply a [volunteer company] with rations or food," the governor later wrote. "The regular employees of the Indian Service only can be rationed, and rations will be issued to Indians only in case of necessity."[483]

After four months of riding together, Company M, with its 52 men mustered to protect Craig in the Nez Perce country, was formally dissolved.[484] Craig gave the officers the usual time to settle their affairs.[485] The Nez Perce warriors loyal to William stayed with him, the disgruntled white men went their separate ways.

The next day, Robie's pack train, along with Craig, left the Walla Walla Valley bound for the Lapwai Valley. Spotted Eagle and the Nez

Perce warriors provided escort and, in military fashion, the adjutant of Shaw's company inspected their rifles and sidearms before they left, declaring them in "generally good order."[486] The journey was accomplished without incident, and the food arrived safely in the Lapwai Valley. But waiting at the Craig home was a great gathering of Indian people, and they were in a stormy mood. Not just Nez Perces had gathered, but Cayuses and others. Craig guessed about 2,500 Indians were at his place.[487]

Craig had earlier been concerned that when the buffalo-hunting families returned to Nez Perce country, they would not be happy with the tumultuous situation their people were now facing. His concern was well founded. He listened in a council to find out the feelings of some of the Indians gathered at his place. Even though they had been far away, the buffalo-hunting leaders had received reports of events in their homelands, and they did not like what had been happening. It was, above all, the hanging of Indian men by white men that would sever the Nez Perce alliance to Americans.

Man-with-the-Rope-in-His-Mouth recalled that, when he was on the other side of the mountains, they received news by letter that once again white men were "hanging people in this country." He was still disturbed by the events years ago that led up to Cayuse men being hanged to avenge the Whitman mission deaths.[488]

Thunder's Eye, staunchly loyal to the Americans, is not reported to have returned from buffalo country to lend his voice to the debate. But, according to Craig's later report, others just back from east of the Bitterroots voiced strong dissatisfaction not only with the white men, but also with the goods they brought.[489] Eagle From the Light spoke, saying they had kept their friend (Robie) there so he could hear their hearts. The hangings of Indians by white men without calling a council to decide their fate had, he believed, broken the treaty. He said:

> ...three...people...[had been] killed and hung; that has been in my mind ever since...the man who was hung at Red Wolf's Ground was also a relative of mine. I thot he was hung for burning a house; I know not whether it is so. Property is not equal to a man's life...[490]

Eagle from the Light recalled that the previous year they and the Americans had talked in friendship, but "from that talk this blood has run." Eagle from the Light warned the Americans to move off. Although he had always thought a great deal of the Americans and thought they would "do everything justly and by Council," he now knew their hearts and wanted them to know his. "I wish the Americans to stay away, and not come to my country."[491]

It was an edgy situation for *so·yá·po·*. Robie and his crew quickly returned to the volunteers' camp in the Walla Walla Valley. Craig stayed, however, and listened to "excitable tales," later recalling that four or five Nez Perce leaders "did not wish any more provisions sent into their Country neither did they wish any Whites to come among them."[492] After the council, Craig relayed the Nez Perces' feeling to Shaw, who sent a messenger to the Lapwai, confronting the Nez Perce leaders who were, it appeared, thinking of going to war.

Craig again called a council, and the talk of war abated somewhat. He probably reiterated a well understood fact: if the Nez Perces went to war with the United States, they would be done. Like the Cayuses, they would be driven from their homelands and the graves of their ancestors—their women and children would be crying in their tepees. Craig thought he had averted the talk of war, for he reported that during the council they reached "a very fair understanding and as the Cayuses had left for their own Country everything resumed the usual quietness and we got along very well."[493] Weeks passed and tensions eased in Nez Perce country.

Meanwhile, Shaw's volunteers drew rations, checked their weapons, and marched southeast toward the Grand Ronde country, seeking hostiles. Stevens' orders to Shaw were to "strike the hostiles wherever he finds them…[and] to spare no exertion to reduce to unconditional submission any hostiles within reach."[494] With Captain John acting as guide, the volunteer army of 190 soldiers with provisions for ten days climbed out of the valley heat into the Blue Mountains.[495] On July 17 they saw dust rising near the Grand Ronde River and soon came upon an Indian camp (near present-day Elgin, Oregon). Shaw ordered his men to attack the camp, and they killed at least sixty people – many of them women and children who were run down and shot as they fled in terror. Shaw's men destroyed the food they found in the camp; "about 150 horse loads of camas, dried beef, tents, some flour, coffee, sugar." Also found and destroyed were the tools and cooking utensils of the lodges, about 100 pounds of ammunition, and about 200 horses, "most of which were shot, there being about 100 serviceable animals."[496] The occupants of the camp had been mainly non-combatants, for most of the able-bodied men were out hunting or fishing.

Stevens was delighted when Shaw reported a great "victory" over a "large hostile force," for he believed a victory was what he needed to justify his war policy and bring the fighting to a quick end. The details of the massacre were not divulged to Stevens, however, and he moved ahead with earlier plans (those urged by the Nez Perce leaders) to hold a second council at the Walla Walla grounds. What he believed was a victory at the Grand Ronde in fact cast a darker pall than even the actions of the Oregon volunteers.

A growing number of Nez Perces had been ready to fight the Americans, but they stopped talking war when they learned of the massacre at Grand Ronde. After the attack, Shaw had sent a challenge: "he was tired of trying to persuade people to be peaceful who would not be—that if they wanted war they should have it."[497] The Nez Perce leaders backed off, unwilling to subject their families to the suffering the Cayuses, Wallawallas and other families camped on the Grand Ronde would suffer when winter came and those that survived the attack had no food.[498]

When Craig heard from Shaw about his "great victory" in the Grand Ronde country, he sat down to write a congratulatory letter. Craig said the victory had come at a most proper time and he was pleased that Shaw had given them a "damned good thrashing."[499] As he sat at his desk with pen and paper, he knew he would have to leave the Nez Perce country if things didn't change; the only white person the Nez Perce leaders wanted to see was Governor Stevens himself. A decisive victory for the Americans would straighten out those who advocated fighting.

But before Craig finished writing his congratulatory letter to Shaw, a messenger arrived with alarming news: the war party had learned of the Grand Ronde massacre and had come to kill him. With a shaky hand (and perhaps with "Blue John," his whiskey keg, nearby[500]) Craig sat again at his desk and added these lines:

Now it is getting dark and the news comes of a large party of Indians in the mountains about three miles from this place. [The person I talked to] tells of a great many being killed by you in the grand round and says the[y] will charge on this place in the morning 29th.[501]

Thus was Craig informed that Shaw's troops accomplished a massacre of noncombatants rather than a victory over armed fighters. Angry warriors were gathered in the mountains above the Craigs' place, waiting for daylight before attacking his house.

But the attack did not come, at daylight or later. It is impossible to know why. Perhaps, when warriors gathered the night before to prepare for war, enough leaders spoke about not risking the wrath of the U.S. Army upon their people—which would surely come if they killed Craig—a point that altered enough hearts to change their plan. Perhaps some talked of the years that he had been their friend and interpreter and decided to spare his life. For whatever reason, a war party did not arrive at William and Isabel's house at dawn to avenge the Grand Ronde deaths.

When their fear was diluted by the dawn, William finished writing his letter:

We have passed the night and has had no charge from the war party. Capt. John is starting and I will close.

Yours truly -- Wm Craig
Lt Col

—PS The cheaves say Gov Stevens will visit them when there is peace any message from him the wil [they will] be glad to Receive[502]

The massacre of old men, women, and children by American volunteer soldiers sent a strong message to the anti-*so·yá·po·* faction of Nez Perce leaders (Old Looking Glass, Old Joseph, Three Feathers and Eagle from The Light)[503] and others who were ready to drive out the white men. The anger of the Nez Perces made the area a dangerous place for settlers, and most of the white people living between the Walla Walla Valley and the Clearwater country packed up and moved away. Henri Chase and his family resettled in the Bitterroot Valley, not far from John Owen's trading post.[504] The Raboin family, as well as Al Tallman, settled nearby.[505] With the exception of William Craig and a few agency employees, the farms in the valleys of the Lapwai and Tucannon soon sheltered no white people.

Craig had been directed to take a reconnaissance trip north to the Spokanes, to see if they and their neighbors were close to joining the war against the whites. He was about to do so: "with a few Nez Perces but the[y] said I had better not go in to that country," as the war party dominated the prairies and plains and they blamed Craig for "having that Indian hung last winter" and were determined to kill him if they got the chance. Craig told Stevens that he did not ask Shaw for an escort; "It would take a Strong one as the greater part of the hostile Indians"—all the Yakamas, some of the Cayuses and Wallawallas—

were on the prairies north of the Snake River, camped in three places.[506]

Lansdale, now agent for the Flatheads, was making a trip from the Bitterroot Valley to The Dalles and asked Craig to furnish a Nez Perce warrior escort. Craig was prepared to meet Lansdale as requested, with an escort of Nez Perces, but they told him he had better not do that—they offered to go and bring Lansdale to Lapwai. Craig was not one to shirk his duty and had his share of courage. But, heeding advice, he instead asked George Montour to escort Lansdale; Montour brought with him Antoine Plante, two Spokane chiefs, and one Coeur d'Alene chief who met the Nez Perce escort and traveled together to Lapwai.[507]

While it was a difficult summer, a bit of Craig's wry humor (honed, perhaps, when he was a mountain man) crept in when he was composing a letter to Stevens. While he was at his desk, a courier arrived bringing letters. Craig opened the letters and added this line to the one he was writing: "Just now there has an express come in from the Spokans. But all the letters is written in french and as I cannot read french you may suppose I do not get much News."[508]

Because his Nez Perce allies wanted to meet with him, Stevens made plans to travel to the Walla Walla Valley for a second council with the plateau tribes. Fearing for his safety, he asked Col. Wright to accompany him with soldiers—for even though the Spokanes hadn't joined the hostilities, the Nez Perces seemed to be on the brink of war.[509] He did not think the Nez Perces would attack the whites immediately, but he did think strong measures were needed to prevent it.

Wright and Stevens met August 13 in Vancouver and agreed to a plan that would change the course of the hostilities on the plateau. Wright was to send four companies of men under Lt. Col. Edward J. Steptoe to build a U.S. military fort in the Walla Walla Valley; in return, Stevens was to raise no more militia and to muster his volunteers out of service by September 9.[510]

Meanwhile, the Craig family was going about business as usual. The Craig ranch provided fresh mounts for the express riders going back and forth between the Bitterroot Valley and Olympia. Craig hired (at $60-month salary) Green McCafferty and William Simpson as herders for the government livestock.[511] Now that his son, Joe, was almost grown, the younger Craig often served as his father's express rider: the job of courier in the Nez Perce tribe was one filled by young, athletic, unmarried men, for the work was both physically demanding and dangerous.[512] In early August 1856 Joe delivered a letter from his father to Shaw in his Walla Walla Valley camp.[513]

Many of the Nez Perces had moved off to their fishing, berrying, and hunting grounds and those who farmed were threshing wheat when word came that Stevens was calling another meeting. Stevens had informed Shaw of his council plans; Shaw passed the news on to Craig, along with an invitation to Lawyer and other Nez Perce chiefs to attend the council and a promise that the hostiles could come and go in peace.[514]

Andrew Dominic Pambrun, now 33 years old, was delighted when Governor Stevens asked him to join his staff for the council: the job paid five dollars a day in gold coin and he needed the money. Col. Shaw was back in the Walla Walla Valley camp with about sixty volunteers, and a forty-wagon ox train of supplies had arrived safely. Pambrun had heard of Shaw's recent Grand Ronde attack and knew the tribes were angry about what the whites had done, but he nonetheless took the job. Years later, he would write in some detail about his experiences.[515]

As Stevens traveled to the Walla Walla Valley, the U.S. Army closed the area east of the Cascade Mountains to white settlement. From The Dalles on August 20, 1856, Col. Steptoe issued an order prohibiting any white person—other than Craig ("persons ceded rights from the Indians"), Hudson's Bay Company employees or miners "collecting gold at the Colville mines"—from remaining or settling in Indian country.[516] Stevens was incensed when he learned of the closure and argued that the U.S. military had no authority to keep white people out of the interior.[517]

Nez Perce warriors, along with William, left the Clearwater country August 23 and took seven days traveling to the Walla Walla Valley; they brought with them Dr. Lansdale. While they were en route, on the evening of August 28 a select group of twelve Cayuse and Walla Walla warriors attacked an incoming pack train (near modern Milton-Freewater, Oregon).[518] If memory served him well, Pierre Pambran recalled that the volunteers who were escorting the train shot off all their ammunition and then abandoned the horses and the packs to the warriors, who happily took possession.[519] The supplies included clothing and two kegs of whiskey; the whites hoped the warriors would get drunk on the whiskey and be easy prey, but their leader was smarter than that. He tapped one keg, gave his men a drink and then "threatened if any of them took any more, he would destroy it all."[520] The volunteers and packers escaped to the Walla Walla camp and reported the fight to Stevens, who gave them a good dressing-down.

Stevens was embarrassed; he believed that the volunteers had forfeited "much of the prestige" of the Grand Ronde by the only loss of animals and supplies in the whole of the volunteers' services.[521]

Once again the Waiilatpu area was filling with people. Col. Steptoe arrived with troops and construction material for the new post. Antoine Plante, along with George Montour, rode in from the Spokane country and reported the Spokanes still friendly though not planning to attend the council, as they needed to lay-in fish for the winter. When the main delegation of Nez Perces entered, the volunteers honored them with a salute. Robie and crew successfully brought a pack train and a wagon train of goods from The Dalles. Homlie, chief of the Wallawallas since Yellow Bird's death, arrived with his people; some of the bands hostile to the Americans came and set up their camps. The whites were quite provoked, Pambrun recalled, when braves who had attacked the supply train rode in on pack mules wearing the clothes "intended for the poor and almost nude volunteers."[522] By September 9 the major council participants were ready and waiting.

Council commenced two days later, but it was obvious that the mood of most tribes was ugly. A rumor was circulating that the Cayuses were coming to attack Stevens' camp. In formal council, Stevens found that half of the Nez Perces and almost all the other tribes were hostile. Groups of unreceptive bands were camped in the outlying areas, not willing to commit themselves to the valley; Qamáya'qin was camped with his followers on the Touchet (tu'se) River. Stevens requested Col. Steptoe to bring his troops and camp at the council grounds. When Steptoe, who was under orders from Gen. Wool not to participate in affairs of Stevens and his volunteer army, refused to move to the council grounds, Stevens proceeded to move the council site five miles to Col. Steptoe's camp.[523]

As the army and wagons were moving on the main road, Stevens, Craig, Lawyer, Pambrun, and a Dr. Burns took an adjacent trail in order to keep an eye on the Yakama group. Soon they saw Qamáya'qin and his warriors, riding abreast and heading their way. As Pambrun remembers it, Craig and the men drew their guns and made ready to fight, but Qamáya'qin changed from threatening to friendly, "cooled down and wished to shake hands." Pambrun cautioned the Governor not to let Qamáya'qin get close enough to shake hands with the teamsters at the wagons, as his party outnumbered Stevens' at least five to one and they might try to stampede the animals. "Mr. Craig and others agreed with [Pambrun's] views, but the Governor…was a man who unwillingly took any suggestion not emanating from himself, and was also ignorant of Indian character…" Stevens followed his advice, however, and Pambrun told Qamáya'qin that they were anxious to get to camp, but would meet them there and happily shake hands as they had come to make peace. When they reached camp, Qamáya'qin and his warriors did not arrive to shake hands; Lawyer told Stevens and Craig that they had been wise to keep them at a distance out there on the trail.[524]

The council was reopened on September 16, but after just a day of talk it was clear there would be no agreement. Stevens was nonconciliatory and rigidly militant, later telling Secretary of War Davis that his "propositions were unconditional submission to the justice and mercy of the government, and the rendition for trial of murderers."[525] Qamáya'qin had come to the council to see if Stevens' words jibed with those of the U.S. Army's negotiator, but he found the two white men had different hearts. Qamáya'qin's brothers had already pledged the Yakamas to peace with Col. Wright, as had Quiltaneenock of the Rock Island (Isle de Pierres) band of Sinkiuse.[526] None of the tribes' leaders would surrender anyone to Stevens' soldiers when there was an option of peace offered by Wright. Pambrun recalled that a dangerous addition to the mix was a large supply of bourbon among the officers in Steptoe's camp, which "kept the Governor half shot, and indifferent to danger…"[527] (Stevens drank excessively at times but, according to a biographer, alcohol seldom affected his productivity.[528])

Although the talks were not going well, the agents distributed treaty goods. To the "friendly Indians" Craig issued gifts of provisions from the government pack train that Robie delivered: bacon, beef, flour, peas, coffee, sugar, vinegar, candles, soap, salt, 220 pounds of saleratus (baking soda), and 66 pounds of tobacco.[529] He kept the bulk of the tobacco (234 pounds) on hand for future council smokes, to pay spies, and to have some left over for his pipe. No clothing or blankets were handed out. Craig distributed the food and supplies to the headmen, who saw that it went to the most needy of their people.[530]

The council was a complete failure. Craig and the Nez Perce headmen loyal to Stevens had wanted the council to bolster their alliance with the Americans, but the opposite occurred. Stevens reported to Secretary of War Davis that, "all my efforts, both to make arrangements with the hostiles, and to do away with the disaffection of the Nez Perces…proved abortive."[531] After closing the council, Stevens met with the Nez Perces separately:

...all, both hostile and friendly Nez Perces, advised the sub-agent Wm. Craig, not to return to the Nez Perce country, as his life would be in danger, and they were afraid he would be killed.[532]

It saddened many Nez Perce people to have Craig think of leaving their country, for he was a Nez Perce by marriage and continued to have the friendship and trust of many. Spotted Eagle spoke what was in his heart:

If you do not return with me, we shall go back as if our eyes were shut. I think my people will not go straight if Craig gets up from that place. But, my friend Craig, on account of the talking I have heard at this place, I am afraid for you.[533]

Years later, Hazard Stevens recalled that the friendly chiefs feared Yakama warriors might kill Craig as a way to involve the Nez Perces in the war.[534]

Stevens arranged for Craig to operate the Indian agency from a new location near Steptoe's military installation, at least for the winter, a relocation that would actually last for several years. Steptoe spoke with the Indians and informed them he came not to make war but to build a post, and he hoped they could get along as friends.

Although he did not publicly admit it, Stevens knew that most of his Indian policies east of the Cascades had failed.[535] He had handled the treaties he sent to Congress in an arrogant manner. His volunteer militia had won few battles, although he had spent lavishly to conduct Indian wars. Now a majority of America's interior Northwest Indian allies had given up on what Stevens offered them and his liaison to the Nez Perces, William Craig, was in danger of death if he returned to his home. And, as though he had not had enough challenge, a further confrontation was about to be visited on Governor Stevens.

On the morning of September 19, Stevens departed camp accompanied by Craig, Pambrun, Perrin Whitman, about fifty Nez Perce warriors led by Lawyer, and sixty-nine volunteers commanded by B. F. Shaw.[536] They were heading for The Dalles. Some three miles from Steptoe's camp, Stevens' party was attacked by a group of warriors led by the young Yakama leader, Qualchan, and Rock Island leader Quiltaneenock. About 450 Yakama, Sinkiuse, Nez Perce, Palouse, Umatilla, and Wallawalla warriors were observing the attack, including Qualchan's uncle, Qamáya'qin, and his father, Owhi.[537] Before they attacked, the warriors told the 50 Nez Perce men who were accompanying Stevens (he had assigned them to hold the ridge on the east side of the corral) to leave: "[We] come not to fight the Nez Perces, but the whites, go to your camp, or we wipe you out."[538] The camp with their women and children was about a mile away. Stevens ordered the Nez Perce guard to leave, as he was afraid his men wouldn't be able to distinguish them from the attacking warriors and the Nez Perce might fall to friendly fire.[539]

The attackers had prepared for this moment; their faces, bodies and horses were painted for war, and Stevens' men just had time to circle their wagons and run the stock inside before the warriors galloped down from the hills. Stevens took charge and deployed Pambrun with six or seven men in a thicket about 75 yards distant, while Craig, wagon-master Higgins, Whitman, Stevens and others fired their weapons from inside the enclosure.[540] The battle went on the entire day and both sides suffered casualties.

The fighting continued until about ten o'clock the following morning and ended when Moses, the Rock Islands' headman, was badly wounded. His companions got him off the battlefield and took him home.[541] Moses died upon reaching Rock Island in the Columbia River (near present-day Wenatchee). Governor Stevens reported his party "had one man mortally wounded, one dangerously, and two slightly. We killed and wounded thirteen Indians."[542] Many of the warriors in the attack party were from tribes who had been told to move from their land by the 1855 treaty.

Stevens' party started a second time for The Dalles on September 23. They must have had a bitter taste in their mouths from the disastrous council and its follow-up attack, but the journey was pleasant. Stevens, Craig, Whitman, and a few others, probably having tapped the quartermaster's stores, were riding along, "singing merrily and enjoying themselves generally."[543] They bucked a stiff wind from the west, as was common to the Columbia-carved gorge.

7
White Men Conquer Plateau People (1856~1859)

After escorting Stevens to The Dalles, Craig continued to Portland to take the oath of office as a local agent to Indians of Washington Territory.[544] He had been hired as a subagent, probably because the law authorized only a limited number of full agents while subagents could be appointed at the president's discretion.[545] Craig's duties and responsibilities were those of a full agent. Joining him in Portland were a number of the Nez Perce warriors who had helped escort Stevens back from the Blackfeet treaty council; about a week later Lawyer joined them, traveling by boat from The Dalles to Portland.[546] On October 10, Craig and his companions appeared in the office of the United States attorney, where Craig posted a $5,000 bond and took the oath of office:

I William Craig do solemly [sic] swear that I will support the Constitution of the United States and well and faithfully serve the United States in the office of Local Agent for the Indians in Washington Territory. That I will carefully attend to all such orders and instructions as I shall from time to time receive from the President of the United States, the Secretary of the Interior, the commissioner of Indian Affairs, or the person under whose direction I am or may hereafter be placed, and that in all things belonging to my said office, during my continuance therein I will faithfully, justly and truly, according to the best of my ability, skill and judgement, do equal and impartial justice, without fraud, favor or opposition.

William Craig[547]

On the return trip from Portland to Walla Walla, and before disbanding the volunteers pursuant to the Stevens-Wool agreement, Craig went shopping at The Dalles. Stevens' warrior escort to The Dalles as well as Craig's former Lapwai area volunteers were furnished "a good fit-out of clothing to wit Coat, Pants, Vest, shirt and one pair of Blankets...Hats & shoes..."[548] He bought clothing for about seventy-five men.[549]

The volunteer units of Washington Territory were disbanded October 30, 1856.[550] Enough officers and line personnel were retained beyond that date to finish the paperwork, but Craig was not one of them. He had served only ten months as aide to the Commander in Chief of the Washington Territorial Volunteers.

The "Superintendency of Indian Affairs," as it was called, now had Perrin Whitman on its payroll. He was a young man with an excellent command of the Nez Perce language, and earned a salary of $100 per month as interpreter.[551] The Walla Walla agency also owned a wagon and mules to pull it, all the agent's responsibility. In The Dalles, Craig put the team up in Bigelow's corral (cost of oats and corral: $25) and saw to it that the wagon was repaired and the mules shod ($47.50), bought a new whip and had the harness straps replaced ($7.50).[552]

His business finished at The Dalles, Craig then joined the government wagon train for the journey back to the new Fort Walla Walla garrison and his new agency. In the past month Col. Steptoe had moved his fort a few miles from the old Hudson's Bay Company site to the location of the 1855 treaty council and he had moved the blockhouse and Indian agency property there as well.[553]

Wright and Steptoe met in October with Red Wolf, Eagle from the Light, and three Cayuse headmen and agreed to peace. Wright made a speech that included the phrases, "The bloody shirt shall now be washed and not a spot left on it. ...All past differences must be thrown behind us. ...Let peace and friendship remain forever." Craig's family and friends believed that all the Nez Perces were now ready to go back to their alliance with the Americans; it was reported that Old Looking Glass "had ordered all of the war party out of his country" and asked Craig to come back home. But Craig was not sure that the friendship of the disillusioned chiefs would hold; unless "the Indians come in & talk very fair," he would send for his family and spend the winter in the Walla Walla Valley.[554]

With regular army troops stationed nearby and peace agreed to between Wright and the hostile contingent, settlers thought it safe to return to their homes in the Walla Walla Valley. The returning settlers included A. D. Pambrun and his family, who camped with other returnees on the brow of the hill and looked over the valley with their burned-out farms. They built bonfires, and a few "who had firewater for the occasion, dozed away a few hours in happy inebriety."[555] They then moved nearer to the garrison for the winter, and the tenuous peace combined with winter snow left them undisturbed until spring.

Meanwhile, Isaac Stevens was winding down his tenure in Washington Territory. His aspirations were not in the West. He wanted to be in Washington City, District of Columbia, and had won the election as Washington Territory's delegate to the U.S. Congress.[556] Not wanting to leave unfinished business, Stevens pushed for (and succeeded with Leschi) having leaders of hostile bands in Washington Territory tried and hanged as murderers.[557] Before departing, Stevens worked to organize the underfunded and understaffed Indian service so that the needs of the subjugated Indians—some of who were now starving—might be met. When in the spring of 1857 he turned the Superintendency over to James W. Nesmith (now responsible for Indians in both Oregon and Washington Territories), no shooting wars were taking place and the departmental accounts were in order.[558]

Craig knew war parties had wintered in Nez Perce country: Cayuse war chief Big Belly and his band were with Joseph's people, and Qa·máya'qin, Quiltaneenock and their families were together in Lapwai Valley to reclaim horses. Col. Wright might believe the war was over, but William heard that there were still plenty of people ready to drive away the whites. Col. Steptoe instructed Nez Perce leaders that they must force the war party out of their area or they would all be considered guilty by association. Craig doubted if Lawyer was strong or brave enough to carry out Steptoe's instructions; he didn't think Lawyer:

...has got the Sand to drive [the war party] out of his Country as myself and Col. Steptoe told them they must do. I think different from Col. Wright, I think things are as far or further from being settled than last Spring.[559]

Stockwhitley, leader of the Deschutes band of about twenty families, came to Craig because his people were hungry, but Craig refused him food until he gave up his arms.[560] By denying Stockwhitley, Craig was carrying out long-standing government policy to withhold food (and later annuities) from Indians not allied to America.

In mid-December Richard (Tackitonitis) brought Craig news that about half the Cayuses and Wallawallas were still in Wallowa country with Old Joseph's people and Qamáya'qin and Quiltaneenock were still at Lapwai.[561] Stockwhitley told Col. Steptoe that Qamáya'qin and the Cayuses were killing cattle belonging to the warriors who had accompanied Governor Stevens to The Dalles.[562] Such news from the

Lapwai region led Craig to believe the coalition against the whites was growing.

Craig was struggling to support his family far away from his Lapwai fields, garden, horse herd, and farm stock. While he was building a house, he rented one—for $20 a month—near Steptoe's camp.[563] He requested permission from Stevens to plant some fields of grain, promising that he would not let farming interfere with the time he devoted to the tribes under his care; but "there is a heavy expense accrued living at this place." Stevens was preparing to leave for the East, and Craig must have felt a spark of sentiment for the little man who had been his leader for the past tumultuous year. In his most emotional written words found to date, Craig closed his letter to Stevens with: "Your Friend and Well Wisher, Wm. Craig."[564]

The year 1857 began with frigid temperatures and a shortage of food. Nobody moved around much unless it was unavoidable. The food supply was desperately short for Indians and whites alike, as Stevens' ill-advised August-September 1856 council had interrupted gardening before crops were preserved for winter and hunting, fishing, and berrying had been cut short. Since official food and supply allotment to the tribes would begin when the treaties did, the long delay in Congressional ratification of the 1855 treaties seriously complicated health and life itself, not to mention Indian-white relations.

Captain Cain of Steptoe's troops brought two oxen as food and Craig issued 1,000 pounds of beef to the "Friendly Nez Perces and Cayuses."[565] Robie had brought a train carrying emergency food for the Indian Agency to the Walla Walla Valley in December and Craig dispensed it to the Nez Perces who traveled there. Again rewarding the thirteen warrior leaders who escorted Stevens to The Dalles, Craig gave them more than 1,300 pounds of flour and 350 pounds of sugar; he also distributed beef, peas, coffee, candles, soap, and tobacco sparingly to the entire group.[566] Were it not for the government provisions, the "friendly" Nez Perces and Cayuses could not have fed their families through the winter.

Craig had a new superior—James W. Nesmith, in charge of both Oregon and Washington Territorial Indian matters—and theirs was to be a testy relationship. The Indian Superintendency office in Salem returned Craig's January 1857 supply paperwork to him for correction after he made a mistake adding columns of figures.[567] Having his work questioned and rejected by departmental superiors had not happened to Craig before—and his was a minor and understandable error. He likely was being targeted because he was a southerner and the issue must have been of more consequence than he realized. A group of anti-slavery Oregon Territory politicians—Nesmith was one of them—was building political momentum for Oregon to seek statehood as a free state.

As fall moved into winter, Craig tried to keep track of the hostile bands of Indians as well as his stock left in the Lapwai Valley. The families of Five Crows and Young Chief were reported to be near Fort Boise, Big Belly's band was on the Snake River at the mouth of the Salmon, and Qamáya'kin's band was on the Palouse.

The Snow is very deep in the Nez Perce Country. I fear much for my Stock as the Indians have taken some of the best of them they are there now starving and I cannot go or send after them as the Snow is very bad. I have written to Higgins to send up a Small Pack Train. The military are almost out of supplies.[568]

Since the provisions of both the Indian agency and Steptoe's garrison were running short—the garrison had only a ten days' supply left—Craig needed to retrieve stock from his Lapwai Valley ranch. But his friends advised him not to go as "all the Hostile Cayuses in the Country are at my place." He sent his son Joe, who reported a number of his animals, including some belonging to Washington Territory and two belonging to the federal government, could not be found.[569]

Soon Stevens instructed Craig to visit the Nez Perces in their country and report "the feelings of the Indians" to him.[570] After learning that the Yakama bands had left his Lapwai Valley place, Craig set out January 24, 1857, to visit his beloved Clearwater country. He did not seem to fear for his life; and he sent word ahead by courier to the Nez Perce leaders to come for a talk. Upon arrival he found that the war party had taken all but two of the Washington Territory horses from his place, along with an Indian Agency horse and mule. His own stock came up short thirteen head of horses and fourteen head of cattle (the cattle he supposed were killed by the war party). Since some of the Nez Perces were completely out of food, Craig—in an action mirroring the responsibilities of a *miyó·xot* (leader, chief)—"offered the remainder I had on hand since last summer at that place and some 20 bushels of corn and wheat." Craig called a council and sat down with Old Looking Glass, Old Joseph, and other Nez Perce chiefs. His instructions from Stevens had been to remind the Nez Perces to stay separate from those who were fighting; but that reminder only served to insult some chiefs, who had never wavered in their loyalty to the Americans. They told Craig that the war party had no influence over them. However, the "Nez Perces that were Fighting gave me to understand that they did not wish me to be their agent or to live in there country any more."[571]

Fighting the Indians with volunteer and regular troops had already cost the territories an enormous sum of money (and Stevens was now lobbying Congress for payment of the debts), but Congress was hesitant to approve the treaties until questions were answered about the war. Until ratification, there would be no funds appropriated to fulfill treaty obligations except in emergencies or to sustain native people whose traditional economy had been disrupted.

In the flurry of activity aimed at leaving Nesmith a solvent Indian department, Stevens had—at the same time he instructed Craig to meet with the Nez Perces—directed him to cut down on staff and to keep only one man (likely a herder) and his interpreter (Perrin Whitman) on the payroll. Craig continued to receive no provisions for distribution to the allies, and at one point he complained, "the Government [pack] Train is on the way [from The Dalles] and nothing for the Indian Dept."[572] With no government money to cover expenses, Craig issued certificates (in lieu of cash) totaling, from January to July, $3,388.75 to pay for herding, Perrin Whitman, blacksmithing and ferriage charges, plus his own salary and expenses.[573]

When, hungry plateau people came into the Walla Walla Valley in February 1857, needing food and clothing, Craig requested instructions from Stevens since the "Indians that are coming in are all out of Provisions and they belong to the Umatilla Reservation."[574] The Walla Walla, Cayuse, Umatilla reservation was in Oregon Territory, the Nez Perce reservation in Washington Territory, but hunger recognized no boundaries.

As the grass greened up in the spring of 1857, the white settlers who had returned to the Walla Walla Valley began rebuilding their houses and planting gardens. Col. Steptoe encouraged the settlers to raise as much produce as they could (even though there were few tools) so that they could help feed the soldiers.[575] Spring also brought a new crop of miners heading for the gold mines in Colville country. Craig reported that by mid-April about 100 miners had already passed through the Walla Walla Valley and that "they do not call at either the post or my place [but] pass right on asking no advice from any one." White miners on the way through the Indians' lands often led to trouble; Craig added, "there is some hard cases...such as Jack Hull and others from the Dalles."[576]

Hope continued to build in the Indian communities that they could get their land back. It had been almost two years since the treaty council; none of the money, goods or services had been paid for the land the whites were already moving onto, the U.S. Army had kicked the volunteer soldiers out and stopped new settlers from coming in, Col. Wright was expected to come to the military Fort Walla Walla in June, and the anti-American factions of the tribes were anxious to hear what Col. Wright had to say. Billy and his band of Nez Perces visited Craig in April, bringing news that some of the Nez Perces, along with the Cayuses, Wallawallas, and Palouses, were talking of war or of Colonel Wright returning their country to them.[577] For the time being, Steptoe's garrison remained in the Walla Walla Valley and the plateau bands went about their lives without harassment, other than the constant danger from white men traveling to and from the Colville mines. An armed truce reigned and no fighting occurred in 1857.

Craig submitted a report, dated July 21, 1857, on the allied Cayuse and Nez Perce people. He estimated the Nez Perces and friendly Cayuses numbered about 3,500 people. He said they owned many horses and some cattle and had until the summer of 1856 been responsive to the whites. But in 1856, Craig reported, about two-thirds of them had joined the hostile bands, although they had since returned home. He did not mention the hangings and Grand Ronde massacre that had contributed to the Nez Perces' anger toward whites and had threatened his life. He noted that his people were now working their gardens as they had done before the fighting and had forty to fifty acres under cultivation in wheat, peas, potatoes, and corn. If they had farm implements, they could raise their own food, Craig believed, for they are "enterprising and industrious." The big issue was the treaties:

A part of them appear anxious that the treaties should be kept, and a part do not wish it. As soon as they learn the treaties are not sanctioned they will all be at rest.

Craig believed a $25,000 appropriation would be enough to build mills, school the children, and keep the peace.[578]

Craig's characterization of the Nez Perce people as "industrious" and "enterprising" was descriptive of what the government wanted the Indians to be, as current policy called for "civilizing" them on self-supporting reservations using schools of manual labor.[579] However,

Craig's boss, James Nesmith, believed that it was "utopian and impractical" to think the Indians could ever be civilized or Christianized; he advocated putting them on reservations to keep the peace and control the liquor while waiting for "starvation, disease and bad whiskey" to relieve the government of its responsibility to them.[580]

Congress in 1857 hired a journalist, J. Ross Browne, to investigate and report on causes of the war in Oregon and Washington Territories. The war had driven settlers away from Washington Territory and the stagnant economy brought about by nonratification of the treaties was stalling any new immigration.[581] Congress wanted a report on not only the causes of the war but how the Indians were handled and the Indian department's expenditures.[582]

Browne and Craig came together on two occasions. Browne visited reservations and agencies, talking with headmen and agents. Craig interpreted for Browne's meeting at The Dalles with Lawyer as well as at a well-publicized meeting on the Siletz reservation at Yaquina Bay (near present Newport, Oregon).[583] At Siletz, Craig would have used Chinook jargon and English to interpret between the headmen and Browne. Ten years later, a reminiscence in the Port Townsend, Washington Territory, newspaper noted that Browne made frequent use of a pocket flask of whiskey during the council and the veracity of both Joseph Lane and James Nesmith was in question.[584] The product of Browne's investigation—two reports that added to the turmoil—found conditions on the reservations quite unsatisfactory and the U.S. Treasury responsible for costs of the recent war.[585]

Both Indian and white politicians grappled with the question of whether the 1855 treaties should be scrapped. A majority of the plateau tribes wanted the treaties forgotten and their land back. Most of the white politicians wanted the treaties to be stopped short of ratification (as Anson Dart's had been) and new treaties negotiated. Col. Steptoe and some army staff agreed that the treaties would not be ratified while General Newman S. Clarke (General Wool's replacement) believed if the treaties were ratified, there would be all-out war. J. Ross Browne was of the opinion the treaties would be ratified and enforced; Craig hoped that would be the case.[586]

It was during the relative peacefulness of 1857 that Craig met Thomas B. Beall who was to be a friend the remainder of his life. Beall recalled their meeting:

*I first met Craig in the latter part of September 1857. He was at
The Dalles, Oregon, for the purpose of purchasing his winter supplies
accompanied by several Nez Perce Indians, among them Chief Lawyer
and Reuben. As I wanted to see the Walla Walla country, my
cousin...gave me a letter of introduction to Craig which I tendered on
my arrival at The Dalles.*

*Craig was the sub-Indian agent for the Nez Perces at that time and
the agency was at Walla Walla. I was at The Dalles two days...[and
was] soon informed that Craig would not be able to return to the
agency for several days and as I was anxious to proceed I...[traveled
with a party of Hudson Bay people as far as old Fort Walla Walla, now
Wallula.] I there...proceeded to Cantonment Stevens in the Walla
Walla valley. Occupied by...U.S. army, under the command of Col. E.
J. Steptoe. I was there nearly two months and saw a great deal of
Craig nearly every day during my stay, and our intercourse with each
other soon ripened into an ever lasting friendship.*[587]

It was also in this time period that Perrin Whitman accused Craig of
not paying his salary as the agency's interpreter. Isaac Stevens, who
was leaving the West aboard the ship *Commodore*, wrote to Nesmith
about Whitman's claim that Craig had not paid him in the spring of
1857.[588] Nesmith checked Craig's records and found Craig had
"charged the amount of $1000 as paid to said Whitman for his
services."[589] Nesmith was furious. Craig had certified his accounts to
be true on his honor. If they were accurate, then Whitman had perjured
himself; if Whitman was correct, then Craig was culpable. When later
confronted by Nesmith, Craig stated that he had taken vouchers and
issued certificates "as other Agents were then doing which I thought
was the proper course to pursue in the absence of funds."[590]

From that point on, the Salem office demanded that Craig's
paperwork be submitted in triplicate, sent many accounts back to him
for correction, and questioned lateness of reports and noncompliance
with procedures.[591] In April, Craig personally brought his accounts to
Nesmith's Salem office.[592] It appears that groundwork was being laid
for Craig to be replaced.

There was frequent trouble between whites and Indians as more
miners headed to the Colville and Fraser River gold mines and plans
progressed for the Mullan Road, which would link Fort Walla Walla
with Fort Benton on the Missouri River.[593] In the spring of 1858 white
miners killed Quiltaneenock, the young leader of the Rock Islands, as
he rode down a trail in his country (near modern Wenatchee).[594]

Qamáya'kin and Quiltaneenock had tried to rally the Nez Perce warriors to join Yakamas, Rock Islands, Spokanes, and Coeur d'Alenes in a unified fight against the Americans. Craig had known the two leaders and their followers to be in Clearwater country at times, and it was their presence that had caused him to fear for his life.

Craig wrote to Isaac Stevens in Washington D.C., urging him, as Washington Territory's Congressional delegate, to influence a United States military strike against the hostile Columbia Plateau bands:

I think it the most favourable time to do anything with the Indians in this valley as they are rather poor at present. But it does not appear to be the wish of the commanders…to do anything with them…All the country from White Salmon on the North side of the Columbia and the river DeChutes on the South side is Indian Country and no person is allowed to settle with the exception of the Hudson Bay Company servants…I understand from reliable Indians that all my fencing and buildings and fruit trees are destroyed in the Nez Perce country.[595]

That Craig urged the Americans to send troops against enemy Indians shows his interest in putting both the Nez Perces and himself not only on the winning side of the conflict but in a position to gain economically. His thinking is understandable, for he would be killed if the hostile plateau Indians beat the Americans. Yet it was not only survival that motivated Craig; he had been making a good living at trading, innkeeping, farming, and stockraising before war ended such enterprises. The interior's poor economy juxtaposed with its wonderful possibilities undoubtedly frustrated him. He yearned to return to a stable income or, better yet, expand his trade to include new settlers, for his experiences to date confirmed that thousands of white people in the United States wanted to settle in Oregon and Washington territories. Although he had fled the United States long ago, the nation and its free-enterprise system was now coming to him. Just a few bands of angry plateau Indians stood in his—and the allied Nez Perce people's—way.

Col. Steptoe was becoming increasingly irritated by the stock-stealing raids in the Walla Walla Valley and by reports of more conflicts between miners and Indians to the North. In April, while Craig was in the Willamette Valley, Palouse warriors had captured settlers' horses and cattle, along with 13 head of cattle belonging to the U.S. Army at Fort Walla Walla.[596] Steptoe considered taking troops north of the Snake River to demonstrate the military might of the U.S.

Army, crossing, as it were, the figurative line in the sand drawn by the tribal coalition.

Therefore, on May 6, 1858, Steptoe led about 160 men out of Fort Walla Walla in a show of strength to the anti-American alliance. According to some reports, although Steptoe took two mountain howitzers, he had his men leave their sabers at the fort and had issued only 40 rounds of ammunition per man, obviously not expecting a major engagement.[597] Timothy, his brother Levi, and other Nez Perce men ferried the troops across the Snake near the mouth of the Alpowa, then accompanied them on their march.[598] As Steptoe's troops rode north over the undulating grasslands of Palouse country, news of their coming preceded them and warriors congregated and prepared for battle. Just northwest of *yamástas* (now Steptoe Butte, near the town of Rosalia, Washington), Col. Steptoe's troops fought a battle against several hundred warriors. The troops were surrounded and defeated but with the aid of Timothy's warriors escaped in the night back toward the Snake River.

News of the defeat and the ignominious retreat was delivered to Craig at Fort Walla Walla, and on May 20 Craig notified J. W. Nesmith:

I drop you a line to let you know how things are going on in these parts. On the 6th Inst. Col. Steptoe moved after the Indians who have been committing depredations on people and property. He crossed the Snake River at the same place that we crossed in the Cayuse War and [went] on beyond where we turned back.

On the 16th he fell in with a large body of Indians Say Spokanes Coeur d'Alenes, Palouses, Yakimas, Rock Islands and some of the Walla Walla and some of the Cayuses about 9 hundred so report says.

When I heard from Col Steptoe he had been fighting 3 days and was very much cut up had lost his pack train and all his pack animals.

He has sent only one express in and that was before he commenced fighting.

Another express man was killed and he [Steptoe] is on the retreat there has been about 85 men sent to his relief this is the last account I had from that quarter.

Report says that the Nez Perces have taken some beef cattle to the command how true it is I cannot Say but I believe the Nez Perces are still friendly.

It is expected the Umatillas and Cayuses have an idea of attacking this place as there is very few troops left to guard the post.

When I learn more I will write again.

I am Sir Your most Obdt –
Wm. Craig
Sub Ind. Agent
Washington Terry[599]

Two days later Col. Steptoe and his surviving troops returned to the fort. The American army had been whipped and plateau people were ready to take their land back. Craig observed, "They have gained one victory which will give them great encouragement."[600]

Earlier, during the relative quiet of 1857, white residents of the Walla Walla Valley had applied to the federal government for a post office. The new Fort Walla Walla was now a permanent institution housing hundreds of men, Craig's Indian Agency did a lively express business, and the number of settlers around the fort was increasing. On June 2, 1858, a post office was officially established, the location was called "Wailepta," and William Craig was appointed postmaster.[601] The Craig family's log house, sitting on a quarter of an acre, served as the post office.[602] Documents from Washington City authorizing the post office could have arrived at Fort Walla Walla by August or September; therefore—just as Craig had served as an Indian agent for months before paperwork made it official—he probably was serving as postmaster of Wailepta before the paperwork caught up. Wailepta's second postmaster, Francis L. Worden, was appointed on October 1, 1858.[603] In 1862 the name "Wailepta" was changed to "Walla Walla."[604]

After Steptoe's decimated troops returned to Fort Walla Walla, the white people in the valley feared Indian attack even more than before. Although plans had been made for Craig to take his agency paperwork to Salem in June, he cancelled the trip, unwilling to leave his family unprotected. In a letter to Nesmith, Craig reported that:

The Indian news is that they are still collecting to fight the troops there is a great number now waiting for another battle. They say if Col Steptoe does not go to them they will come over in a large body and wipe us all out.

The Nez Perces still remain friendly there are a number of them in this place employed as spies and herders. I have Some of them employed. They caught a palouse indian this morning running off mules & horses...[605]

The defeat and embarrassing (to the United States) withdrawal of Steptoe's troops brought immediate reaction from General N. S. Clarke and the U.S. military. Clarke put Col. George Wright in charge of more than 600 fighting men (many reinforcements coming from California) and ordered:

...the punishment and submission of the Indians engaged in the late attack on the command of Lieutenant Colonel Steptoe, and the surrender of the Palouze Indians who murdered two miners in April last...You will attack all the hostile Indians you may meet, with vigor; make their punishment severe and persevere until the submission of all is complete.[606]

The troops under Col. Wright engaged and defeated the combined forces of Spokane, Coeur d'Alene, Palouse, and some Yakama warriors in early September 1858, at what became known as the Battles of Four Lakes and Spokane Plains. Rather than their traditional guerrilla warfare, the warrior-army had developed distinct war plans. But, they "met their enemy in open battlefield encounters, in which they were decisively defeated." Casualties were light on both sides, for the long range of the U.S. military's new weapons—Sharpe's long-range minie-ball rifles—neutralized Indian offensive action.[607]

The army captured a herd of close to 1,000 horses belonging to Snake River people. Women and children had been driving the horses north from Wahwahwai when they were discovered by the troops. Wright reserved the best horses for army use and ordered the remainder shot; killing the horses took the better part of two days.[608]

Accompanying Col. Wright's troops were 30 Nez Perce warrior-scouts, dressed in blue army uniforms, under command of Lt. John Mullan.[609] Wright had been authorized to employ as many friendly Nez Perces as he wished and to outfit them with arms, ammunition, and obsolete uniforms.[610] The Nez Perce scouts served the army well; but it is reported that they also performed as a Nez Perce secret-service organization by sending information about the white camps to the Indian people.[611] The Nez Perce scouts were, in effect, double agents.

Clarke had authorized Wright to accept surrender of the Spokane and Coeur d'Alene tribes if they delivered the Indians who fought Steptoe and if they retrieved the abandoned howitzers.[612] After accomplishing those objectives, Col. Wright carried out a series of hangings that picked up momentum daily. His anger and embarrassment after the 1856 Yakama campaign—when he was not successful in brokering peace after repeated negotiations with Qamáya'qin's followers—was now vented on Palouses and anyone with connections to Qamáya'qin.[613] He sent word to meet and council at Latah Creek (now known as Hangman's Creek, near Spokane, Washington), then imprisoned and hung warriors who came into his camp. Thomas Beall, packmaster with Wright's supply train—who had in Walla Walla become friends with William Craig—acknowledged that he knew how to fashion a hangman's noose, and he thus acted as hangman.[614] Wright executed men accused of provoking attacks: among those he hung was the young Yakama leader, Qualchan. Qualchan's father, Owhi, was later shot while a prisoner. As Wright's troops headed back to Fort Walla Walla, he ordered Palouse, Wallawalla, and Yakama men hanged as they came upon them. By October 1858, the leaders of hostile interior Washington Territory tribes were almost all dead, the remaining chiefs submissive, and their people dominated by Americans. The American offensive that began in August 1858 was finished by November. Qamáya'qin did not come in to talk with Wright, and as a result he survived. He traveled with his family to Canada, then Montana, and returned to the Palouse Country about 1860. He lived out his life in poverty and died about 1877.[615]

Col. Wright deposited at Fort Walla Walla the prisoners taken on his conquering sweep north of the Snake. Some of the prisoners were soon hanged: three Wallawalla men on charges of murder, one for "exciting to war."[616] The majority of the prisoners were being held as hostages to insure the good behavior of their people, and Craig was responsible for releasing them in due course; meanwhile he was ordered to provide tobacco and other items to keep them comfortable while locked up at Fort Walla Walla.[617]

After the defeat of the plateau Indians in the fall of 1858, events in and around the Walla Walla area moved quickly. General W. S. Harney took over the command of the northern district from General Clarke and at the end of October ordered the Walla Walla Valley open to white settlement.[618] Wright, promoted to general, was assigned command of the Department of Oregon.[619]

The 1855 treaties were at last moving toward Congressional ratification, a move Craig thought long overdue. Craig maintained that the treaties should have been ratified in the next session after they were signed, saving two years of wars. Similarly, Craig thought the treaty negotiated with the Nez Perces was a good thing, stating the negotiations "cannot be made more just or better calculated to promote the true interests of the Indians and our government."[620] He looked upon the treaties as tools toward peaceful coexistence of Indians and white people and the eventual melding of two cultures into one, as he had blended into Isabel's Nez Perce family and the greater family of the interior tribes. It would take but a few years, a gold strike, and a national civil war to shake Craig's faith in Isaac Steven's treaty with the Nez Perce people.

Craig's Annual Report for 1858 was, among other things, another plea for Congress to ratify the 1855 Walla Walla treaties so the Nez Perces could move to their reservation, grow food and—an element now demanding attention—be protected from whiskey peddlers.[621]

Writing the report before Col. Wright took to the field, Craig stated that the Nez Perces had stayed allies of the whites even though "nearly all the other tribes residing in Washington Territory east of the Cascade Mountains are now in open hostility against our government." The Nez Perces were and had always been reliable friends of the white people. He reported that they had been offered strong inducements by the hostiles to join the coalition fighting the Americans, and "at one time it was supposed a portion of the tribe were strongly disaffected," but in the past year the Nez Perces remained allies of the whites even though they were surrounded by hostile tribes who threatened to destroy their crops and take their stock if they did not join them in fighting.

Craig maintained that credit and praise should be given the Nez Perces by the U.S. government for their friendship and that approval of their 1855 treaty would reward them for continued alliance with the Americans and prove to disbelievers that the white people could be trusted.

The government's current Indian policy was to segregate them on self-sufficient reservations while teaching them to live like white people. With those goals in mind, Craig wrote that, if the government kept its treaty promises, the Nez Perce people could raise their own food and, when protected on reservations that had schools for the children, they could be self-supporting. Protection on reservations was critical:

Lately some evil disposed persons have begun to introduce whiskey among them, the pernicious and bad effect of which have become most glaringly apparent within the past few months…many of the Cayuses and Walla Wallas living in this valley have been leading a most dissolute and renegade life lately under no control whatever.

Despite past governmental experiences with alcohol control, Craig evidently believed that placing the tribes on reservations would enable the agency staff or military to prevent whiskey being peddled to them.

He ended his report with a recommendation that $5,000 be spent for a few presents, to buy some provisions to keep some of the poorer families from suffering, but especially as a reward for the Nez Perce people's "gallant behaviour and good conduct and to maintain further peaceable relations."

In late December 1858, Craig reported whiskey-trafficking problems to Superintendent Nesmith. There were a "number of persons…engaged in the traffic of whisky in this valley and…the effect upon the indians is very injurious…"[622] The problems caused by Indians drinking alcohol dated from the earliest white settlement in America, leading one scholar to conclude that "the Indian propensity toward strong drink and the disastrous results that inevitably followed were universal phenomena."[623] The colonies, and later the United States, restricted liquor trade early on in well-intentioned if ineffective attempts to keep their frontiers peaceful as they methodically moved onto lands belonging to Indians.[624] Craig hoped Nesmith would enforce the law, now that whiskey was being stocked in a Walla Walla trading house and sold openly. But Nesmith was to have no better luck than other territorial officials, who continued to be either unwilling or unable to cope with the whiskey problem. In years to come, a number of Craig's own descendants would be among those affected by the alcohol the government could not control.[625]

Craig turned his attention to straightening up affairs at the Indian Agency. He inventoried supplies on hand and found a number of unneeded tools, equipment, and even some food. He listed the items and recommended they be sold at public auction: "Most of this property was unfit for service when I received it…I have no suitable place for storing it and the expense of a storehouse would far exceed its value." Among the items listed were forty-four gallons of vinegar, almost two hundred pounds of saleratus, two Navy revolvers, an ox yoke, a powder horn, a powder flask, a drawknife, and a shot pouch.[626] So ended the year for Washington Territorial Subagent Craig as he put the agency in order for a new year and a new agent.

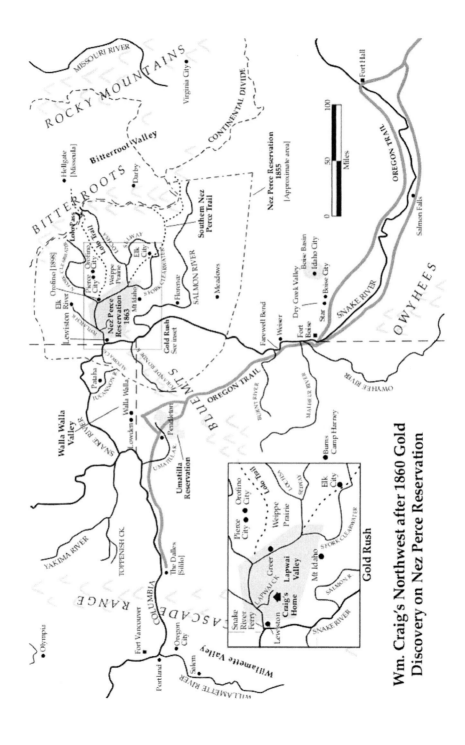

Wm. Craig's Northwest after 1860 Gold
Discovery on Nez Perce Reservation

8
Gold in the Clearwater (1859~1862)

Early in 1859 William Craig was officially notified that he was no longer a Washington territorial Indian subagent. Isaac Stevens saw to it that the Interior Department "removed Craig, agreeable to [Nesmith's] recommendation and appointed John Owen Sub Agent in his place."[627]

What had precipitated Craig's removal as agent? It was not Craig's relationship with the Nez Perce leaders; although he disagreed with some, he seemed to be largely trusted and regarded somewhat like a *miyó·xot* (leader, chief). It was not Perrin Whitman's accusation of fiscal impropriety, for there was likely no intentional wrongdoing on Craig's part and, although the matter had gone to the Department of the Interior, no further action ensued. The reasons for Craig's dismissal may be found in the national political climate.

The very union of the United States of America was being threatened over the issue of slavery, and some southern states were (again) considering secession. At the same time, Oregon Territory was preparing to apply for admission to the union as a free state. Craig's Virginia roots and pro-southern sentiments placed him at odds with, among others, his boss, James Nesmith, one of the settlers working to have Oregon Territory admitted to the union. Nesmith, who had emigrated from Ohio, was one of many transplanted anti-slavery Democrats in the Oregon country. Craig was active in Walla Walla County's Democratic party; the Democratic Central Committee of Washington Territory had appointed both William Craig and A. H. Robie to be part of Walla Walla's "Corresponding Committee."[628] But Craig was a southerner. America's emotions ran high on both sides of the slavery issue; in the Northwest those pushing for Oregon's admission as a free state viewed southerners with suspicion. Former Kentuckian Joseph Lane and Virginian Joe Meek, along with many other influential southern-born settlers and homesick miners, had short or non-existent futures in Oregon's politics. John Owen, a native of Philadelphia, although temporarily assigned Craig's job, would within a few years be released from the Flathead agency after being "suspected of disloyalty to the Union."[629] And Craig, who had started in 1848 as a governmental agent to the Nez Perces, lost his job.[630]

In mid-February Craig turned over agency property and funds totaling about $4,000 to Andrew J. Cain, the new Indian agent for Washington Territory. A Walla Walla Valley neighbor of the Craig family, Thomas Hughes, was within months appointed local agent to the Nez Perces.[631]

Thus, when in March 1859 Congress at last ratified the treaties of 1855, it was not Craig who brought the news to the Nez Perce people but Cain. After Craig's removal, Cain was the first of many agents to be assigned to the territory as a whole or the tribe in particular. The Nez Perces were getting the impression that agents were being used like decoys, sent out to make everything look peaceful until there were "soldiers and citizens enough…to drive them off their lands without paying them for them."[632] Headquartered in Walla Walla, Cain informed Lawyer and the other visiting Nez Perce headmen that the treaty was at last ratified, then arranged to meet with all the people at the Weippe root grounds. He also posted a notice for the white people, warning them not to try to take over land outside the reservation that was being farmed by Nez Perce people until they were formally removed by the government, reminding them not to conduct trade on the reservation, and requesting their cooperation in suppressing liquor traffic.[633]

On the Weippe prairie, where fifty-four years earlier members of the Lewis and Clark party had emerged, starving, from the mountains – most Nez Perces and many from nearby tribes attended a general council and met Cain. Eighteen-year-old Joe Craig served as interpreter.[634] Cain reported a "highly satisfactory" council attended by all the chiefs other than Eagle from the Light; he noted that "Thos. Hughes, Local Agent, and Jas. [sic] W. Craig Interpreter, rendered me very important service which it is due them to acknowledge."[635] Cain announced that the treaties were confirmed and the reservations secure and that (since money was no longer given to satisfy annuity payments) they could expect delivery soon of annuity goods and services

When a Nez Perce man named Tipyahlahnah Oikelazikin—known to white people as Reuben—returned from the buffalo country, he noticed more *so·yá·po·* in his country than when he left. Reuben was one of the signers of the 1855 treaty.[636] He saw the *so·yá·po·ná·wit* (white man's way) as opportunity for expanding his trade in horses and other entrepreneurial ventures. Before long he built a log house within the boundaries of the reservation.[637] The structure stood on the south side of the Clearwater above its mouth (the current location of Clearwater Paper and lumber mill [formerly Potlatch Corp]. Reuben's log house, fronted by the Clearwater River and backed by stark basalt bluffs dividing the highlands from the river valley, was to be a notable landmark to many white men in the days ahead: it was visible from both trail and river, and the traffic on both was soon to increase.

Since the November 1858 opening of the plateau to settlement, land and gold seekers had hurried across the mountains from Puget Sound; newspaper reports told of 2,000 whites who had been waiting to exploit Walla Walla Valley's grasslands or ready to claim lands east of the Cascade Range.[638] The village of Waiilatpu (Walla Walla) already had two saloons, a store, a tin shop, a boarding house, two trading companies, and a meat market. The Craigs' home was about a half-mile from the new town, on the south side of the creek, and was described as "quite a tract under squatter's right…"[639] With many white people arriving in Waiilatpu to look for land or passing through on their way to the Colville or British Columbia gold mines, the Craigs were in a position to profit from the suddenly vibrant economy. One of their enterprises was opening their house to boarders.

A medical doctor from Canada, Augustus J. Thibodo, rode into Waiilatpu in 1859 and noted that where the previous year there had been but three "log shanties" there were now about fifty frame buildings. Needing a place to stay, since there was no hotel or boarding house, he was directed to

a Farmer a Missourian [sic] named Craig who lives a mile & a half from the village & procured board & lodging for me price not fixed yet. I have no blankets & they can't furnish me with a bed, they have none… an old miner…Ray Albro he boards with Craig also, he told me that I might sleep with him until I could do better. Craig's wife is a Nez Perce squaw, rather good looking he has some fine looking half breed daughters, he appears to be a bluff good jolly fellow, had an excellent supper beef, coffee & cornbread. Slept very comfortably up in the garret, the floor below is all occupied by fellows sleeping on it…[640]

One clear, cold morning about a dozen people took a ride to the fort in a sleigh pulled by four horses, and "Col. Craig" remarked it was the first sleigh ride he had taken for some thirty years. Thibodo noted the extreme cold of December (minus ten degrees at night), the large number of men in the valley, and that "Sundays not observed here, Drinking & gambling, buying & selling even more than on a week day." After a couple of weeks he settled up his bill and left the Craig house for better quarters. Craig charged him $10 a week "and I had to

furnish my own blankets. I paid him $10 & still owe him ten more."[641]
In the spring Thibodo left Walla Walla for the gold diggings, but he
and the Craigs would meet again in the coming months.

The Craig home near Waiilatpu was the site of several family
weddings, and the first of record was held January 29, 1860. Justice of
the Peace John M. Cannady administered marriage vows to James M.
Holt and Mary Adams.[642] Mary Jane Adams was then fifteen years old
and the daughter of former Hudson's Bay Company man, Charles
Adams. Many years later, Mary Jane's mother was recorded as
"Louise Craig."[643] While Mary Jane Holt's ancestry is here
undocumented, the fact that she and James Holt were married in
William and Isabel Craig's home points to a familial connection.

By February 1860 the weather had improved to the point where a
few miners hefted their packs and started northward for the gold fields
in Colville and British Columbia and the men who slept on the Craigs'
floor gradually cleared out to search for homesteads or gold. A gold
seeker named Elias Davidson Pierce was about to undo in a matter of
months the Nez Perce treaty that had taken Congress almost four years
to ratify. Like many of the men who left their homes to look for gold,
Pierce was a bold entrepreneur whose desire to be wealthy may have
overwhelmed latent principles. Pierce had for years eyed the Nez
Perces' mountains as a possible source of gold, and the fact that their
reservation was guaranteed safe from white intrusion meant nothing
more to him than an obstacle to be dodged.

The Craigs knew of Pierce's Clearwater country prospecting plan
and tried to dissuade him. Pierce—with former HBC employee Charlie
Adams as his guide—had since 1852 traded with the Nez Perces for
horses, which he then sold in California. He had come through the
Walla Walla Valley in 1857 when Craig's house—"the only house in
the place"—was under construction. Calling on the Craigs, Pierce had
asked about white people going into the Lapwai area. Craig told him
no white person had been in the Nez Perce country since he had been
ordered to leave, and he didn't believe it to be safe for a white person to
go among the Nez Perces. "I will have to shift my plans and take a new
track," Pierce wrote later. Col. Steptoe and Perrin Whitman also
advised Pierce against entering Nez Perce country, and Isabel Craig
("Col Creigs woman") reportedly said:

*I am a Nez Perce, was raised and always lived there. That was the
home of our people many years before we knew any thing about the
whites. A part of our people are all [for] war with the whites, and a*

*portion friendly. They ordered us to leave the nation or they would kill
us. And if they would kill us, and we their people, they will also kill
you.*[644]

Pierce had stored his goods with the Craigs, and Craig had arranged in
April 1857, for a Nez Perce man called George to guide Pierce to
Lapwai.[645]

Pierce had been horse-trading in the Lapwai region at the same time
Qamáya'qin and his band were there rounding up stock. During his
stay with the Nez Perce people, Pierce apparently fathered at least one
child: in 1911 one James McConville deposed that he was a grandson
of "Capt." Pierce.[646] Pierce "kept trading in stock and lingering…with
a view of getting into the clear water and salmon river country" until
troops under Col. George Wright crushed native resistance and the
country was opened to white settlement.[647] Finally, in February 1860,
feigning a horse-trading trip, Pierce and a companion rode from Walla
Walla to the Clearwater country. They camped on the north side of the
Clearwater River and bought some horses from the people whose
headman was an elderly gentleman named Wislenéqe (Half-Shorn).
Wislenéqe and his people cooperated as they tested gravel upriver,
finding gold in every place they tried. The two white men, Wislenéqe,
and eight other Nez Perce men rode to Walla Walla to buy outfits,
planning to return and mine for gold.[648]

While Pierce was spreading the word in Walla Walla that gold was
in Clearwater country, activities of another nature were taking place at
the Craig home. Martha Craig and Albert H. Robie decided to marry.
During the same period, Joe Craig had often been with the Cayuse
people near the Catholic mission (Frenchtown, now Lowden,
Washington) in company with a young woman named Temáha.
Temáha was a daughter of Theentheenmeetsa and Inzazinatwai of the
Catholic Cayuses.[649] Joe and Temáha were probably married according
to Indian custom; John Cannady also married them in a double wedding
with Joe's sister and according to Washington Territorial law. The
weddings were reported in the Albany, Oregon Territory, newspaper:

*Married: On the 4th of March, 1860, at the residence of the bride's
father, (Col. Wm. Craig,) by [Mr. Kennedy, [sic] J.P], Capt. A. H.
Robie and Miss Martha Craig, both of Walla Walla, W.T.*

*At the same time and place, by the same, Mr. Joseph Craig and
Miss Wapi-tan-ion Th-in-mitsa, both of Walla Walla, W.T.*[650]

Now that the Nez Perce treaty had been ratified, funds were appropriated for new buildings to house the Nez Perce Indian Agency. A site at the mouth of Lapwai Creek was chosen, near where the Spaldings had once lived. Tom Beall, the teamster who had accompanied Wright's troops and served as Wright's hangman, hauled building supplies in *bateaux* up the Columbia, Snake and Clearwater Rivers to the mouth of Lapwai Creek.[651] The towering, stark hills and dramatically chiseled landscape must have appealed to Beall, for he would make the region his base for many years to come.

About this time, an (alleged) unpaid debt—coupled with North-South polarization soon to culminate in the U.S. Civil War—caused Craig some legal problems. Sidney W. Moss, a prominent Oregon City Democrat and associate of James Nesmith, had done business with Craig on at least two occasions. In 1857 Craig had purchased on credit a "Gold Cased Chronometory Watch" valued at $200 and the next year a chestnut stallion worth $600. On August 2, 1860, Sheriff Lycurgus Jackson served on Craig a complaint for nonpayment of his debts, with notice to appear in the Walla Walla court; the judgment Moss sought against Craig was $920, including interest and costs of the suit.[652] No judgment in the matter has been found and its settlement is unknown.

Meanwhile, Elias Pierce ignored Cain's disapproval, outfitted his party of four at The Dalles for a four-month expedition, and rode to the new Nez Perce reservation agency on Lapwai Creek. There he talked a clerk into writing him a permit to go on the reservation and picked up Wislenéqe and his men to accompany him. Wislenéqe was, however, having misgivings about allowing white men to mine for gold. He justifiably worried that the news of gold would bring a flood of whites who would steal stock and build towns in the mountains. On the other hand (his thinking reflected that of William Craig), it was tempting to think of the goods whites would bring so that the Nez Perces could buy anything they wanted right at home; and Nez Perce people could get rich from *so·yá·po·* buying their horses, cattle, and produce. Wislenéqe sent for Lawyer who, although he seemed receptive to the idea, gave no approval. Pierce and his men returned to Walla Walla where they again left their outfits at the Craig place, telling Craig they would wait and try again later.[653]

In the months that followed, tension and excitement rose among both the whites and the Nez Perces. Craig, who traveled back and forth between his homes in the Walla Walla and Lapwai Valleys, said that the Nez Perces knew Pierce was coming back to their country and were preparing for war. Craig advised that Pierce could not go into Nez

Perce country "without one hundred armed men, but he could go alone and not one word would be said about it."[654] Craig's words cooled the enthusiasm of many men, and some who had been ready to accompany Pierce changed their minds.

By mid-August 1860 Pierce was again ready to make his move into the forbidden country. With ten men and a guide, the party rode from Walla Walla to the mouth of the Tucannon River and northeast across Palouse country and then entered timber and mountains. (Their route took them about where Elk River, Idaho, now is located.) They prospected for more than a month. Near the end of September they camped on a creek in high country where they found "gold in every place in the stream—in the flats and banks and gold generally diffused from the surface of the bedrock."[655] Excited men shouted for joy, but the U.S. Army patrol out looking for them was not near enough to hear. Pierce and his companions re-named *tawá·nmwa·wam*, the largest stream, Oro Fino creek; they laid out a town site with "nice building lots" that they named Pierce City. They then returned to Walla Walla, where they displayed their gold dust in a showcase in Sam Ball's saloon so all would know of their discovery.[656]

While Pierce and his party were busy with gold, officers at Fort Walla Walla asked Craig to be one of their guides for an expedition south into Shoshone country. Reports had just come in that, almost a month earlier, an emigrant wagon train had been attacked near Salmon Falls on the Snake River; there might be starving survivors still wandering on the plains.[657]

Rumors were rife and facts sparse about what had happened. A survivor, an ex-soldier, made it over the Blue Mountains and was found by agency employees on the Umatilla reservation. Within days two more survivors made it to the reservation. The agency sent men with supplies back on the trail to pick up other survivors, but none were found. Newspapers from the west coast to the east picked up the story; what the newspapers lacked in accuracy they made up for in enthusiasm. The Army knew only that, weeks earlier, Shoshones had attacked an emigrant wagon train and that some survivors had reached a populated area; there could be others who were lost and starving.

Captain Frederick T. Dent (a brother-in-law of Ulysses Grant) led a large enough force to the Snake River Plain to both punish those responsible and rescue any survivors. When Craig joined the expedition as a scout and guide, he, in his early fifties, was the oldest member of the party. There were more than 100 soldiers and four officers. One of the officers was Second Lieutenant Marcus A. Reno, who years later would serve with General George A. Custer at the battle of the Little Big Horn. On the evening of October 11 the relief party left Fort Walla Walla and rode south to pick up the Oregon Trail.

After crossing the Blue Mountains, Captain Dent ordered Lt. Reno and his forty dragoons, with Craig as scout, ahead to comb the Burnt River area. They covered much of the territory without finding anyone, but on the evening of October 19 the detachment came upon two men. The men were emaciated, almost naked, with no fire and less hope. Lt. Reno had them fed and clothed, then continued the search. The first of the emigrants from the Utter-VanOrnum wagon train had been rescued.

With just five soldiers and Craig, Lt. Reno rode the remainder of the night and into the next day to the Malheur River. Not locating any emigrants, they traveled back toward Farewell Bend. At some places on the trail Craig found tracks of women and children, but following them was almost impossible since the terrain was rocky and it had recently rained. Finally, on high ground between the Burnt and Snake Rivers, Lt. Reno, Craig and the soldiers came upon six bodies, stripped, mutilated, and "gleaming in the moonlight." The bodies were those of a woman and five men. They were identified and buried where they were found. Tracks leading away from the site included a small barefoot track among the moccasin prints. Craig and Reno followed the tracks until Captain Dent decided not to continue.

Dent then sent a detachment ahead of the main company to search the Malheur and Owyhee Rivers. Within a day the fast-riding detachment came upon a young, wasted woman out searching for fuel near the Owyhee River. Before sunset, the soldiers were in the camp of survivors who were in advanced stages of starvation. Roasting on the fire was human flesh, for they had stayed alive only by eating the remains of people who had died.

Dent learned from survivors that everyone who escaped the initial attack was now accounted for except four VanOrnum children; he felt sure that they had been made captives. It was their trail that Craig and Lt. Reno had followed to where they had crossed the Snake River at Indian Head Mountain. With snow in the mountains and weak survivors to transport, pursuing the Indians was out of the question. On November 7, 1860, after a painfully slow journey, the relief expedition arrived back at Fort Walla Walla.

The expedition had performed well. Dent commended the men for the "zeal, skill, energy, and humanity" they all displayed in bringing to Fort Walla Walla, "alive and safe, the wrecks of fellow beings we found on the Owyhee and Burnt rivers"[658] William Craig had once helped to wrestle the first wheels across what was to become the Oregon Trail; now, twenty years later, he helped transport starved immigrants, recipients of Shoshone rage at American invasion, over the same trail.

Not long after Craig returned from Shoshone country, the family celebrated the wedding of daughter Adeline.[659] In a Christmas Eve ceremony in Walla Walla, 15-year-old Adeline Craig was married to Samuel Phinney, then 28.[660] A native of Susquehanna County, Pennsylvania, Sam had in 1855-56 served a year in the Oregon volunteers under Colonel Kelly.[661] Sam and Adeline Phinney made their first home in the Walla Walla Valley.

By the time the wagon train survivors returned to Fort Walla Walla, word of the gold strike had spread to California and beyond. Newspapers carried items of rescuing the wagon train "massacre" victims along with news of the gold discovery.[662] Miners in camps from Calaveras to Fraser River and beyond made ready to travel in the spring to the Nez Perce mines. Anticipating a rush of miners onto the reservation, and certain a war with the Nez Perces was coming, Cain recommended changing the treaty of 1855 to give the federal government the gold-bearing lands.[663]

Pierce's party, meanwhile, had not waited until spring to return to the Clearwater region. Prospectors (Elias Pierce not among them) with enough food to last the winter re-entered the Nez Perce reservation and spent the winter at the site of the gold discovery.[664] Upon arrival at Canal Gulch in early December 1860, the party was almost immediately snowed in; the snow kept a U.S. Army detachment from following and evicting them as illegal trespassers on the reservation.[665] Before the snow fell—knowing they would soon be unable to sustain their pack mules and horses in the mountains—some men had taken the animals down to the Pataha country (present-day Pomeroy, Washington) to winter.[666] The miners built cabins and sluice boxes and made ready for spring, when they would begin serious gold mining.

By the winter of 1860-61 William, Isabel, and their family were back in their Lapwai Valley home after an absence of four years. Wright's defeat of the hostile tribes and Congressional ratification of the 1855 Nez Perce treaty had cleared the way for the Craigs' return to Clearwater country. The gold discovery not seventy miles from their Lapwai home may have sped their return, although William, son Joe, and most Nez Perce people did not appear to exploit the earth's resources for personal wealth.[667] However, like Pierce, the Craigs planned to profit from trade with the hordes of people expected to rush to the gold discovery.

As white population increased in the Lapwai Valley, one of the new agency employees, John M. Silcott, hosted what was reported to be the first Christmas celebration in the region. He sent invitations to "every white man within 50 miles of his home"; and the guests included "Col. William Craig," Thomas B. Beall, N. B. Dutro, Thomas Page, Capt. M. M. Williams, Doctor Thibodo, Jake Schultz, Joe Medeau (known as "French Joe"), Henry McNally and a cook they called "Spanish Frank." Christmas dinner menu included stuffed bear cub and wild goose; Thibodo, now employed as the agency's doctor, donated a five-gallon can of the government's pure alcohol he had lifted from the agency's dispensary. The guests were "equal to the occasion of enjoying raw alcohol with water," and before the effects of this had worn off, William Craig invited everyone to his home on Waha Creek for a New Year's party.[668]

Since the alcohol was gone and there was still time before the Craig family's New Year party, Jake Schultz and French Joe volunteered to go to Walla Walla to buy whiskey. Silcott furnished the money to buy ten gallons, while Craig furnished the horses for the trip. Schultz and Medeau broke the record for fast freight service, for they covered the round trip of more than 200 miles in just three days.

The Craig home was "a pretentious dwelling for that day and age," rather large and with a smooth floor; William and Isabel planned a dance. The females at the party were all Indian wives and mixed-race daughters of the white men, and after an elaborate dinner the men competed for the women and girls as partners. The native girls were "too modest to make lively dancers, but they were induced to join in the mazy waltz and the bewitching quadrille while the liquor held out."[669] The Craigs' New Year's party was an event long remembered.

When travel became possible in the spring of 1861, white people made their way up the Columbia, Snake, and Clearwater Rivers toward the gold mines. An Olympia newspaper reported more men coming through on their way to the Clearwater country than had come for the rush to Similkameen, British Columbia (which disappointed) and each was determined to reap a rich harvest.[670] As the closest settlement selling mining provisions, Walla Walla was booming. Most people traveled as far as possible by boat, then bought horses to transport equipment into the mountains; there was thus a high demand for Nez Perce horses.[671] White men already in Nez Perce country encouraged others to follow. Newspapers regularly reported that the mines were substantial and the Indians "well disposed," but a Portland newspaper article stated frankly that "the miners [at Oro Fino Creek] were extremely anxious for more men to come up there to keep the Indians in check."[672]

Early in the spring Craig joined Captain C. H. Armstrong, who was a special agent, and Thibodo on a mission to the Oro Fino Creek mines. Before he asked the Nez Perces for a new treaty, Cain wanted information about the geology of that part of the reservation and an update on whether the miners and Indians were getting along with one another. The men left the Lapwai Creek agency and traveled up Craig's Mountain; Thibodo, upon reaching the summit, said he was "agreeably surprised to find a pretty rolling tableland." They then descended into a deep canyon that contained granite and quartz[673] (likely Big Canyon, now home to Peck, Idaho). At the mouth of the canyon, Thibodo, Armstrong, Craig and their party found two Nez Perce lodges. Although most of the men were absent, Craig interpreted for Armstrong, who questioned two men still at home. They learned that the others were helping a white man find a route for wagons into the gold mines. The Nez Perces voiced no particular objections to white people traveling though or mining in their country, nor had their headman, Wislenéqe, who lived upriver at *téwe* (present-day Orofino, Idaho).[674]

Stopping next at *téwe*, Armstrong, Thibodo, and Craig talked with Wislenéqe. White men mining gold in his country did not upset him, but he complained bitterly about liquor being introduced to his people. "He has reason to do so too. I am informed—though not by him—[that] one of his daughters was induced to drink to excess, and was debauched by some unprincipled white man."[675] Armstrong suspected the liquor had come from former mountain man Jim Conner, for he found liquor in Conner's camp and heard that Conner had a history of making his own.[676] But Conner assured Armstrong that he had not traded liquor to Indians and, after Armstrong talked with both Indians and whites, Armstrong took Conner at his word.[677] The Nez Perce reservation was now fraught with the "ardent spirit" problem that had plagued Indians since whites settled their land.

At Pierce City, Armstrong saw to it that the miners addressed the issue of alcohol on the reservation. They called a meeting and drew up resolutions governing the liquor problem in order to comply with federal law. Armstrong later recommended a "sufficient force be…stationed at the ferry over Snake river or at some better point…and that no liquor be allowed to enter the Indian Territory."[678] Had there been sufficient forces to stop liquor from entering the reservation, the white people carrying the liquor and looking for gold could also have been stopped, except that no one knew the exact location of the reservation borders.

During Craig's travels with Armstrong and Thibodo, the men discussed Craig's piece of land in the Lapwai Valley. It was a prime piece of land, they all agreed, and would become valuable with all the people pouring into the country. Craig was confident his claim to it was good, but Armstrong promised to check on the claim's status at the Olympia Land Office.

Armstrong kept his promise, for not long after returning from the trip, Craig received a letter from the Land Office. The letter assured Craig his papers were "perfect," except that Henry Crosbie had neglected to affix the Seal of the District Court (which they would immediately correct). Craig was informed he had completed the residency and cultivation requirements, but that a certificate could not be issued until the property was surveyed. And a survey could not be done until "Township lines are extended over the Reservation." Yet it was the Land Office's opinion that Craig could sell the claim if he wished, since he had strictly complied with the law.[679] Craig was reassured that the land given him by the Nez Perce people was legally his in the eyes of the United States government.

In the winter of 1860-61, Washington Superintendent of Indian Affairs Edward R. Geary and Agent Cain called another treaty council with the Nez Perce leaders. The government's goal was either to exclude gold-bearing land from the reservation outlined in the 1855 treaty or to allow whites to mine gold on the reservation. After waiting so long for the treaty to be ratified, celebrating its ratification as proof that the U.S. government was, after all, trustworthy, then watching their "secure" reservation fill with *so·yá.po·*, Nez Perce warriors were on high alert to defend home and family. It was hard when people you trusted—people like Craig—told you the treaty would be a good thing but events continued to prove otherwise.

Two distinct strategies for coping with the miners' invasion had coalesced among Nez Perce leaders. The first was found in Lawyer, now at Kamiah, and the headmen of other bands who accepted him as their spokesman. Believing Craig's advice was the best approach, and knowing they could not win a war against the *so·yá·po·*, they opted to profit from the new arrivals' business and become wealthy by trading their vast herds of horses and other items needed by miners. A consortium of Nez Perce bands living further from *simí·nekem* and the routes to the gold mines adopted a different approach to the problem.

These leaders planned to avoid the white men: they would neither fight them nor do business with them but continue their traditional lives in their traditional home territories.

White men representing the U.S. government labeled the two Nez Perce groups: Lawyer and his followers from the lower Clearwater region were seen as "friends" while leaders of bands from the upper Clearwater, Salmon, and Wallowa regions were labeled "disaffected" or "hostile." Before the Grand Ronde massacre, "hostiles" had meant tribes or coalitions not allied to the Americans. Never before had "hostiles" been applied in such a wide swath to the Nez Perce people, the United States' perennial allies. But political divisions had often been left in the wake of the federal government's dealings with Indian people.[680] The differences between the two Nez Perce groups became more pronounced during the 1861 gold-bearing land council and would lead, in less than two years, to a split in the Nez Perce Nation.

Just weeks before the 1861 council, a journalist interviewed Lawyer. Lawyer said he was not happy so many whites had come into his country; his people were rich now, and if they went to war with the whites they would lose all their horses and cattle as the Cayuses had. Lawyer's people liked the business the whites brought and, in order not to suffer the fate of the Cayuses, he and his followers were ready to sell the gold-bearing land to the government.[681]

Held in the Lapwai Valley in April 1861—as early as weather allowed for travel—the 1861 "gold treaty" council did not result in the Nez Perce leaders selling land but, rather, in a compromise. The Nez Perce leaders agreed to allow miners access to the gold-bearing land *north* of the Clearwater River for mining purposes. They provided a route for miners across the reservation (again on the *north* side of the Clearwater), specified that the opened portion of the reservation be subject the U.S. trade and liquor law, and further called for a "sufficient military force" to be placed on the reservation to protect the Nez Perce people.[682] Lawyer, Joseph, Looking Glass, and Big Thunder (Thunder's Eye's replacement) were among the forty-seven Nez Perce leaders who signed the treaty, as did Geary and Cain.[683] Craig was present as friend and advisor to the Nez Perces. Robert Newell, who had come from Oregon to regain his lost wealth in the new gold mines (but been disappointed), had stayed to help Craig negotiate a peaceful solution between the Nez Perces and the government.[684]

However, because of entrenched miners and the U.S. Civil War, the 1861 treaty was doomed. Miners had been recording claims to gold-bearing ground since February, entering their claims in a leather-bound book that contained no recognition of either the Nez Perces' or United States government's title to the area.[685] Miners who had built enough houses and businesses to create two towns—Pierce City and Oro Fino City—were already selling them to others as though they had legal title to land and structures.[686] Even worse, before the 1861 Nez Perce treaty could be sent to Congress, another rich prospect of gold was found to the south of the Clearwater River. Miners rushed from Oro Fino-Pierce City mines to the new diggings. The treaty was worthless almost before the ink dried.

Life changed drastically for the Nez Perce people. Fearing "a collision" with the miners traveling the trail near the *qémes* prairie just southwest of the gold mines, the headmen told their people not to gather roots at the Weippe root grounds.[687] It was hard on the *ni·mí·pu·* to have their annual *qémes* camp discontinued because of miners: young and old looked forward to the yearly trip where families and friends met and camped together. The women worked hard digging and preparing roots for winter food; everyone socialized, held races, sweated, gambled, drummed, and danced. Each season when they returned to the root grounds the family *kápoy* (mortars) and *piley* (pestles) were waiting for them on the high prairie. This season, although the tools waited, no *ni·mí·pu·* came.

A new white settlement appeared at *simí·nekem*. In July Cain had posted a notice in which he informed the white men that "the settlement made at the junction of Snake and Clearwater rivers is in violation of United States law and cannot be permitted..."[688] No one paid any attention. Despite Cain's weak efforts and some Nez Perce leaders' strong opposition, the number of tents and shanties at *simí·nekem* continued to increase.

The war between the North and the South that had begun April 21 took most of Congress's attention and funds, leaving few provisions in the Nez Perce agency and no credit with which to buy any. Moreover, most funds that were received by Agent Cain in Walla Walla did not reach their intended target on the Nez Perce reservation: of the almost $60,000 reportedly spent on the Nez Perce people in 1860-61, little improvement was made to the agency buildings, no fencing nor plowing was done, and employees made off with what little harvested grain there was.[689] Nonetheless, when annuity goods—53 packages— arrived on the Walla Walla landing at the end of December 1860, Cain acknowledged receipt of the boatload and made arrangements to distribute them to the Nez Perces in the coming summer. He complained that *goods* were sent instead of what was actually wanted—help with "agricultural and mechanical pursuits," and predicted that the annuities "will in fact prove an entire failure."[690] Cain was correct.

The first "annuity council" was held in July 1861 and it was a much-anticipated event. The 1855 treaty, made almost six years earlier, was finally coming to fruition. But the occasion became noteworthy not because it was the very first annuity council pursuant to the treaty, but because the annuities provided by the U.S. government were so unsatisfactory that war was barely averted. Most bands traveled many miles to the meeting site, and a prodigious amount of food was necessary to feed the multitudes of people: about ten beeves were slaughtered and eaten each day.[691] The *ni·mí·pu·* dressed in their best clothing and decorated their horses; they were an elegant sight as they accepted the blankets, sheeting, trinkets and farming tools.[692] But it soon became apparent that the annuities were not worth much. About two-fifths of the Nez Perce people, determined to stay clear of government gifts, refused them entirely. The overwhelming reaction was one of disgust with the quality and quantity of the goods, and tension filled the air.[693]

Cain and the U.S. troop commander worried that the warriors in the bands independent of Lawyer's influence would paint for war. They devised a plan to keep the people in council longer "to gain time for their passions to cool and have some of their bitter objections explained away."[694] But to keep the people in one place, they must have food— and the government had none. Craig, generous and affable, donated some of his cattle to feed the people so they would stay in the valley, discuss the problems, and not go away angry. According to a participant, Craig's generosity forestalled war:

> *...the treaty was peaceably inaugurated and a horrible Indian war was averted. For the accomplishment of this end, the Government and people are indebted to William Craig for his confiding generosity in advancing his bands of cattle for such subsistence...when not another man east of Walla Walla but him was willing to open his plethoric hoards and thus give succor to his country.[695]*

Cain was relieved of his duties as agent shortly thereafter and replaced by Charles Hutchins, who would soon be an eloquent Craig defender in a plot by an old friend to besmirch Craig's reputation.[696]

It was the last time that documentation has been found showing William Craig participating in a council between the

federal government and the Nez Perces, and it was during this
period that Craig's disillusionment with the government seems
to first become evident—and that it did so during the Civil War
is probably no coincidence. There were soon too few U.S.
military in the West to enforce the new gold mining treaty as
entire regiments were reassigned East to fight the Confederate
Army. Many U.S. Army officers serving in the West gave up
their commissions and headed to their eastern homes to fight
for their cause, be it for the North or for the South. At the same
time, an enormous number of men in the East evaded military
service by running West to the gold fields. As the West
emptied of career military men, it was filling with rough ne'er-
do-wells and thousands of other gold seekers.

A writer with an eye for detail arrived on one of the early steamers.
Cincinnatus Heine (also known as Joaquin) Miller left Siskiyou
County, California, after a bench warrant—for assault with intent to
commit murder—had been issued for him.[697] As he watched the
countryside go by from the steamer out of Portland, he took notes on
what he saw—and he was a keen observer.

> *The first place on Clearwater worthy of notice is "Reuben's" farm.*
> *Reuben is a "big Injin" up here. He is proprietor of a log house. He*
> *owns twenty-five hundred horses. The rapids, three miles up*
> *Clearwater, are named after him. He owns a ferry at the mouth of the*
> *river, and hires white men to run it.*[698]

Miller spent about a year in Nez Perce country. He rode the mail
express line between the Oro Fino mines and Oregon and he partnered
with Isaac V. Mossman to form an express company.

People kept coming, and to fill the demand for more lumber for
sluice boxes, cabins, fences, and towns, Craig put up a lumber mill
south of his house in the Lapwai valley.[699] Son-in-law A. H. Robie
came with his wife from Walla Walla to run it. The Craig place had
since spring been a stopping-over place for some of the miners on their
way to the Clearwater mines: they could spend the night, eat a meal,
buy a horse or mule, pasture their animals, stock up on produce—and
now they could buy lumber as well.

Thomas Beall offers a rare personal vignette of William Craig
during these times, telling of his ability as a hunter. Craig had some
hogs feeding up what was later known as Mission Creek. One day Jake
Schultz rode to the Craig home, very excited, having spotted a cougar

stalking the hogs. He found Craig reading and told him about the cougar. Craig reportedly told Jake to ride back and "tell that cougar I'll mess with him." The next morning, according to Beall's recollection, William saddled his horse, grabbed his rifle, whistled up his dogs; and before long he returned to the house with the hide of the cougar across the back of the saddle.[700]

When Reuben had first started his entrepreneurial activities, miners noted that "a young and intelligent chief of the Nez Perces" was preparing to build a warehouse on the Clearwater and had a ferryboat on the Snake River near the mouth of the Clearwater that was advertised in Walla Walla.[701] Reuben's partner in the ferry business venture was William Craig.[702] Craig was involved in building at least two other ferries. One was the "Spalding" ferry on the Clearwater just upstream from the mouth of Lapwai Creek. There the oarsman would force the ferry away from the bank and into the rapids, then row hard across the current toward the ferry landing before being swept past it. The user charge was $1 for a footman and $1.50 for a horse and rider.[703] Craig's third ferry was established in 1861 over the Clearwater River on the trail leading to the mines, downriver from *ne'we* (Lolo Creek, near present-day Greer, Idaho). Craig built the ferry in partnership with his friend, Jacob Schultz, and Tom Beall was also involved.[704] The constant traffic of miners heading up the Clearwater generated a stream of income from each ferryman to the owner and "seldom it was he did not pass the $250 per day mark in receipts, and sometimes double."[705]

The summer of 1861 brought developments around Fort Boise and the Snake River plains that worried the agency staff. The four VanOrnum children that Craig had helped track from the unlucky wagon train were not yet rescued. Cain sent Shoshone Indian men south (keeping their wives as hostages) to learn where the VanOrnum children were and what was going on with the hostile Snakes; one of the Indians returned and reported the children had been killed.[706] The spy also reported that a very large council was being held near Salmon Falls and that Eagle from the Light was waiting to hear the results; the Mormons expected many people to join them this year and "the Snakes and the Mormons are to have an understanding soon."[707] Cain believed the Mormons and Shoshones were working together against the mainstream white emigration while the Civil War occupied American soldiers.[708] He was convinced that Eagle from the Light was trying to work an alliance with the Shoshones and that the Mormons were providing ammunition and encouragement to the Indians to wipe out the Americans.[709]

Joe Craig was on the government payroll as Nez Perce agency interpreter.[710] After Cain and his hirelings were relieved of their positions, Charles Hutchins toured the reservation with young Craig. He was appalled at what he found. Almost 15,000 white people were on the reservation; "shebangs" (inns) were operating near most downriver villages as well as at busy stream crossings "ostensibly for the entertainment of travellers, but almost universally used as a den for supplying liquor to Indians."[711]

The tent settlement holding whites and mining supplies at *simí·nekem* grew until, by October 1861, white men platted a town at the site of the Reuben and Craig's warehouse and ferry. Doc Newell described the collection as a "cotton town" because of the preponderance of tents.[712] Rumor held that the laying out of the town was "done with the consent of Lawyer and his headmen...[and they] received some compensation for their reasonable attitude." There was a report when Cain was still agent of a secret nighttime meeting among Lawyer, a few headmen, an interpreter (likely Joe Craig), and Cain, wherein a bribe of gold coin offered by miners and other interests bought the townsite.[713] Notwithstanding its nebulous genesis, the white men involved agreed to name the town in honor of Meriwether Lewis and the settlement was called "Lewiston."

In a transaction aimed to buy out Reuben's share of their ferry, Craig on December 1, 1861, had paperwork prepared to sell a one-third interest in the *simí·nekem* ferry to Homer Sanborn. Although Reuben's name did not appear on the business transaction, it follows that the $1,000 selling price went to him. A. H. Robie was the third partner, and Vic Trevitt (whose suggestion it was to name the town Lewiston), signed as a witness.[714] The ferry continued operation, still known as "Craig's Ferry."

Within a short period, Craig was told to re-apply for the permit to operate the ferry at *simí·nekem*. Craig applied to the local Indian agent stating that the ferry had been in constant use since its construction and benefited everyone in the area—apparently the necessary criteria.[715] Hutchins granted permission for Craig to continue ferry operations until the Indian Bureau in Washington, D.C., could review his application, since the ferry was of service to the government and since Craig resided lawfully on the reservation.[716]

Meanwhile, on April 27, 1862, at the Lapwai agency where he was now employed as Superintendent of Farming, Robert Newell wrote a very long letter to his "Dear Old Friend and Senator," James Nesmith, in Washington, D.C. [717] Nesmith and Newell had fought with the Oregon volunteers in Yakama country back in 1855; in the ensuing years both had become prominent in Oregon territorial government.[718] But Newell had suffered a number of setbacks and the most recent left him financially strapped, for the Willamette River had flooded and carried away his Champoeg store.[719] Another reversal had been brewing longer and the hurt ran deeper, for his and Kitty's sons—like Joe and Jinny Meek's children—faced racism from many Willamette Valley settlers.[720] To help him out, some of Lawyer's group –who valued Newell's advice and wanted his Nez Perce wife's sons back among their people—had given him about five acres of land along the Snake River at *simí·nekem.*[721] All of these things, plus more, were on Doc Newell's mind when he wrote to Nesmith.

Asking that he not be divulged as the informant—and professing that he did not like to complain or get personal—Newell complained that there were many men in the Clearwater country who were "disunionist" in their beliefs and were influencing the Indians to turn against the government.[722] Then Newell offered that his "Old friend Craig on this Reservation" was one of those, that Craig's "whole soul is with the South and the news of a Rebble defeat makes him quite sad" and that the government made a mistake when it donated a land claim to Craig.

I expect you will be surprised at what I say about Craig but really if he were my Brother it would make no difference. Scores of people are speaking about his secession proclivities but they can be borne by the Whites but there is something else that makes Sesesh ashamed of itself—besides as he is an old resident and runs with the damndest hard unprincipled crowd on earth his influence is great and I hope he will mend his ways…[723]

In another letter to "Nes" the next day, Newell warmed to sharing his opinion of Craig and included his old friend Joe Meek in his aspersions:

Craig has got a ferry on Snake River near Lewiston that is worth I presume $300 per day in income and the expence per day is small as it is a bail and wire suspension…I am sorry to say the old fellow drinks hard and is quite a hard case. …I am sorry land was given him on this Reservation, though he has no sertificate of it. …Joe Meek passed here

*a few days ago on his way to the Mines on foot poor as piss and don't
amount to a pair of trays he is as low nearly as Jo Lane or Teuvault.*[724]

William Craig soon received a letter signed by B. F. Kendall, the
new Superintendent of Indian Affairs for Washington Territory,
informing him that he was no longer permitted to keep a ferry on the
Nez Perce reservation.[725] Craig reacted firmly, writing to Lapwai
Agent Hutchins that Kendall's order was "harsh, tyrannical and unjust,"
that he could stand to lose thousands of dollars, and that, since Kendall
had already been removed from office, he was reapplying for
permission to run his ferry "confidently believing that I shall receive
justice at the hands of [Kendall's] successor."[726] Hutchins agreed with
Craig, saying his office believed that the service provided by Craig's
ferry was required for the public good and gave Craig permission to
continue the ferry service until "the Indian Bureau, the Superintendent
of Indian Affs. Or this office" revoked permission.[727]

The Washington Territorial Legislature had, in its last session in
Olympia, granted franchises to certain constituents to operate roads and
ferries; among the franchises was one to G. Hays, Esq. for the ferry on
the Snake.[728] However, a territorial legislature had no jurisdiction on
the Nez Perce reservation, since the reservation had been established by
treaty between the United States of America and the Nez Perce Nation.
Nonetheless, based on the territorial franchise, Calvin Hale—Kendall's
replacement as Superintendent of Indian Affairs—was ready to put
Judge Gilmore Hays in the Lewiston ferry business.[729]

So Newell's attack on Craig began bearing fruit. Craig would be
made to suffer both for his prosperity and his allegiance to the South.
Hale advised Hutchins that permission was denied for Craig's ferry—
and that Judge Hays was to be approved to operate a ferry at that
location. Hutchins came immediately to Craig's defense and,
responding to Newell's allegations, stated:

*It is undeniably true, that William Craig is not a highly educated
man, perhaps his selection of companions and associates are such as
would not be of our selection, of such private and personal matters we
are not to be the censors. William Craig did not concur with our
political theorems in 1860, but that fact does not ostracise him from his
rights as a loyal American citizen. ...You further allude in your letter to
the signal favor Craig has received from the Government in its ceding
to him so valuable a tract of land as is held by him under the treaty. It
is true that he has so acquired a valuable homestead from the*

*Government, but his indebtedness is not greater than the hundred of
thousands who have been the like recipients at the hand of a liberal
and intelligent Government. At least his loyalty is not so mendacious
as to consider that the price of it, nor does he hold his particular
privileges in this Indian country as the sine qua non of his loyalty.
Living here as he did for many years before the Treaty—married
lawfully to a daughter of the tribe—having a large family of children
growing up around him and possessing the entire confidence of the
Indians by numberless deeds of kindness assistance and integrity, it
was but natural that he desired to spend the winter of his life here
among his children; . . . this, too, long before that especial value was
attached to the land, which has occurred since the discoveries of the
gold mines.*[730]

Hutchins reiterated that in the time Craig's ferry had been running
across the Snake River, the U.S. military, Indian agency, tons of
merchandise, and thousands of whites going to find gold had been
transported. He had constructed "an excellent ferry at a cost
approximating $4500…[and] he has not charged any Indian fare for
crossing."[731]

As if his defense of William Craig were not enough to shorten his
Lapwai tenure, Hutchins also pointed out to his superior that the
Washington Territorial Legislature dispensing franchises to run roads
and ferries on federal Indian reservations was "as stupid" as if they
passed laws governing the Sandwich Islands (Hawaii). He pointed out
that Judge Hays had neither the tribe's nor the agent's approval to live
on the reservation and that, unless the treaty was to be considered a
joke, the man could not qualify for ferry privileges.[732] On August 23,
1862, Charles Hutchins was removed as agent to the Nez Perce tribe
and transferred to relieve John Owen in the Bitterroot Valley.[733]

Hutchins's successor, John Anderson, was told to settle the ferry
business immediately and instructed to "recognize the right of Gilmor
Hays Esq. to the ferry franchise across Snake river at Lewiston."
Anderson was unsure that he could stop Craig from operating his ferry
and give the right to Judge Hays, particularly since Hays had informed
him that the Territorial Legislature had earlier given still another
party—Judge Francis Chenoweth—a charter to run a ferry at
Lewiston.[734]

Anderson reviewed the ferry background and determined that Craig
had been operating the ferry legally; if he lost it, he would lose the

several thousand dollars he had invested, for "this ferry is valuable property to any one having the right to run it."[735] Unable to deny Craig's ferry permit on legal technicalities, Anderson asked people in Lewiston about Mr. Craig's loyalty to the United States. From what he heard in Lewiston, Agent Anderson believed Craig's ferry permit could be denied on grounds that Craig was disloyal to the government for, when under the influence of alcohol, Craig reportedly "used language that might well be construed as unfriendly to the government..."

I have not been able to get the exact import of any of his expressions, so as to repeat them. I think however, that men often disclose the real state of their feelings more fully and unequivocally when intoxicated than in their more sober and guarded moments. I have heard no imputation thrown out against Mr. Robie's or Sanborn's loyalty. Mr. Craig's however I should consider very doubtful.[736]

Agent Anderson wrote a terse letter notifying William Craig that the license granted to Gilmore Hays April 3, 1862, was valid, that Craig's ferry was in the way, and that Craig was to stop operations at Lewiston and remove from the Snake River "all your boats, buoys and other obstructions" that could interfere with the privilege the Indian department had just granted Judge Hays.[737] Craig read the letter, may have voiced his sentiments about its author, and went on with business as usual.

As if expecting to be ignored, Anderson asked that Major J. S. Rinearson of the Oregon Volunteer Cavalry send soldiers to remove Craig's ferry equipment.[738] But no detachment was deployed. Instead Rinearson wrote a short note to Craig, informing him that the army had been asked by the Indian agency to remove the ferryboat and appurtenances operating without authority in the Snake River near Lewiston: "Perhaps this notice may save further trouble."[739]

Craig was highly puzzled. He knew he had fulfilled treaty requirements, for before starting to build the boat he had asked for and received permission to proceed from Lawyer and subordinate chiefs, and he did not think the U.S. government would grant him land on the reservation without a way of crossing the river to get to it.[740] He was being unfairly targeted, but he did not know why:

What good reason for pressing these charges I am a loss to know as I never have to my knowledge refused to cross any one for the want to pay the charges.[741]

Now that it seemed like the government was taking his *simí·nekem* ferry privilege, Craig recalled having spent over $7,000 to establish it and make it safe, having ordered the cable and other fixtures from California. Craig's parting words regarding his Snake River ferry were: "I hope that those who wish to deprive me of this ferry have other reasons than pecuniary ones."[742] In Newell's case, the reason was an unhealthy dose of jealousy, which, in the histrionic Civil War atmosphere, was almost lethal to Craig's ferry.

Craig held on to the ferry, but it took help from a person with a strong moral compass and high station. Brigadier General Benjamin Alvord of Fort Vancouver, when notified of the doubt raised about Craig's loyalty, thought Craig was being unjustly assailed; he asked that Major Rinearson give the U.S. government's oath of allegiance to Craig and forward the results back to Vancouver.[743] That done, Craig's reputation was cleared and pressures eased on Craig's ferry business. In 1864, in his own good time, Craig sold the ferry over the Snake River to Theodore Schenk.[744]

After gold was discovered in the Salmon River country, the primary route to the new towns of Elk City and Florence went through the Lapwai Valley. Directions to the mines had often included reference to the Craig place: in December of 1861 the *Walla Walla Statesman* reported that from "Robie's mill, near Col. Craig's to the Camas prairie" there was snow on the ground and that, when coming down from the Salmon River mining area, the express rider had "met about three hundred pack animals and two hundred or more men on their way to Salmon River."[745] The snow was deep and the temperatures cold between the Columbia and the Salmon River mountains; three weeks later, "[t]he trail from Lewiston—via Craig's and Robie's mill—is the only one now traveled and it is said to be in good condition, and will probably be kept open…"[746]

The Northwest winter of 1861-62 was severe. Miners in the Oro Fino and Florence areas came close to starving when they ran out of food before running out of winter, and travel conditions kept new miners out of the high country until well into the spring. Mossman and Miller reported in March 1862 that there were about two hundred men and their horses at the foot of Craig's Mountain near the mill, waiting for better weather so they could travel to the Salmon River mines.[747]

As soon as travel was possible, more miners headed for Lewiston and the gold strikes beyond. Stagecoach service was begun from Walla Walla to Lewiston, the trip taking just 30 hours.[748] Steamers plied the waters of the Columbia and Snake all spring, bringing to Lewiston full complements of passengers and cargo. About $10 million worth of gold was estimated to have been taken from the Nez Perces' mountains before mining ceased for the winter of 1861-62, an activity that employed at least 30,000 people altogether as miners, traders, and others.[749]

The West was rapidly changing. In 1862 Congress passed the Homestead Act, enabling white settlers with pre-emption (squatter) claims to change their surveyed lands into homesteads. Congress also authorized the Union Pacific and Central Pacific companies to build a transcontinental railroad along the 42nd parallel, or central route. The military road from Fort Walla Walla to Fort Benton on the Missouri was opened to traffic. The Washington Territorial Legislature at Olympia counted the white population east of the mountains and created four new counties, which they named Shoshone, Missoula, Nez Perce, and Idaho.

Meanwhile, the Nez Perce people on their reservation were trying to survive in the midst of thousands of so·yá·po·. Brigadier General Alvord in October 1862 told the assembled chiefs: "You [have] my respect and regard. Could I have had my will, I would have raised a wall as high as the heaven around you to keep intruders out."[750] Alvord was a scholar with wide interests who had come to the West on an early wagon train and knew the region well.[751] Reacting to the government's inability to keep gold miners off the Nez Perce reservation, the U.S. Senate, in an amendment proposed by Senator Nesmith, appropriated $50,000 to negotiate a treaty with the Nez Perces for the relinquishment of "a portion or all of their present reservation, or its exchange for other lands."[752] Senator Nesmith advocated buying the Nez Perce reservation and moving the people elsewhere: "Washington Territory extends to the summit of the Rocky mountains, nearly to the Missouri river. They can be sent up in that region."[753] He proposed having them "taken to some valley which will be more remote than the present position which they occupy," in country that Isaac Stevens had wrested from the Flathead people.[754]

While miners poured into the Clearwater region, Civil War battles continued in the East. In the autumn of 1862 news reached Washington Territory that Isaac Stevens was dead. He died fighting for the Union, leading a unit of volunteers in a charge at Chantilly, Virginia.

President Lincoln later remarked that people like Stevens had given their all to the cause of the Union, even though often denounced as secessionist sympathizers.[755] The Walla Walla newspaper eulogized Stevens as "an honored citizen of this Territory…[whose] talents were [just] being appreciated…"[756] Some Nez Perce people remembered Stevens as a man with more talents than scruples.[757]

One can only guess how William Craig felt about Isaac Stevens. He had worked closely with Stevens to broker treaties at the 1855 Walla Walla council, helping devise a multi-faceted deal that they thought would serve the Nez Perce tribe, Stevens and himself well. In the war that followed, Craig had obeyed Stevens' orders, adhered to his militaristic goals, taken the initiative to carry out Stevens' Indian policies and believed Stevens considered him a friend. But since that time Stevens had played a role in Craig losing his job as agent, the Nez Perce people were on a reservation full of gold miners and the government was ignoring its treaty terms. Craig may have faced the possibility that Stevens had used him, the Nez Perce leaders—even Washington Territory's Indian war—to make a name for himself that could be attached to a brass nameplate in an office on the Potomac. And it must have been a bitter pill for Craig to swallow that Stevens died leading northern volunteers in a charge against southern soldiers.

Although the eastern portion of the nation was being savaged by war, people in the Northwest were, for the first time in a number of years, free of military operations; the Nez Perces were, however, about to gain a military presence.

Brigadier General Alvord notified the Nez Perces in November 1862 that the U.S. wanted a new treaty and would arrange a council in the spring.[758] That only two killings of white men had occurred was a miracle, Alvord thought, and the alleged murderers were members of the bands always hounded by the white men: "if guilty, it is the very first Nez Perces known to kill a white man in the scores of years Craig & Newell have known that tribe…"[759] To serve as a supply base for the gold country to the east, and to protect the Indians from the gold seekers that he termed a "throng of the very worst white men," Alvord established a military post on the reservation, a few miles south of the agency building in the Lapwai Valley, which he garrisoned with volunteers.[760] The volunteers at Fort Lapwai were governed by the same rules and regulations as soldiers in the regular army, and drew the same pay.

After gold was discovered in the Boise Basin and south of the Wallowas in the Powder River valley, the Nez Perce reservation was hemmed in on three sides by gold miners. Anticipating a new council in the spring, the Nez Perces were in no position to bargain. They were almost surrounded by throngs of white men and protected only by the volunteer military garrisoned just north of the Craig family's house.

9
Passing the Reins (1862~1870)

In the summer of 1862, Craig had two wagonloads of sacked barley from his farm to sell in the new little town of Lewiston which had about 200 "tenements of various descriptions" and a population of about 1,200 white people.[761] The barley was being sold to Mssrs. Gamble and Weisgerber, partners in a brewery. Thomas Beall visited Craig at his home and Craig asked him to drive one of the two wagons. Beall agreed, and they started the next morning. Craig drove the team of mules, Beall the team of horses. They delivered the barley to the brewery and then put the teams up at the White Front stable. "Craig went to the different stores to make his purchases, not forgetting Blue John…to have it replenished."[762]

After eating their noonday meal, they thought to arrange the empty wagons so that they could ride together back to the Sweetwater. Since Beall's wagon was the heaviest, they hitched Craig's mules to Beall's wagon, put the team of horses in the lead and tied Craig's wagon behind. Beall drove and Craig sat beside him. They traveled without trouble, keeping company by swapping yarns, until a front wheel ran off the side of the road into an irrigation ditch. The jolt knocked Craig off the wagon seat and, long legs flying, he landed in the ditch. He climbed out unhurt, shook the mud off his coat, and told Beall if that was the way he drove a team he'd be damned if he would ride with him. Craig then lay down on the empty grain sacks in the tow wagon.

Beall took up the reins. It wasn't till he was halfway down the canyon that he looked behind him. The tow wagon had come loose and was not in sight. Tying the team to some trees and dropping the wagon tugs, he walked back up the road. At the top of the hill he found the wagon, with Craig asleep on the barley sacks.

Not waking Craig, Beall picked up the wagon tongue and started down the road until he came to a steep incline. He stopped and set the wagon brake, but he "could not move the vehicle with the brake on and it would move too fast with it off." He released the brake and tried again to hold the wagon back, but the pitch was too steep—it rolled ahead of him as he jumped aside. The wagon went off the side of the road and turned over, and Beall could hear Craig yelling from under the grain sacks. Beall lifted the wagon up and Craig crawled out, took a look at the situation, and "exploded with laughter from which the canyon replied in echo." A young man passing by helped them get the wagon back on the road. Craig and Beall positioned themselves in the "off" and "nigh" positions like a team of mules and managed to nurse the wagon down the road.

They had their two wagons safely re-attached when Craig asked Beall if he didn't think the situation demanded "a sentiment." Beall agreed that it did, so Craig found Blue John, lifted the keg, and gave his usual toast: "How" (in Chinook jargon, "listen" or "attend").[763] He took a drink then passed Blue John to his friend.[764]

It was not unusual for Craig to keep his whiskey jug at the ready; alcohol was a fixture of Euro American frontier life. Men in the fur trade earned a reputation for opportunistic drunkenness, yet that begs consideration alongside the months the mountain men lived virtually alcohol-free. There is enough evidence to indicate that Craig drank frequently, and it is highly probable that Craig drank to excess on occasion. But it is unlikely he could have been a successful trader, an Indian agent, a postmaster and a guide for both a military rescue expedition and a government survey party and create and maintain successful businesses had he been a habitual drunk. Considering his Scottish roots, character and accomplishments, William Craig was without doubt not a "tee-totaler," nor was he probably an alcoholic.

Reservation farming and family life went on as usual in 1862, but it was under a cloud of dread over a new treaty. James Nesmith had told the Senate that the Nez Perces were "anxious to dispose of the reservation and remove to some point where they will not be intruded upon," but that was ludicrous rhetoric given the Nez Perces' ties to the land of their ancestors.[765]

New treaty "negotiations" were set for early May 1863, and the usual governmental preparations took place, but William Craig was not an official part of them. Appointed to serve as commissioners were Washington Territory's Superintendent of Indian Affairs, Calvin Hale and agents Charles Hutchins and S. D. Howe; Hale met with Lawyer and several other headmen at the Nez Perce Agency to appoint an interpreter.[766] Craig, Newell and Henry Spalding (who was back with the Nez Perce people but not as a missionary) were all considered as interpreters; but the job went, at the request of Lawyer and his constituency, to Perrin Whitman. According to Hale, Lawyer wanted to avoid any possibility of the interpreter not being a "neutral" party. Craig and Newell were both connected with the Catholics, a fact that likely influenced Lawyer's opposition to their employment. Newell did, however, serve the commissioners as a "stool pigeon" (his words) to pick up what information he could from the Indians; he received $1,000 from the government for his "services in negotiating."[767]

Not only did the commissioners propose removing all gold-bearing land from the reservation, but they also proposed an even more drastic reduction in the size of reservation, freeing up additional land for American settlement. With a smaller reservation, the commissioners said, they could better protect the Nez Perces from bad white men and their liquor.[768] While Craig was not hired to interpret for the 1863 treaty council held in the Lapwai Valley, he was there and, with his people, heard Lawyer refuse the commissioners' proposal.

They heard Lawyer remind the new crop of government employees of the reasons the Nez Perce Nation deserved fair treatment from the United States. How could the government not keep its contracts with its allies when the Nez Perces had sacrificed so much by staying loyal to the Americans? Lawyer ticked off seven events over the past fifteen years that proved the loyalty of the Nez Perce Nation to the Americans. Lawyer read them into the record from a list; Craig had been involved in many, either directly or as an interpreter.

(1) The Nez Perces had delivered up the murderers of Dr. and Mrs. Whitman to be put to death;

(2) Captain John and Jason had helped Major Haller against the Snakes [likely as scouts serving the U.S. Army against their perennial enemies, the Snakes];

(3) warriors had helped Governor Stevens after Mr. Bolon was killed, "we called upon Craig for his advice, and he took the lead in directing us;"

(4) they furnished over forty horses to Col. Cornelius after his were taken;

(5) Timothy and some Nez Perces went with Col. Steptoe – two warriors "mingled their blood on the ground";

(6) they furnished Col. Wright with warriors so they could defend the country together;

(7) under Col. Craig, eighty warriors gathered and defended Craig and [Henri] Chase.

Lawyer argued that, instead of being asked to forfeit their lands, the Nez Perce allies should be rewarded for the help they had given the Americans.[769] The Nez Perce leaders offered to sell only the parts of their country where gold had been discovered as well as where

Lewiston was situated, plus the country around Lewiston for ten or twelve miles.

The commissioners refused the Nez Perces' proposal.

The difference of opinion between the two factions of Nez Perce people remained unchanged. Lawyer's group was ultimately ready to acquiesce to the government's terms, but those for whom Big Thunder spoke—bands led by Old Joseph, White Bird, Eagle from the Light, and Qilqilsenena (of present-day Kooskia, Idaho)—refused. The government had a long history of influencing appointment of an English-speaking head chief in order to ease treaty making, and Lawyer was one such office-holder. Given their sharp division, the Nez Perce leaders decided to dissolve the arrangement that allowed Lawyer to speak for the entire tribe.

The formal end to the political system foisted on them in 1842 by Elijah White came in an after-hours council. Leaders of the Big Thunder faction and the Lawyer faction met, talked, and agreed to dissolve the Nez Perce nation and become two separate peoples—still friends, but distinct.[770] Lawyer's position as *wiyá·taqismiyo·xat* (head chief) was gone.

Lawyer should have informed the commissioners that he was no longer "head chief" of the people, but he did not. Old Joseph, whose band's home was entirely outside of the proposed new reservation boundaries, now believed that since no one could speak for him, his homeland was safe from the treaty-makers. He withdrew from the council. However, the commissioners continued to operate in the belief that Lawyer was the only signer they would need for a legal treaty, and soon Lawyer's party accepted their proposals.

A newspaper account stated the new reserve "will embrace within its limits the present homes of three-fourths of all the Indians...and will not include over one-twelfth of the area of the old treaty." Onlookers hoped the new treaty (referred to as the "thief treaty" by Nez Perce people for years to come) would end the talk of war.[771] In fact, the new treaty would be a contributing factor leading to war in 1877.

One cannot help but wonder how the gold rush would have affected the Nez Perce reservation had it been home to not only the Nez Perces but also the Spokanes, Umatillas, Wallawallas, and Cayuses, as Isaac Stevens had originally planned. The original reservation might not have been drastically reduced in size in 1863 had it accommodated five tribes rather than one.

No written record has been found revealing William Craig's stance on the 1863 treaty, but the Portland *Daily Oregonian's* editor was convinced that Robert Newell's influence over the Nez Perces was the predominant reason they agreed to the treaty terms. Newell, the newspaper reported, had "labored long and earnestly with the leaders to persuade them that the propositions of the Government were wise and generous..."[772] The fact that Craig was not included in the accolades for Newell leads to the conclusion that Craig distanced himself from the proceedings and was not involved in the 1863 treaty.

One of the consequences of the new treaty was that the Nez Perce village at the confluence of the Snake and Clearwater Rivers was no longer within the reservation. Chief Eagle Shirt, a signer of the new treaty, thereafter relocated his village.[773] They moved to land by *'áysnima* [now Mission] creek, nearer the mountains, not far from William and Isabel Craig's ranch. Other consequences of the new treaty would be less easily handled.

Meanwhile, life returned to normal for the Craig family. In the summer, Newell and Craig traveled together to the Republican Party convention at Mt. Idaho.[774] That little community had sprung up at the end of the wagon road and the beginning of the pack trail to gold mines at Florence; Brown's Hotel was the meeting site. (The Democratic convention was held at Packer John's large log cabin—it had several rooms and a cookstove—at the Meadows to the south.[775]) Newell, an experienced Willamette Valley statesman trying to carve a niche in his new home, was seeking the Republican nomination as Idaho Territory's delegate to the U.S. Congress.

The first night of Craig and Newell's journey was spent at a roadhouse in Durkeeville on Craig's Mountain.[776] The place was full of men heading for the convention. Newell went upstairs to bed; Craig stayed downstairs and played cards. When Craig left the card game and went to the room he shared with Newell, he saw Newell's handwritten speech sticking out of his coat pocket. Craig, either as a joke or to exact a measure of satisfaction, took Newell's speech downstairs. He read it to the men, evidently embellishing it. The next morning, when Newell came down for breakfast, he was the center of attention. The men praised him as a "good fellow," shook his hand, offered him a drink and a cigar. What Craig had added to Newell's speech must have sweetened the settlers' pots.

. As the story goes, Newell mused as they rode on to Mt. Idaho that, if he were nominated, he would win the election and go to Congress and all hell wouldn't stop him. To which Craig replied that, more likely, Newell would go to hell and all of Congress wouldn't stop him. They arrived at Brown's Hotel, and the convention went well. Newell made his speech, but many told him they had already heard it. The convention nominated territorial governor Wallace.

Later that autumn, Craig was among the first men to vote in a formal election in Lewiston, Idaho Territory. On October 31, 1863, at the house of A. J. Lewis, the voters elected their delegate to Congress, a member of the territorial Council (equivalent to Senate), and a member of the territorial House of Representatives and voted on whether to levy a tax to erect a county jail. Craig was the 27th voter of the 216 (white) males registered in the Poll Book.[777]

Gold dust was being hauled out of the Nez Perce country on the riverboats that brought people and supplies to Lewiston. About the time of the fall 1863 elections, sternwheelers were again able to dock in Lewiston after low water of late summer had kept them out. On October 29 a small sternwheeler, the *Nez Perce Chief,* carried a record payload of gold dust worth $382,000 from Lewiston to Portland.[778] (Almost one hundred years later, the Nez Perce tribe filed a claim— ultimately adjudicated for $3.55 million – against the U.S. government for the millions of dollars worth of gold removed from their reservation during the "trespass period."[779]) The gold mines in the Boise Basin and Alder Gulch had drawn many miners away from Clearwater Country; those who stayed continued to find gold.

Gold mining attracted many people who preferred stealing from others to working for a living. Very near the Craig ranch (in the vicinity of present day Culdesac, Idaho) was a headquarters, or safe house, of Henry Plummer's gang of robbers, and another "shebang" was across the Alpowa hills from Lewiston on the road to Walla Walla that followed Pataha Creek.[780] All robbers were not to gain the notoriety of the Plummer gang, however. A miner named Jim Ford stole three cows from a Nez Perce family who lived on the Clearwater River. Ford sold the cows to a butcher at Oro Fino City but agent Hutchins was unsuccessful in his efforts to have Fort Lapwai troops arrest Ford so he could be brought to trial.[781] (A creek, known to the Nez Perces as *mi'se,* currently bears the name "Jim Ford Creek.")

Because they had riverboat service from Portland, Lewiston businessmen now pressed for a wagon road linking them to new gold discoveries to the east, across the Bitterroot Mountains. They, as well as riverboat entrepreneurs, wanted a more direct route to supply the new mines. On May 26, 1864, President Lincoln signed an act making Montana a U.S. territory, and a few months later he signed an omnibus road-building bill that included $50,000 for a wagon road between Lewiston, Idaho Territory, and Virginia City, Montana Territory.[782]

Idaho Territory's first and second legislatures met in Lewiston under governors Wallace and Caleb Lyon, respectively. Before Idaho Territory was created, Lewiston had been the center of the white population. But soon gold drew more miners to the Shoshone tribe's country in the Boise basin than had filled the Nez Perce reservation. When the territorial legislature voted in 1864 to permanently locate the capital in Boise City, residents of Lewiston were outraged.[783] Governor Caleb Lyon, an eccentric and deceitful New Yorker, was instrumental in relocating the territorial seal and other government paraphernalia from hostile Lewiston to triumphant Boise City.[784] From the safe distance of Walla Walla, Lyon twice sent Sewell Truax, an unemployed engineer and former commander of the volunteer forces at Fort Lapwai, to Lewiston to seize the territorial records.[785] Sewell Truax and William Craig were soon to work together in a project to connect Lewiston to Virginia City. A few years later, Gov. Lyon would actually steal the Nez Perce treaty money.[786]

Shortly after the territorial capitol left Lewiston and resurfaced at Boise City, so did Albert H. Robie. Still in the lumber business after getting his start from his father-in-law, Robie left the Lewiston area and built a sawmill on the Boise River. With two partners he also started a planing mill and lumberyard in Boise City at 4th and Main Streets.[787] The Robies built a home in the Dry Creek Valley. A. H. and Martha Craig Robie's family prospered along with the new capital of Idaho Territory.

In the spring of 1866, Craig was hired as a guide on the Lewiston-to-Virginia City road-surveying project. In circumstances not unusual in the government's 19th-century spoils system, Craig's boss was an Iowa physician. Wellington Bird, superintendent of the road survey project, hired Iowan George B. Nicholson as engineer and Northwestern University professor Oliver Marcy as scientist/geologist.[788] The men traveled together to New York, sailed to the West Coast and bought some supplies and food in San Francisco, wagons and mules in Portland, and the rest of the outfit in Walla Walla and Lewiston. The trio arrived in Lewiston late in April, and Bird hired three local men to round out the core staff: Sewell Truax as the second engineer, William Craig and a Nez Perce man named Tahatutush as guides. Craig's salary for the project was $417.

Isabel and William's youngest daughter, Annie, was attending St. Vincent's Academy—a new all-girls Catholic boarding school—in Walla Walla.[789] Adeline and Sam Phinney, with their baby son, Fitzhugh ("Fitch"), moved from Walla Walla to the Lapwai Valley about this time, providing more family to help Isabel with the work during William's absence.

While waiting in Lewiston for the snow to melt in the mountains, Dr. Bird met with Craig, Tahatutush, and others knowledgeable about the region's geography. He learned there were five routes from the Columbia River to Montana Territory: from Walla Walla through Boise City to Virginia City; From Lewiston through Elk City on the Southern Nez Perce trail; from Lewiston on the Northern Nez Perce trail, or Lolo Fork; from Walla Walla on Mullan's road past the Coeur d'Alene mission to Hell Gate (Missoula); and from the White Bluffs or Priest Rapids via Pend d'Oreille Lake and Clark Fork to Missoula. Dr. Bird eliminated the Boise City, Coeur d'Alene and Pend d'Oreille routes as too circuitous to be practical, which left only the Lolo and Southern Nez Perces trails to be explored. Of the two routes, Bird believed the Southern Nez Perces trail "seemed most direct, but the one by way of the Loulou Fork was endorsed and recommended by the territorial legislature of Idaho at their last session."[790] He began explorations on the Lolo trail.

It was late May when Bird left Lewiston with his entourage. The group included, besides the engineers, geologist and guides, "camp men packers and axemen" to cook, to care for the wagons, mules, and pack animals, and to cut a swath through the heavy timber expected ahead. They traveled the road up Craig's Mountain, across the highlands and down the steep trail to the Clearwater River (present site of Greer, Idaho). After crossing the river on the ferry (formerly Craig's ferry), they joined Nicholson in camp. By early June they had climbed out of the canyon and made their way across high, timber-rimmed prairies due east to "Muscle" (Musselshell) Creek, where they again camped. They had accomplished a tortuous but scenic journey to this point; the Lolo trail still lay ahead.

It began to rain steadily, and an exploration party sent fifteen miles ahead returned with the news that the snow was still too deep to start up the higher mountains. They were stuck in camp at *se·wi'snime* (Musselshell) for twenty days, waiting for the rain to stop and the snow in the higher country to melt. Finally, on June 26, they packed up and pulled out.

It took the party eleven days to cross the mountains to the Bitterroot Valley near Fort Owen. The route taken was basically that of the Nez Perce trail so well known to Tahatutush and Craig. The *kuseyne'iskit* (bison hunt trail) followed ridges north of the Lochsa River and had been used for untold generations by the Nez Perce people: in places the trail was worn to a deep depression. It was a difficult path, often cluttered with deadfall trees and sometimes wide enough for the passage only of one horse and rider. As it had for generations, the availability of grass for the livestock dictated camping spots, and water was not hard to find. In 1805 the Lewis and Clark party had followed portions of the trail as they struggled west across the Bitterroots, and on their return trip Nez Perce guides led them from the beginning to the end of the trail. Once the snow had gone off, Craig and Tahatutush had no difficulty piloting the Bird and Truax expedition across *kuseyne'iskit*.

In early summer, John Owen unexpectedly came upon his old friend, Craig, with a party of men at Hell Gate. Owen invited Craig, Bird and Truax to spend the night at his home and noted in his diary:

Tuesday 10: [July 1866] retd home after an absence of over two Mos. Met the party at Hell Gate Who are Exploring a rout by the Lolo Fork from Lewistown under the direction of Doct. Bird. The Doct. Col. Craig & Maj. Truax (?) rode up with Me from their Camp on Lolo's Fork...[791]

The scene in the adobe fort that was John and Nancy Owen's home was one repeated often as the men visited one another; they ate, drank, smoked, and talked, sharing the news of the day that kept strong the ties between their distant homes.

Once back at the Lolo Creek camp, Bird split the party. Marcy left for home, while Nicholson, Truax, and Tahatutush were sent to explore the Southern Nez Perces Trail. Bird, Craig, and the packers, axemen, and cooks retraced their steps over the Lolo pass to Musselshell Creek. From there Bird returned to Lewiston, where he learned from Nicholson's report that the Southern Nez Perces Trail was not feasible. Bird sent supplies and laborers, under direction of Sewell Truax, to the Musselshell to begin work on the Lolo Fork route.

Nicholson spent the month of August blazing trail, where often the timber and underbrush was so dense he could not see fifty feet ahead:

The only instrument that could be used was a common hatchet to blaze the way for the woodchoppers through the timber. Every part of the ground had to be carefully walked over. Alignments were made by my assistant and self blazing in many instances toward each other by sound of voice, from points previously selected.[792]

When Nicholson went back to the "Oyipe" (Weippe) prairie to begin the instrumental survey, Craig finished blazing trail for the axemen. The high *qémes* grounds, root garden for people since *ni·mí·pu·* beginnings, sanctuary after Lewis and Clark's close escape from the Bitterroots, now housed transits, axemen, and shovels.

Before winter forced them to quit, they had a 93-mile mile stretch "cleared out [of timber] in sufficient width for a road…[with] enough grading done to make it a good pack trail."[793] The improved trail followed the backbone of the ridges, was graded from saddle to saddle and had reached a creek they named "Takon Creek," one of the streams forming the headwaters of the Lochsa River some one hundred seventy miles from Lewiston (now known as Packer Meadows). Craig and Tahatutush likely contributed the Nez Perce word, *té·kin* (swamp, meadow), for the Bird-Truax map.[794]

The Bird-Nicholson-Truax survey party had tinkered with the most difficult portion of the bison-hunt trail and was just short of the summit and nearby hot springs when work stopped. But Congress did not further fund the project and the Lewiston to Virginia City Road Project was never completed. Some Montana Territory taxpayers felt the money appropriated for the "Lewiston and Montana road" was not put to good use. People recognized the political pork barrel project was funded as a favor to some influential Lewiston merchants, and Montana sentiment held that the money could have been put to better use improving Mullan's road over the Coeur d'Alene pass.[795]

In the spring of 1867, the United States Congress finally ratified the 1863 treaty.[796] Funds, when finally appropriated by Congress to fulfill treaty obligations, were often inadequate to give each Indian more than a few dollars; goods worth less than the debt owed were substituted.[797] The government continued its past post-treaty behavior.

Over the years, the religion brought by the black robes to Thunder's Eye provided a sustaining faith to his descendants. His granddaughters, Annie Craig and Clara Robie, while at school in Walla Walla, were baptized into the Catholic Church. Annie, who would soon be fifteen years old, and her niece, Clara ("Mary Rosa") age six years, were part of a group of young people baptized by Father D. F. Halde on April 28, 1867.[798]

Late in 1867 a man who was to have a close relationship with some of the Craig family arrived at the Lapwai agency. Reverend Joseph Cataldo had been assigned by the Catholic Church to the Nez Perce missionary field—a difficult undertaking given that Lawyer, one of Spalding's Presbyterian converts, had been successful in keeping a Catholic church from being built on the Nez Perce reservation. Agent James O'Neill denied Cataldo's request to build a church, yet a number of Nez Perces (Isabel Craig undoubtedly among them) wanted Catholic services. While waiting for permission to teach at "a small government day school for Indian children" near the agency, Father Cataldo built a Catholic church in Lewiston.[799]

When in October 1868 Robert Newell was appointed Nez Perce agent (replacing O'Neill) he gave Cataldo permission to build a church on land next to the Clearwater about a mile above the agency—land donated by Stuptupnim (Hair Cut Short), who wanted to become a Catholic. Newell stipulated that the church be built at no expense to either the government or himself, and it was constructed forthwith using volunteer labor and trees from a nearby island. Located on the north bank (area now known as Arrow Beach), the small church had log walls, a dirt roof and was prone to spring flooding. Despite his efforts, Newell's tenure as agent was short. In the wake of the Civil War, President Grant saw Indian agencies as a source of jobs for the surplus military officers, and in July 1869—even though the Nez Perce leaders wanted him as their agent and had submitted a petition signed by more than 140 people asking that he remain—Newell was replaced by Lt. J. W. Wham.[800]

Isabel and the children must have been pleased to have a priest and a church close to home, but no record has been found showing William joining any organized religion. What he had seen of churches and missionaries likely convinced him that they were the prime cause of problems between people. Henry Spalding and his methods had, to Craig's way of thinking, done great harm to the Nez Perces. And religion continued to cause contention: the fact that Craig's family was Catholic had likely been instrumental in Lawyer's faction rejecting Craig as interpreter in 1863. Although he had been raised as a Presbyterian, Craig discarded that church along with all others. Many years later, grandson Fitch Phinney was admiring the valley, mountains, and pine trees near old Fort Lapwai and recalled that Craig's spiritual fulfillment was found not in a church but in the land:

...that mountain and those trees were old Craig's religion...yes, sir, they were his very damn religion, he lived his life like that...tall and straight...[801]

Government had long used Protestant missionaries to teach Indians both Christianity and farming. Craig had likely believed, when he partnered with Isaac Stevens, that the government's approach was the only way to save the Nez Perces from being annihilated by Americans. But his firsthand experiences with the government's dealings with Indians had, over time, soured him on treaty promises just as Henry Spalding had earlier soured him on Bible verses. He stayed as free as he could from both.

Early in May 1867, Craig took a little trip to do some hunting and prospecting with Thomas Beall and a man named Mike Mayer. From Craig's Mountain they rode across the prairie and descended to the Clearwater at the big eddy. Four miles upstream they crossed the river, climbed out of the canyon and traveled north to the headwaters of the Potlatch River, where they camped (northwest of present-day Boville, Idaho). Around the campfire at night, Craig often reminisced about his life in earlier times. He called his birthplace, Virginia, the "Old Dominion. He recalled his exploits as a mountain man with "no egotism" invariably saying "we" or "he" rather than "I."[802] Although they didn't know it as they stoked the campfire beside the stream, time was running short for Craig, for within a year he would suffer from a stroke and no longer be able to ride the Clearwater country trails.

The stroke Craig suffered in 1868 knocked him down, as nothing else in life had been able to do. Isabel cared for him, but he was never to regain his strength and physical faculties. Daughter Adeline and her husband, Sam Phinney, began helping on the Craigs' farm when her father fell ill. In return for Phinney's work on the place—and to ensure his continued help, since Craig was getting no better—Isabel and William decided to turn over some of their place to Sam. The old letter from the Olympia land office, the one stating that William's claim was perfect and he could sell the land, was still safe in the trunk.[803] On February 13, 1869, Isabel and William appeared before court clerk S. S. Fenn in Lewiston, there to sell 160 acres to their son-in-law, Sam Phinney, and neighbor, Moses Rice. William signed his name, Isabel made an "X" as her mark; the selling price was $1,000 in gold coin.[804]

Thomas Beall was leaving for a gold mining trip to Moose Creek in the backcountry, and he visited William before leaving. They sat up most of the night talking about good times they had shared. As Beall left the next morning, he recalled, Craig said: "Thomas (he always addressed Beall as "Thomas"), I'll never see you again on this earth." Later, when Beall came down from Moose Creek, he stopped at Weippe and there picked up a letter from Sam Phinney, telling him of Craig's death.[805] He had died at home on October 16, 1869.

Craig had earlier, on a winter day with snow covering the hills, chosen a place for his grave; the site was where the last rays of winter sun lingered on the hillside.[806] Family and friends gathered and buried William on his and Isabel's land, at the place he had selected for a cemetery.

After death, Craig was credited with accomplishments little lauded when he was alive. The eulogy in the *Idaho Triweekly Statesman* reflected the kind thoughts of the white community for mountain man William Craig, along with recognition that they had lost a link to the country's far different past: he used "his influence successfully to prevent the Nez Perces and other tribes from open hostilities…was a man of nerve, kind hearted and generous impulses…"[807] Some forty years later, in a lawsuit over the land, a court found that William had been:

> …*a man of unusual intelligence and activity, and performed large service to the government of the United States as interpreter, inspector and assistant of the Governor Isaac Stevens in the making…of Indian treaties, and as an officer in Indian wars, and as an Indian agent…*[808]

Had the Nez Perce tribal community published an obituary at William's death, it might have read that he was, to many, a trusted friend. They valued the fact that he had not deserted Isabel and their children like so many of the mountain men, that he could read and write and was generous and truthful. Few men could laugh and joke like Craig. Never had anyone gone hungry if he had food to share. Never had a *ni·mí·pu·* paid money to be carried on his ferries across one of the Creator's rivers. And he had given advice to the leaders that basically had proven sound, for they still lived on the land of their ancestors, many had grown rich doing business with newcomers, and their women and children were not hungry and crying in their lodges after their men had been killed in battle with the Americans. William had always told them to join the white people as friends and live together, much as he lived with the *ni·mí·pu·*.

Even before Craig died, Robert Newell had been preparing to leave the Clearwater country. He and his new wife, Mary, had purchased a farm near Dayton, Washington, on the road between Lewiston and Walla Walla. But before the Newells could move to their new farm, Robert suffered a heart attack. On a November day in Lewiston, Doc Newell died at the age of 62.[809] Mary and his many children gathered to bury him on the bluff above the town (present site of Pioneer Park).[810] Old Craig and Old Doc stayed close; their deaths were within a few weeks of one another, their graves less than twenty miles apart. And they were among family.

Left: One of William and Isabel Craig's grandsons, Joseph Anthony Craig, son of Joseph William Craig and Temáha. Undated photo. (Courtesy of National Park Service, Nez Perce National Historical Park; image no. 2261)

Below: Some of William and Isabel Craig's descendants at the October 26, 1946 monument dedication, one hundred years after the Craigs moved onto their donation land claim left to right:

Mayme (Mamie) Phinney Johann (granddaughter)

George Phinney (great-grandson)

Helen Phinney Jones (Peterson) (great-granddaughter)

Minnie Fairfield Caldwell (granddaughter)

Mary Ellen Phinney (great-great-granddaughter)

Fitzhugh Phinney (grandson)

Ermith Phinney Freeland (great-great-granddaughter)

Archie Phinney (great-grandson)

Permission to use Lewiston Morning Tribune photo given by Nez Perce County Historical Society.

(Nez Perce County Historical Society)

Afterward (1870-1886)

No matter what strategy the U.S. government tried with its Indian policies, nothing seemed to accomplish its perpetual goal of bloodlessly moving Indian people aside so that white people could own and farm the land. Before the end of William Craig's life, angry Minnesota warriors in 1862—and at Colorado's Sand Creek two years later—had retaliated against trespassing settlers and triggered horrific military retaliation.[811] Additionally, it was generally known that, in many cases, payments for lands ceded by the tribes were not reaching them: on the Nez Perce reservation, former agent James O'Neill had admitted to pocketing some $10,000 sent for education simply by hiring no teachers and keeping the funds.[812] But it was the Sand Creek massacre that became a rallying cry to change federal policies from those based on military power to ones based on kindness and decency.

Redressing the wrongs of slavery had culminated in the Civil War. After the war, some Americans in the East came together to right the wrongs done to Indians. However, over the next thirty years—through policies calling for segregation, Christianization, education, assimilation, and allotment—reformers, however well intentioned, compounded the wrongs. They repressed Indian culture, violated treaties, and subjected Indians to pressures aimed at separating them from their heritage—all ostensibly for the Indians' own good so that they could be molded into American citizens.

The first approach involved the government inviting churches to staff the Indian reservations: Ulysses Grant's "peace policy" (it might have been labeled the "religious policy") called for Indian agents supplied by Christian denominations.[813] Of the reservations established at the 1855 Walla Walla treaty council, the Catholics were given responsibility for the Walla Walla Cayuse Umatilla reservation, Methodists the Yakama reservation, and Presbyterians the Nez Perce reservation.[814] John B. Monteith, a young, Presbyterian clergyman from the Willamette Valley, was appointed U.S. Indian Agent for the Nez Perce agency.

When Sam Phinney in 1872 auctioned some of the Craig land to pay his father-in-law's estate debts—and a white man purchased the land—Agent Monteith became aware of privately held land within the Nez Perce reservation.[815] He soon became involved in what was to be a lengthy dispute with some of the Craig family.

The 1863 treaty called for allotment of 20-acre parcels to each adult male in the tribe. In the next few years, a series of events took place involving J. Monteith, representing both the government and the Presbyterians, and the Craig family, who were in the unique (albeit uncomfortable) position of being Catholics who had inherited private land on an Indian reservation administered by Presbyterians.

The Craig descendants' roles were further complicated by the fact that Adeline had married a white man who, along with her brother, Joe Craig, was associated by Monteith with the element he labeled "whiskey men."[816] A feud developed between the agent and a number of men on the reservation that included Sam Phinney, William Caldwell (the agency farmer and operator of an express way-station), two of Robert and Kitty Newell's sons, and Joe Craig.[817] Monteith's efforts to rid the reservation of Craig and Newell descendants attracted the attention of settlers, and over three hundred of them joined in a petition for agent Monteith's removal.[818] More than 50 Nez Perce men signed a separate petition requesting Monteith's replacement and Idaho's congressional delegate, John Hailey, asked the Interior Department to investigate.[819] Monteith was not removed.

The legality of the Craigs' claim to the Lapwai Valley land came under scrutiny. Sam Phinney, aided by a Lewiston attorney, eventually proved its legality with the help of two people: Perrin Whitman (who attested he had known William Craig since 1843, that Craig lived on the Lapwai Valley land until his death, and that Sam Phinney was married to a daughter of William Craig) and his mother-in-law, Isabel Craig.[820] Isabel deposed as to her children's relationship to William and William's claim to the Lapwai Valley land; she then deeded her 320 acres of the claim to son-in-law, Sam Phinney.[821] Questions remained, however, about the boundaries of the Craig donation land claim. Over the years several surveys were made and protracted litigation by descendants lasted into the twentieth century, ending in the United States Supreme Court.[822]

In 1874 Joe Craig was reported to have avenged the murder of a Nez Perce man by another tribal member and Monteith had him arrested.[823] Monteith wanted to "place him in the hands of the military and have him saw wood for the garrison," the same way he punished full-blooded Indians for being drunk or bringing liquor onto the reservation.[824] The treaty-Presbyterian Indians wanted him prosecuted under U.S. law, but the Lewiston judge doubted that he had jurisdiction in the case and released Craig.[825]

The little Catholic Church near the river was so flood-prone that Eagle Shirt offered different land (not far from the Craig home) on which to build a new church; by late 1874 Father Cataldo's church, St. Joseph's Mission at Slickpoo, was built.[826] Two of Adeline and Sam's daughters were baptized in the church and Joe Craig, when 36 years old, was baptized there on Christmas Day 1876.[827] After having married John Seeds in Ada County in 1875, Annie Craig Seeds on March 19, 1880, married Charles Fairfield at the Slickpoo Mission; their baby son, Innes Fairfield, was baptized there the same day.[828]

When the U.S. government opened the Wallowa Valley to white settlement in 1875, Monteith talked with Young Joseph about moving his people from the Wallowa Valley to the reservation.[829] Almost two years went by and Young Joseph's band continued living in their homeland, where the graves of their ancestors were, rather than follow the dictates of the 1863 treaty. (The "thief treaty" still invites scrutiny: in 2000 it was argued that the 1863 treaty was illegal in that it violated the 5th Amendment to the U.S. Constitution, and that forcing Joseph and his people from the Wallowas was punitive.[830]) Finally, in late winter 1877, Monteith sent a message to Young Joseph to move to the reservation by April 1.[831] At the same time, Monteith also served notice on Joe Craig and the Newell brothers to be off their farms in the Lapwai valley by April 1.[832] If he could remove Catholics Joe Craig and the Newell brothers from their farms on the reservation, Monteith was sure he would have enough land for the Wallowa band—and he wished likewise to free up the good land farmed by Phinney and Caldwell.[833]

The off-reservation leaders were told there were 60 20-acre farms on the reservation waiting for them.[834] A tour was arranged with General Oliver O. Howard, who hoped to settle Young Joseph's band on Phinney and Caldwell's land. When the off-reservation leaders stopped for lunch at the Caldwell farm, however, Young Joseph declined the property, believing that he had no right to what belonged to white men.[835] The deadline was moved back and other places were chosen on which the off-reservation bands could settle.

Ultimately, however, the off-reservation bands did not settle on the reservation as planned, for hostilities erupted after some young Nez Perce men killed white people along the Salmon River. The remaining years of Monteith's tenure as Nez Perce agent were spent dealing with war and its aftermath.[836] And no *ni·mí·pu·* were unaffected by the events that followed, when the bands under leadership of Whitebird, Young Joseph, Young Looking Glass, Hushhushcute, and others fought the U.S. Army in June 1877 and then fled Idaho with the U.S. Army in pursuit.

For the Craig family, the War of 1877— some people called it Joseph's War—was experienced within the sway of the Catholic Church. Joe Craig stayed west of the Rocky Mountains and was sent out by the army to try to avoid widespread war. He rode with Father Joseph Cataldo and served as his interpreter. The two Joes—Cataldo and Craig—covered a circuit of hundreds of miles over many weeks, talking to leaders in villages to the west and north, convincing them not to join the Nez Perces, who were sending couriers asking for help fighting the whites. Less than a year after the October 1877 surrender by young Joseph, Idaho's congressional delegate, S. S. Fenn, spoke to the U.S. House of Representatives and memorialized Cataldo's and Joe Craig's contributions towards averting all-out war.[837]

The extended Craig family's roles in the 1877 war played out from the Cascade Mountains to the Bear's Paw in Montana. Yellow Wolf recalled Thunder's Eye the Younger being captured by the army after crossing into Montana with the Nez Perce families.[838] Thunder's Eye the Younger (also known as Amos George) in later years said that he had served as a scout for Capt. Logan's troops and was given the name "Capt. Long."[839]

Craig family legend (undocumented) holds that another young man caught up in the flight of the Nez Perces, Seeyakoonilpilp (Red Spy, Red Scout, Red Courier), was a son of William Craig. Because of his place in the Craig family tradition, Seeyakoonilpilp is given a place in this work. Early in the conflict, Red Spy reportedly killed army scout Charles Blewett and took his spyglass; he then scouted for the fleeing Nez Perce families and fought the U.S. Army from Idaho to the Bear's Paw.[840] He was reportedly with Poker Joe (Lean Elk) at Yellowstone Park.[841] It was said that he was disgusted with preachers, blaming them for most of the current troubles and saying he was neither Catholic nor Protestant.[842] It is reported that Assiniboines killed Red Spy and his companions at the close of the Bear's Paw battle and his body is buried near the Milk River (near present Havre, Montana).[843] Seeyakoonilpilp's name was later passed on to Joe Craig.[844]

Martha Craig Robie

After Joseph's War ended, William and Isabel's eldest daughter, Martha Robie, continued to live in the Boise City area with her husband, A. H. Robie, and their children. Robie was a prominent civic leader, including a term in the 1874 Idaho territorial legislature.[845] The

Robies had five children—four girls and one boy—and owned much of the land on which Boise City was growing. In 1876, Robie sold the lumber business and bought a large cattle ranch near Steen's Mountain in Oregon, although the family continued to live at their Dry Creek ranch (near present-day Star, Idaho). At Camp Harney (now Burns, Oregon), Robie built a sawmill, and on his ranch nearby he had several hundred head of well-bred horses along with his other stock.[846] Robie and a crew of men were rounding up stock at the ranch when Bannock, Shoshone, and Paiute warriors attacked, killing some of Robie's horse herd and driving off others. Robie and his men got away and made a "roundabout 100-mile ride to Camp Harney," where Robie told others about the running fight with the Indians and offered $2,000 for the head of Egan (the marauders' leader).[847] Robie then joined the troops in pursuit of the Indians, trying to recover some of the stock they had stolen. During the chase he suffered from fatigue and exposure, which led to illness and—back at his home on Dry Creek—death. On July 26, 1878, Robie died at the age of 46. His obituary in the Idaho Statesman read in part:

Idaho has lost one of her best and most useful citizens, one who has been permanently identified with her history, and whose name has been associated with all the events and enterprises which have helped to build up the country…a great favorite of Gov. Stevens, who placed the most implicit confidence in his courage, strict integrity and business capacity. …He leaves a wife and five children, two of whom are daughters nearly grown. For his distressed family, his loss is indeed irreparable and the entire community share in a deep sorrow which his death brings to them.

Albert H. Robie's funeral was held at the Masonic Hall on Main Street in Boise and he was buried in Boise's Pioneer Cemetery.[848]

Martha Craig Robie, then a wealthy, 36-year-old widow, continued living on the Dry Creek ranch for a number of years. A neighbor, Hank Vaughan, dealt in stolen livestock and was a familiar visitor to Martha's ranch.[849] Along with Billy Moody and Jim (J. C.) Alexander, Hank used Martha Robie's ranch as a rendezvous point and would sometimes ride into Boise City and terrorize the citizens.[850] The Robies' eldest daughter, 19-year-old Clara (with one marriage behind her), married gang member J. C. Alexander; two years later she married Hank's lieutenant, Billy Moody. In 1883, Martha Robie (Hank affectionately called her "Gus") and the three younger children, Hugh Hall (Huey), Mary (Mollie), and Minnie, moved from the Dry Creek ranch to a farm in Spring Hollow, near Pendleton, Oregon.[851] Daughter Lizzie (Zoe) evidently did not move northwest with her mother and siblings. Soon Hank and Martha were raising the first wheat crop on the Walla Walla Cayuse Umatilla reservation; in 1885 a report noted Hank Vaughn was "a white man who has some 1,500 or 2,000 acres under fence and in wheat," noting that Vaughn's wife was the daughter of a man named Craig, a white man who had lived at times with the Indians, and that the mother of Mrs. Vaughn was a Nez Perce and "in no way connected with any of the tribes on the reservation."[852] On October 7, 1888, Martha and Hank were married at the courthouse in Walla Walla.[853]

Gus and Hank frequently traveled on the Northern Pacific train to Spokane Falls, and Hank, with Gus's help, reportedly foiled a train robbery near Sprague. Although he could be charming, when Hank was drinking he was wild and unpredictable. He had recovered from so many gunshots that, in 1893 when his horse stumbled and he died (at age 42) of injuries from that fall, he reportedly had scars from 13 bullet wounds.[854] Martha Craig Robie Vaughan later resided in Athena, Oregon.

Craig families on the Nez Perce Reservation

Living on the Nez Perce reservation in 1880 were Adeline, Sam, and their children; Joe, Temáha, and their children; and Isabel on the home place with her youngest daughter, Annie.[855] The Craig family stayed connected on the Umatilla and Nez Perce reservations, for young Huey Robie's first marriage was to Julia Rice from the Lapwai Valley.[856] With the exception of Martha's family, the Craig family lived, as they had since William and Isabel built their home in the 1840s, in the valley of the Lapwai.

Early in 1881, the Idaho Territorial Legislature passed an act permitting it to raise revenues by taxing real estate. On August 16, 1881, in accordance with the new law, 640 acres belonging to Sam and Adeline Phinney was, due to unpaid taxes, sold at public auction. John Evans, representing Nez Perce County, was the successful bidder.[857]

On Friday, June 16, 1882, Joe Craig died. He was working on the farm, repairing a hog pen, when he began to feel unwell. He headed for the house but "dropped, choked, and died in his tracks without a struggle or without uttering a word." At 42 years, Joe had "long been a sufferer from quick consumption" (tuberculosis). Joe was eulogized in the press as always a friend of the white man and was given credit for the friendly relations between white and Indian, since he had "sturdy force of character" and the Indians feared him. It was written that Joe was one of the few men on earth who was impossible to frighten, fearless to the point of imprudence, yet with a tenderness that endeared him to others. "Poor Joe!..the sun never shone upon a braver man or upon a truer friend than Joe Craig."[858] Joseph William Craig left his wife, Temáha, and at least six children. He was buried near his father. Some of Joe Craig's descendants relocated to the Walla Walla Cayuse Umatilla reservation where their families continue to reside.[859]

About four years later, on July 6, 1886, Adeline Craig Phinney committed suicide. According to the newspaper report, Adeline shot herself through the heart:

She had been paralyzed for several years, and was barely able to move, and the weapon with which she met so untimely an end was on the bureau in her room, to which she managed to crawl. Long years of suffering is thought to be the cause of her death.[860]

Forty-one years old, Adeline was the mother of at least six children.[861] It is believed she was buried near her father and brother. The fact that Adeline took her own life—and the Catholic Church considers suicide a sin—may explain why no record of her death has been found in church records.

Isabel Craig preceded her daughter in death by almost exactly two months: May 8, 1886. A Lewiston newspaper carried a brief notice of her death: "The venerable wife of Col. Craig died at Sam. Phinny's place on the Lapwai last Saturday."[862] She was buried next to her husband.

Almost everything had changed in Clearwater country during Isabel's long life. Although it was splendidly isolated from main routes of westward white migration, gold mining had drawn a rough element of white men to the land. Some of the early white settlers remained: they, some of their descendants, and others of their ilk, perpetuated the racism earlier aimed at the African Americans during the Civil War reconstruction period. William had died before he saw his children's and grandchildren's spirits pummeled by boarding schools and bigotry; Isabel's faith no doubt gave the family strength during hard times.

In the same issue of the newspaper that printed Isabel's death notice, an article described a pleasure trip of about 300 people who took a steamer up the Clearwater River from Lewiston. The boat stopped at the mouth of Lapwai Creek:

...where the company got off and partook of a basket pic-nic in the Cottonwood groves which line the creek in the vicinage of the agency. There is but little of interest to be seen at Lapwai except a couple of hundred fat and lazy Indians lying on their bellies and staring at the crowd, and so early in the afternoon the company re-embarked and returned to town, benefited by the change of scene and air...[863]

The writing reflected the vacuous arrogance of some who now occupied *simí·nekem*, as well as the fact that—46 years after William Craig first came to live amongst them— *ni·mí·pu·* continued to occupy a portion of their ancestral homelands.

Appendices

Appendix A

AFFIDAVIT OF SETTLERS ON UNSURVEYED LANDS, CLAIMING UNDER THE 4TH SECTION OF ACT OF 27TH SEPTEMBER 1850 AND THE AMENDMENTS THERETO[*]

William Craig of Walla Walla county, in the Territory of Washington, being first duly sworn, says that he is a white settler on the public lands in the Territory of Washington, and that he arrived in Oregon on the 26th day of July, 1829 that he is a native born citizen of the United States and that he was born in Greenbrier county, Virginia, in the year 1807, that he has personally resided upon and cultivated that part of the public lands in the Territory of Washington particularly described in the annexed notification to the Register and Receiver...___ Territory continuously from the 15th day of September, 1846, to the 4th day of June 1855. And he further says that he is intermarried with Isabel Craig his wife and that he was legally married to her on the 6th day of July 1838, in Missouri Territory, and that they have issue: Joseph born Sept. 10 1840, Martha born Feb. 18, 1842, Adeline born May 5, 1845, Mary born Aug. 24, 1850, Anna born June 12, 1855.

Subscribed and sworn to before me this 4th day of June, 1855

(Signed) William Craig

[line illegible]

---

[*] 1913 Appeal of Survey, General Land Entry Files for CRAIG, William and Isabel, Donation Certificate No. 03092, Notification No. 1271, Approximate date of Entry: 9/17/1913, Serial Patent Number: 356234, *Caldwell v. Vaughn.* (Nez Perce County, Lewiston, Idaho)

Appendix B

William Craig's Statement Regarding
Massacre at Whitman's Station*

Question by Hon. P.H. Burnett: State whether you were acquainted with Tom Hill, a Delaware Indian, and when and where, and what statements he made to the Nez Perces, and whether the Cayuses were informed of his statements, and what impression he made on the Indians?

Answer: The first acquaintance was in the Rocky Mountains in the year 1837, and then in 1845, when he came to the Nez Perces country. I frequently heard that he had been telling unfavorable tales of the Americans; how they had treated the Indians in his country. He said the first were missionaries that came to him, and then others came in and settled, and then commenced taking our lands, and finally drove us off; and they will do the same to you. This I had heard of Tom Hill. On seeing him, I asked him what he had told the Indians; if he had told them so and so, as I had heard. He said he had told them how the Americans had treated them in his place, and they had better not keep Spalding there, or it would be the same thing with them; I am acquainted with missionaries; it is only a way of making property; there is nothing in religion, only to make money; you can see that; look how they are selling everything they raise in your own lands; you cannot get anything from them without paying for it, not so much as a piece of meat when you are hungry. After my interview with Hill, he came once in company with some Nez Perces to Dr. Whitman's; after remaining there some twelve or fifteen days, he returned; I asked him how he and the Doctor got along; he told me very well; that he was a heap better man than Spalding; he had asked him into his house sometimes. After that the Doctor told me Tom had done some mischief with the Indians in that place.

Question: Will you state what is the custom among the Cayuses when a medicine man fails to cure a patient and the patient dies?

Answer: Since I have been acquainted with them, it has always been their custom in such cases to kill the medicine man or woman; and every year since I have known them, I have heard of them killing such persons.

Question: How long have you been acquainted with the Cayuses?
Answer: Since the year 1840.

Question: State whether you ever heard any of the Cayuses say anything about the Catholics establishing missions among them, and whether they disliked that they should?
Answer: I heard an Indian, who was left in charge of the Young Chief's business, while the chief was out after buffalo, and which was some time during the summer of 1847, say that the Young Chief told him that if they, the Catholic missionaries, should come there before he got back, to tell them to remain, but not to commence building until his return, and he would show them where to build. It was, however, a common report among the Nez Perces that the Cayuses had asked the Catholics to come among them and to establish missions.

Question: Did you hear Dr. Whitman say anything relative to the Catholics establishing missions among the Indians; if so, state what?
Answer: Dr. Whitman told me that he heard a talk of the Catholics establishing a mission on the Tucannon, about sixty miles off, and said he would rather they would be nearer at hand.

Question: State where you were at the time the massacre took place, and what do you know about a messenger from the murderers to the Nez Perce Indians, and what the messenger said in reference to the cause of the Cayuses killing Dr. Whitman.
Answer: I was living about ten miles from Mr. Spalding's mission, Mr. Camfield [sic] first brought the news of the massacre. On the 8th, after the massacre, being Monday, a great many Indians met at Mr. Spalding's before Mr. S. had returned; a messenger came there from the Cayuses, and the Indians, then assembled, required him to state all he knew about the matter, and to state the truth; I was present; and he said, in substance, that all the chiefs were concerned, except Young Chief and Five Crows, who knew nothing of it; that the cause of the murder was that Dr. Whitman and Spalding were poisoning the Indians. They asked him, are you sure that they were poisoning the Indians? He said yes. How do you know it? Jos. Lewis said so. What did he say? Jos. Lewis said that Dr. Whitman and Mr. Spalding had been writing for two years to their friends in the East, where Jos. Lewis lived, to send them poison to kill off the Cayuses and the Nez Perces; and they had sent them some that was not good, and they wrote for more that

would kill them off quick, and that the medicine had come this summer. Jos. Lewis said he was lying on the settee in Dr. Whitman's room, and he heard a conversation between Dr. Whitman, Mrs. Whitman and Mr. Spalding, in which Mr. Spalding asked the doctor why he did not kill the Indians off faster? "Oh," said the Doctor, "they are dying fast enough; the young ones will die off this winter, and the old ones next spring." Mrs. Whitman said that our friends will be on, and want to settle in this country. A talk then took place between Dr. Whitman and Mr. Spalding, in which they said, how easy we will live when the Indians are all killed off; such an Indian has so many horses, and such an Indian so many spotted horses, and our boys will drive them up, and we will give them to our friends. One of them said that man will hear us, alluding to Jos. Lewis. Oh, no, said another, he cannot hear, he is sleeping sound. They talked rather low, but Jos. Lewis said he could hear all that passed. This Indian messenger stated that Jos. Lewis had made this statement in a council of the Cayuses on the Saturday night previous to the murder, and that Jos. Lewis said he had heard this conversation between Dr. Whitman and the others on the Wednesday before the murder. Jos. Lewis, the messenger said, told the Cayuses in the council that unless they (the Indians) killed Dr. Whitman and Mr. Spalding quick, they would all die. The messenger went on to say himself, that one hundred and ninety-seven Indians had died since the immigration commenced passing that summer. He said that there were six buried on Monday morning, and among the rest his own wife; he said he knew they were poisoned.

Question: Are you acquainted with the fact that the smallpox was spread among the Blackfeet Indians east of the Rocky Mountains? If so, state in what year, and how far it spread, and whether a knowledge of this fact is not familiar with the Cayuses and Nez Perces?

Answer: In the year 1837, the smallpox was spread among the Blackfeet Indians by one Beckwith, who brought the matter for that purpose. Beckwith took it himself, and a clerk at one of the trading posts, Fort Muriah, on one branch of the Missouri river, helped to spread it among the Blackfeet Indians for the purpose of killing them off. A knowledge of this fact is common among the Nez Perces, and, I think, among the Cayuses.

July 11, 1848   (Signed) William Craig

---

* Secretary of the Interior, *Report*, 1857-58, 35th Cong. 1st and spec. sess. 1858, Senate Exec. Doc. No. 40, vol. 12, p. 25-27.

Appendix C

Major Players in the Events*

Alvord, Benjamin	American from Vermont
Beall, Thomas J./B.	American from Washington. D.C.
Big Thunder	Cayuse/Nez Perce from Snake River country
Cain, Andrew J.	American
Camaspello (*Big Belly*)	Cayuse chief from Wallawalla River country
Captain John	Nez Perce warrior
Cataldo, Joseph	Catholic missionary from Sicily
Chase, Henri M.	American from Pennsylvania
Chirouse, Eugene	Catholic missionary from France
Craig, Isabel	Nez Perce from Lapwai Valley
Craig, Joseph W.	Nez Perce/American from Lapwai Valley
Craig, William	American from Virginia
Doty, James	American from Wisconsin
Eagle from the Light	Nez Perce from Salmon River country
Fierce Grizzly (*Umehowlish*)	Cayuse warrior from Wallawalla River country
Five Crows	Cayuse chief from Umatilla River country
Gervais, John Baptist	French/Indian former fur trapper
Gilliam, Cornelius	American from North Carolina
Higgins, Christopher P.	American from Ireland
Hill, Tom	of the Delaware tribe
Hutchins, Charles	American
Jacob	Nez Perce leader
Jason	Nez Perce leader from Asotin on Snake River
Lawyer	Nez Perce/Flathead leader from Clearwater River
Lee, Henry A. G.	American from Virginia
Looking Glass	Nez Perce from Asotin
McKay, William C.	French/Indian from Oregon country
Meek, Joseph	American from Virginia
Miller, Henry (*Joaquin*)	American from Indiana
Monteith, John B.	American from Oregon
Nesmith, James W.	American from Maine
Newell, Robert (*Doc*)	American from Ohio
Old Joseph	Nez Perce from Wallowa country

Owen, John — American from Philadelphia
Palmer, Joel — American born in Ontario, Canada
Pambrun, A. D. — French/Indian from Oregon country
Pearson, William — American from Pennsylvania
Phinney, Samuel — American from Pennsylvania
Phinney, Adeline Craig — Nez Perce/American from Lapwai Valley
Pierce, Elias Davidson — American from Indiana
Qamáya'qin (*Kamiakin*) — Yakama chief
Qualchan — Yakama leader
Quiltaneenock — Rock Island warrior from Columbia River
Raboin, Louis (*The Mosquito*) — former fur trapper, of Illinois French stock
Ravalli, Antony — Catholic missionary from Italy
Red Wolf — Nez Perce from Snake River near Clearwater River
Reuben — Nez Perce leader
Robie, Albert J. — American from Genessee Co., New York
Shaw, Benjamin F. — American from Missouri
Spalding, Eliza — American from Connecticut
Spalding, Henry — Protestant missionary from Prattsburg, New York
Spotted Eagle — Nez Perce from Kamiah on Clearwater River
Steptoe, Edward J. — American from Virginia
Stevens, Isaac I. — American from Massachusetts
Stickus — Cayuse leader from Wallawalla River country
Sublette brothers — Americans from Kentucky
Theentheenmeetsa — Flathead/Cayuse leader
Thibodo, Augustus J. — Canadian
Thompson, Philip — American from Tennessee
Three Feathers — Nez Perce leader from Wallowa country
Thunder's Eye (*Hinmetumsilu*) — Nez Perce leader from Lapwai Valley
Timothy — Nez Perce leader from Alpowa on Snake River
Truax, Sewell — American born in Missisquoi County, Canada
Walker, Elkanah — American from Maine
Walker, Joseph Reddeford — American from Tennessee
Whitebird — Nez Perce from Lamata on Salmon River
Whitman, Marcus — Protestant missionary from Rushville, New York
Whitman, Narcissa — American from Prattsburg, New York
Whitman, Perrin — American from New York
Wislenéqe (*Half Shorn*) — Nez Perce from Téwe on Clearwater River

Wool, John Ellis	(U.S. Army) American born in New York
Wright, George	(U.S. Army) American born in Vermont
Yellow Bird (*Peopeomaqsmaqs*)	Wallawalla chief from Columbia River country
Young Chief (*Tauitau*)	Cayuse chief from Wallawalla River country
Young Joseph (*Hinmahtooyahlatkekht*)	Nez Perce chief of Wallowa Valley

* This list is intended only as a general guide for the reader to help identify the panoply of players; it is not intended for use as a definitive source of each person's origins.

1946 monument by Sons of the American Revolution (photo from the collection of Gloria Manning)

Appendix D

DEATH OF COL. CRAIG

Our friend, Geo. Butler, just down from Lewiston, informs us that Col. William Craig, one of the pioneers in the settlement of the Northwest coast, died at his residence on the Lapwai, a few days since. Colonel Craig was born in Greenbrier county, Virginia, about the year 1810. He went to St. Louis in 1830, and entered the employ of the American Fur Company, and led the wild life of a trapper until 1845, when he came to Lapwai and settled. He was for about two years in the employ of the Mission at that point. During the time of his life as a trapper, he was the comrade of Kit Carson, Sublette, Newell, Meeks, Thompson, Walker, Raboin, and a host of other brave men whose names are indissolubly connected with the early history of this country. He served in the several expeditions of Bonneville, Wythe, and others, and rendered great assistance to General I. I. Stevens in his treaties with the Nez Perces, Cayuse and Blackfoot tribes of Indians in 1855. He was afterwards appointed Indian Agent by Gen. Stevens for the Nez Perces, in which capacity he served until relieved by A. J. Cain in 1859. He also served on Gen. Stevens' staff, holding the rank of Colonel, and stationed at Lapwai. During the last Indian war he rendered the government valuable assistance, using his influence successfully to prevent the Nez Perces and other tribes from open hostilities. The deceased was a man of nerve, heart and generous impulses, and [his passing] will be regretted by all who respect the toil and sufferings endured by the earlier pioneers in opening up the country to settlement.

Walla Walla (WT) Statesman, October 23, 1869, p. 2, col. 3.

Bibliography

Aoki, Haruo. *Nez Perce Dictionary*. Berkeley: University of California Press, 1994.

Bagley, Clarence B., ed. *Early Catholic Missions in Old Oregon*. Seattle, WA: Lowman & Hanford Company, 1932.

Bailey, Robert G. *River of No Return (The Great Salmon River of Idaho): A Century of Central Idaho and Eastern Washington History and Development*. Rev. ed. Lewiston, ID: R. G. Bailey Printing Company, 1947.

Baird, Dennis W., ed. *With Bird and Truax on the Lolo Trail: Building the Virginia City to Lewiston Wagon Road, 1865-1867*. Northwest Historical Manuscript Series. Moscow: University of Idaho Press, 1999.

Baird, Dennis, Diane Mallickan, and W. R. Swagerty, eds. *The Nez Perce Nation Divided: Firsthand Accounts of Events Leading to the 1863 Treaty*. Moscow: University of Idaho Press, 2002.

Beal, Merrill D. *"I Will Fight No More Forever": Chief Joseph and the Nez Perce War*. Seattle: University of Washington Press, 1963. Reprint, New York: Ballantine Books, 1971.

Beal, Merrill D. and Merle W. Wells. *History of Idaho*. Vol 1. New York: Lewis Historical Publishing Co., 1959.

Beall, Thomas J.[B.?] "Pioneer Reminiscences," *Washington Historical Quarterly* 8, no. 2 (April 1917): 83-90.

_____. "Recollections of Wm. Craig." *Lewiston (ID) Morning Tribune*, March 3, 1918.

Brode, H. S., ed. "Diary of Dr. Augustus J. Thibodo." *Pacific Northwest Quarterly* 31, no. 3 (July 1940): 287-347.

Brown, Dee. *Bury My Heart at Wounded Knee*. New York: Holt, Rinehart & Winston, 1970.

Brown, William Compton. *The Indian Side of the Story*. Spokane, WA: C. W. Hill Printing Co., 1961.

Brownstein, Robin. *Scotch-Irish Americans*. The Peoples of North America. New York: Chelsea House Publishers, 1988.

Bunnell, Lafayette. *Discovery of the Yosemite in 1851*. 1888, Reprint, Olympic Valley, CA: Outbooks, 1977.

Burcham, Ralph, ed. "Orofino Gold! E. D. Pierce's Own Story...." *Idaho Yesterdays* 4, no. 3 (Fall 1960): 1-10.

Burns, Robert Ignatius, S.J. *The Jesuits and the Indian Wars of the Northwest*. New Haven, CT: Yale University Press, 1966.

Clark, Robert Carlton. "Military History of Oregon, 1849-59." *Oregon Historical Quarterly*, 36 (1935): 14-59.

Cox, Lloyd M. *In The Days When The Rivers Ran Backwards*. Lewiston, ID: NorBon's Copy Cabin, 2nd ed., 1995. *S*

DeVoto, Bernard. *Across the Wide Missouri*. Boston: Riverside Press, Houghton Mifflin Co., 1947.

Drury, Clifford M. *Chief Lawyer of the Nez Perce Indians 1796-1876*. Glendale, CA: The Arthur H. Clark Co., 1979.

_____. *The Diaries and Letters of Henry H. Spalding and Asa Bowen Smith Relating to the Nez Perce Mission 1838-1842*. Glendale, CA: The Arthur H. Clark Co., 1958.

_____. *Elkanah and Mary Walker: Pioneers Among the Spokanes*. Caldwell, ID: The Caxton Printers, Ltd., 1940.

_____. *Nine Years with the Spokane Indians, The Diary, 1838-1848, of Elkanah Walker*. Glendale, CA: The Arthur H. Clark Co., 1976.

_____, ed. *On to Oregon: The Diaries of Mary Walker and Myra Eells*. 1963. Reprint, Bison Book. Lincoln: University of Nebraska Press, 1998.

Dunbar, Seymour, ed. *The Journals and Letters of Major John Owen Pioneer of the Northwest 1850-1871*. Vol. 1. New York: Edward Eberstadt, 1927.

Elliott, T. C. "Walla Walla and Missoula." *Washington Historical Quarterly* 3, no. 4 (October 1912): 274-76.

Elsensohn, Sister M. Alfreda. *Pioneer Days in Idaho County*. Vol. 2. Caldwell, ID: The Caxton Printers, Ltd., 1951.

Evans, Elwood. *History of the Pacific Northwest: Oregon and Washington*. Vol. 1. Portland, OR: North Pacific History Company, 1889.

Farnham, Thomas J. *An 1839 Wagon Train Journal: Travels in the Great Western Prairies*. 1843. Reprint, Seattle: Pacific Northwest National Parks & Forests Association, 1983.

Ficken, Robert E., Washington Territory. Pullman: Washington State University Press, 2002.

"First Poll Book of Lewiston, Idaho," *Idaho Genealogical Society Quarterly* 3, no. 1 (March 1960): 8-10.

Flanagan, John K. "The Invalidity of the Nez Perce Treaty of 1863 and the Taking of the Wallowa Valley," *American Indian Law Review* 24, no. 1 (1999-2000): 75-98.

Fort Owen State Park. Missoula: Montana Department of Fish, Wildlife and Parks, Montana State Parks, n.d.

Gilbert, Bil. *Westering Man: The Life of Joseph Walker*. New York: Antheneum, 1983.

Goodman, David Michael. *A Western Panorama 1849-1875: The Travels, Writings and Influence of J. Ross Browne on the Pacific Coast, and in Texas, Nevada, Arizona and Baja California*. Western Frontiersmen Series, no. 9. Glendale, CA: The Arthur H. Clark Company, 1966.

Gowans, Fred R. *Tragedy at Pierre's Hole: Revenge vs. Honor or Treachery*. Provo, UT: Mountain Grizzly Publications, 2004.

Hafen, LeRoy R. "Fort Davy Crockett, Its Fur Men and Visitors," *Colorado Magazine* 24, no. 1, (January 1952) 17-22.

_____. "Mountain Men—William Craig," *Colorado Magazine* 11, no. 5 (September 1934): 171-76.

Hafen, Leroy R., and Ann W. Hafen, eds. *To the Rockies and Oregon 1839-1842*. Glendale, CA: The Arthur H. Clark Company, 1955.

Haines, Francis. "Pioneer Portrait: Robert Newell," *Idaho Yesterdays 9, no. 1* (Spring 1965): 1-9.

_____. "Tom Hill: Delaware Scout." *California Historical Society Quarterly* 11 (1946) 139-148.

_____. *The Nez Percés*. Norman: University of Oklahoma Press, 1955.

Hamilton, James McClellan. *From Wilderness to Statehood: A History of Montana 1805-1900*. Portland, OR: Binfords & Mort, 1957.

Harmon, Alexandra. *Indians in the Making: Ethnic Relations and Indian Identities Around Puget Sound*. Berkeley: University of California Press, 1998.

Hartman, Hugh H. *Founding Fathers of Boise 1863-1875*. Boise, ID: the author, 1989.

Holbrook, Robert L., "Col. William Craig, Early Settler of Central Idaho, Paid Homage at Dedication of Memorial Stone." Unpublished. In possession of the author, 1947.

Hoxie, Frederick E., *A Final Promise: The Campaign to Assimilate the Indians, 1880-1920*. Lincoln: University of Nebraska Press, 1984.

Hulbert, Archer Butler and Dorothy Printup Hulbert, eds. *Overland to the Pacific: A Narrative Documentary History of the Great Epochs of the Far West*. Vol. 8. [Colorado Springs]: Stewart Commission of Colorado College; [Denver]: Denver Public Library, 1941.

Hunn, Eugene S., with James Selam and family. *Nch'i-wána, "The Big River": Mid-Columbia Indians and their Land*. Seattle: University of Washington Press, 1990.

Hunt, Aurora. "The Far West Volunteers: The Army of the Pacific and the Unsung Valor of its Men." *Montana the Magazine of Western History* 12, no. 2 (Spring 1962): 49-61.

Huntley, James L. *Ferryboats in Idaho*. Caldwell, ID: The Caxton Printers, Ltd., 1979.

Idaho Territory, 1863-1872. Reference Series no. 682. Boise: Idaho State Historical Society 1982.

Irving, Washington. *The Adventures of Captain Bonneville*. 1895; Klickitat Edition, Portland, OR: Binfords & Mort, Publishers, [1900].

Jackson, John C. *Children of the Fur Trade: Forgotten Métis of the Pacific Northwest*. Missoula, MT: Mountain Press Publishing Company, 1995.

James, Carolyn. *Nez Perce Women in Transition, 1877-1990*. Moscow: University of Idaho Press, 1996.

Johansen, Dorothy O., ed. *Robert Newell's Memoranda: Travles in the Teritory of Missourie; Travle to the Kayuse War; together with A Report on the Indians South of the Columbia River*. Portland, OR: Champoeg Press, 1959.

Josephy, Alvin M., Jr. *The Nez Perce Indians and the Opening of the Northwest*, New Haven, CT: Yale University Press, 1965.

"Journal of E. Willard Smith While With the Fur Traders, Vasquez and Sublette, in the Rocky Mountain Region, 1839-1840." *Quarterly of the Oregon Historical Society* 14 (1913): 250-79.

Kappler, Charles J., ed. *Indian Treaties 1778-1883*. 1904. Reprint, New York: Interland Publishing Inc., 1972.

Karson, Jennifer, ed. *Wiyaxayst/Wiyaakaa'awn = As Days Go By: Our History, Our Land, and Our People—The Cayuse, Umatilla, and Walla Walla*. Pendleton, OR: Tamástslikt Cultural Institute; Portland: Oregon Historical Society Press; Seattle: University of Washington Press, 2006.

Kip, Col. Lawrence. *The Indian Council at Walla Walla*. 1897. Reprint, Seattle: Facsimile Reproduction, 1971.

Kowrach, Edward J., ed. *James Doty, Journals of Operations of Governor Isaac Ingalls Stevens of Washington Territory in 1855*. Fairfield, WA: Ye Galleon Press, 1978.

Lavender, David. *Let Me Be Free: The Nez Perce Tragedy*. Norman: University of Olkahoma Press, 1992.

Limerick, Patricia Nelson. *The Legacy of Conquest*. New York: W.W. Norton & Company, 1987.

Location of Idaho's Territorial Capital, Reference Series no. 344. Boise: Idaho State Historical Society, 1964.

Madsen, Brigham D. "Edward J. Steptoe." In *Utah History Encyclopedia* (Salt Lake City: University of Utah Press, 1994.
http://www.media.utah.edu/UHE/s/STEPTOE,EDWARD.html

Malone, Michael P., and Richard B. Roeder. *Montana: A History of Two Centuries*. Seattle: University of Washington Press, 1976.

Maxwell, Starr J., comp. "Memorial of the Nez Perce Indians Residing in the State of Idaho to the Congress of the United States." Northwest Historical Manuscript Series. Moscow: University of Idaho Library, 2000.

McBeth, Kath. *The Nez Perces Since Lewis and Clark*. New York: Fleming H. Revell Company, 1908. Reprint, Moscow: University of Idaho Press, 1993.

McDonald, Duncan. "Indian Feelings." *The New Northwest (Deer Lodge, MT)*, June 14, 1878.

———. "The Inside Story from Indian Sources." *The New Northwest (Deer Lodge, MT)*, February 7, 1879.

McWhorter, L.V. *Hear Me, My Chiefs!* Caldwell, ID: The Caxton Printers, Ltd., 1952, 1986.

———. *Tragedy of the Wahk-Shum: The Death of Andrew J. Bolon, Indian Agent to the Yakima Nation, in mid-September, 1855*. 1937. Reprint, Fairfield, WA: Ye Galleon Press, 1968.

_____. *Yellow Wolf: His Own Story.* 1948. Reprint, Caldwell, ID: The Caxton Printers, Ltd., 1983.

Meacham, Jon. *American Lion: Andrew Jackson in the White House.* New York: Random House, 2008.

Merk, Frederick A. "William Craig." In *The Mountain Men and the Fur Trade of the Far West.* LeRoy R. Hafen, ed. Volume 2. Glendale, CA: The Arthur H. Clark Company, 1965.

Miles, Jo N. "The Life and Death of A.J. Bolon, 1826-1855." *Pacific Northwest Quarterly* 97, no. 1 (2005-2006): 31-38.

Miller, Henry. "Letters from the Upper Columbia," *Idaho Yesterdays* 4, no. 4 (Winter 1960-61): 14-25.

"News from the Nez Perce Mines," *Idaho Yesterdays* 3, no. 4 (Winter 1959-1960): 18-29.

Nez Perce: St. Joseph's Mission Site at Slickpoo, Idaho. Spalding, ID: Nez Perce National Historical Park, National Park Service, U.S. Department of the Interior, n.d..

Nez Perce Country Official National Park Handbook. Washington, DC: U.S. Department of the Interior, National Park Service, 1983.

Nidever, George. *The Life and Adventures of George Nidever (1802-1883).* William Henry Ellison, ed. Berkeley: University of California Press, 1937.

"Notes and Documents [Letter from Isaac I. Stevens to J.W. Nesmith November 16, 1858]. *Pacific Northwest Quarterly* 31, no. 4 (October 1940): 403-459.

The Official History of the Washington National Guard, Vol. 2, *Washington Territorial Militia in the Indian Wars of 1855-56.* Washington National Guard Pamphlet. Camp Murry, Tacoma, WA: Office of Adjutant General, n.d.

Oliphant, J. Orin, ed. "Journals of the Indian War of 1855-1856." *Washington Historical Quarterly* 15, no. 1 (January 1924): 11-31.

Pambrun, Andrew Dominique. *Sixty Years on the Frontier in the Pacific Northwest.* Fairfield, WA: Ye Galleon Press, 1978.

Partoll, Albert J., ed. and Intro. *The Blackfoot Indian Peace Council (1855).* Sources of Northwest History, No. 3, Missoula: Montana State University, 1937.

Peterson, Helen Phinney. "A Tale Told by Helen Phinney Peterson about William Craig," *Craig Links* 13, no. 3 (July-September 1993): 1122-1124. This newsletter is published by Ann and C.L. Burton, 43779 Valley Road, Decatur, MI.

Powell, Barbara V., abstractor. *Citizens of North Idaho, Newspaper Abstracts 1862-1875.* Vol. 2. Medical Lake, WA: the author, 1986.

Prichard, Robert. "President Ulysses S. Grant's Peace Policy Toward Native Americans and the Ministry of the Episcopal Church." At http://www.vts.edu/resources/classnotes/CH205/Grants Peace.htm

Pringle, Catherine Sager. *Across the Plains in 1844.* http://www.isu.edu/~trinmich/00.ar.sager1.html

Prucha, Francis Paul. *The Great Father: The United States Government and the American Indians.* Lincoln: University of Nebraska Press, 1984.

Quaife, Milo Milton, ed. *Narrative of the Adventures of Zenas Leonard Written by Himself.* The Lakeside Classics. Chicago: The Lakeside Press, R.R. Donnelley & Sons Co., 1934.

Raufer, Sister Maria Ilma. *Black Robes and Indians on the Last Frontier.* Milwaukee: The Bruce Publishing Company, 1966.

Rich, E. E., ed. *The Letters of John McLoughlin from Fort Vancouver to the Governor and Committee [of the Hudson's Bay Company].* 2nd series, 1839-1844. Toronto: Champlain Society, 1943.

Richards, Kent D. *Isaac I. Stevens: Young Man in a Hurry.* Provo, UT: Brigham Young University Press, 1979. Reprint, Pullman: Washington State University Press, 1993.

Roberts, A.B. "Walla Walla Fifty-One Years Ago." *Up-To-The-Times Magazine.* January 1910: 2414-2417.

Robertson, Frank C. *Fort Hall: Gateway to the Oregon Country*. New York: Hastings House, 1963.

Rogers, Cornelius. *The Journey to the Rocky Mountains, the Plains and Rockies*. Boston, 1838.

Ruby, Robert H., and John A. Brown. *The Cayuse Indians: Imperial Tribesman of Old Oregon*. Norman: University of Oklahoma Press, 1972.

St. Joseph's Mission Site at Slickpoo, Idaho. Spalding, ID: U.S. Department of the Interior, National Park Service, Nez Perce National Historical Park, n.d.

Sanford, Gregory R. "The Nez Perce Nation Was Betrayed." *Pacific Northwesterner*, Vol. 6, no. 4 (Fall 1962): 56-63.

Sanger, George P., ed. *Proclamations of the United States of America, from March 1871 to March 1873 and Treaties and Postal Conventions*. Vol. 17. Boston: Little Brown and Co., 1873.

Scott, Darrell, ed. *A True Copy of the Record of the Official Proceedings at the Council in the Walla Walla Valley 1855*. Fairfield, WA: Ye Galleon Press, 1985.

Shannon, Donald H. *The Utter Disaster on the Oregon Trail: The Utter and Van Ornum Massacres of 1860*. Caldwell, ID: Snake Country Publishing, 1993.

Simon-Smolinski, Carol. "River History of Nez Perce County." *Journal of Nez Perce County Historical Society* 1, no. 1 (Spring 1981): 7-17.

Skovlin, Jon M., and Donna McDaniel Skovlin. *Hank Vaughan (1849-1893): A Hell-Raising Horse Trader of the Bunchgrass Territory*. Cove, OR: Reflections Publishing Co., 1996.

Slickpoo, Alan P. *Noon Nee-Me-Poo (We, the Nez Perces): Culture and History of the Nez Perces*. Vol. 1. Lapwai: Nez Perce Tribe of Idaho, 1973.

Splawn, A.J. *Ka-Mi-akin: Last Hero of the Yakimas*. Portland: Binfords & Mort for the Oregon Historical Society, 1944.

Stern, Theodore. *Chiefs and Chief Traders: Indian Relations at Fort Nez Perces, 1818-1855*. Vol. 1. N.p.: the author, 1993.

_____. *Chiefs & Change in the Oregon Country: Indian Relations at Fort Nez Perces 1818-1855*. Vol. 2. Corvallis: Oregon State University Press, 1996.

Stevens, Hazard. *The Life of Isaac Ingalls Stevens*. Vol. 2. Boston: Houghton Mifflin Co., 1901.

Thomas, Edward Harper. *Chinook: A History and Dictionary*. Portland, OR: Binfords & Mort, 1970.

Thompson, Erwin N. *Historic Resource Study, Spalding Area: Nez Perce National Historical Park*. Denver: Denver Service Center: U.S. Department of the Interior, National Park Service, 1972.

Thwaites, Reuben Gold, ed. "Part I of Farnham's Travels in the Great Western Prairies, etc., May 21-October 16, 1839." In *Early Western Travels 1748-1846*. Vol. 28. Cleveland: The Arthur H. Clark Company, 1906.

Tobie, Harvey. *No Man Like Joe*. Portland, OR: Binfords & Mort for the Oregon Historical Society, 1949.

Toland, John. *Adolf Hitler*. Vol. 2. Garden City, New York: Doubleday & Company, 1976.

Trafzer, Clifford E., and Richard D. Scheuerman. *Renegade Tribe: Palouse Indians and the Invasion of the Inland Pacific Northwest*. Pullman: Washington State University Press, 1986.

Victor, Frances Fuller. *The River of the West: The Adventures of Joe Meek*. Vol. 1, *The Mountain Years*. Vol. 2, *The Oregon Years*. 1870. Reprint, Missoula, MT: Mountain Press Publishing Company, 1983.

[Victor, Frances Fuller.] *History of Washington, Idaho, and Montana 1845-1889*. Works of Hubert Howe Bancroft. Vol. 31. San Francisco: The History Company, 1890.

Walker, Ronald W., Richard E. Turley, Jr. and Glen M. Leonard. *Massacre at Mountain Meadows*. New York: Oxford University Press, 2008.

Wallace, Anthony F.C. *The Long, Bitter Trail: Andrew Jackson and the Indians*. New York: Hill and Wang, 1993.

Weibel, George F., S.J. "Rev. Joseph M. Cataldo, S.J.: A Short Sketch of a Wonderful Career." Reprint from *Gonzaga Quarterly*, March 15, 1928.

Weisel, George F., ed. *Men and Trade on the Northwest Frontier as Shown by the Fort Owen Ledger*. Vol. 2. Missoula: Montana State University Press, 1955.

West, Elliott. *The Last Indian War: The Nez Perce Story*. New York: Oxford University Press, 2009.

White, Elijah. *List of Settlers West of Rockies, 1842*.
http://www.orednet.org/~clenzen/1842st.html

White, Richard. *"It's Your Misfortune and None of My Own": A New History of the American West*. Norman: University of Oklahoma Press, 1991.

Wilkinson, Charles. *Blood Struggle: The Rise of Modern Indian Nations*. New York: W.W. Norton & Company, 2005.

Williams, J. Gary, and Ronald W. Stark, eds. *The Pierce Chronicle: Personal Reminiscenses of E.D. Pierce as transcribed by Lou A. Larrick*. Bicentennial edition. Moscow: The Idaho Research Foundation, [1976].

Wood, C. E. S. "Private Journal, 1878," *Oregon Historical Quarterly* 70, no. 1 (March 1969): 5-38.

Young, F.G. "Ewing Young and His Estate," *The Quarterly of the Oregon Historical Society* 21, no. 3 (September 1920): 171-315.

FEDERAL DOCUMENTS

"Indian Appropriation Bill," *Congressional Globe*, 37th Cong., 2nd Sess, May 13, 1862.

Indian Hostilities in Oregon and Washington Territories. 34th Cong., 1st Sess., 1856, Exec. Doc. 118.

Memorial of the Nez Perce Indians Residing in the State of Idaho. 62nd Cong., 1st sess., 1911, S. Doc. 97.

Message of the President of the United States, Report of the Secretary of the Interior, 34th Cong., 3rd sess. 1856, H. Exec. Doc. 1, pt. 1.

Message from the President of the United States, Report of the Secretary of the Interior, 35th Cong., 1st sess. 1857, H. Exec. Doc. 2, vol. 2.

Message from the President of the United States to the Two Houses of Congress at the Commencement of the First Session, 35th Cong., 2nd sess. 1857, H. Exec. Doc. 2.

Message from the President of the United States, Report of the Secretary of War, 35th Cong., 2nd sess. 1857, Exec. Doc. 2, vol. 2.

Message from the President of the United States to the Two Houses of Congress at the Commencement of the Second Session, 35th Cong., 2nd Sess. 1858, H. Exec. Doc. 2.

Message of the President of the United States to the Two Houses of Congress at the Commencement of the Third Session, Report of the Secretary of the Interior, 37th Cong., 3d sess. 1862, H. Exec. Doc. 1 Pt. 2.

Nez Perce 1863 Treaty Council Proceedings. 38th Congress, 1st Sess. 1864, S. Exec. Doc. T.

U.S. Census. 1860 Washington Territory, Walla Walla County.
http://www.rootsweb.com/~cenfiles/wa/wallawalla/1860/pg01.txt

U.S. Census. 1870 Idaho Territory, Nez Perce County.
http://www.rootsweb.com/~cenfiles/id/nezperce/1870/nezper-2.txt

U.S. Census. 1880 Idaho Territory, Nez Perce County.
http://www.familysearch.org/Eng/Search/census/individual_record.asp?INDI_CODE=1880 (National Archives File Number T9-0173)

NEWSPAPERS

East Oregonian (Pendleton).

Eugene (OR) Register Guard.
Lewiston (ID) Morning Tribune.
Idaho Signal (Lewiston, IT).
Idaho Tri-Weekly Statesman (Boise).
*The New Northwest (*Deer Lodge, MT).
The Nez Perce News (Lewiston, IT).
Oregon Statesman (Albany).
Oregon Spectator (Oregon City).
Pioneer and Democrat (Olympia, WT).
Walla Walla (WT) *Statesman.* [Was named *Washington Statesman* in 1861-64.]
The Weekly Message (Port Townsend, WT).
Weekly Oregonian (Portland).

REPOSITORIES VISITED

Catholic Church, Diocese of Boise, Boise, Idaho. [Early Baptismal Records]

Catholic Church, Diocese of Spokane, Spokane, Washington. [Early Baptismal Records]

Clearwater County Historical Museum, Orofino, Idaho. [Early Mining Claims Collection]

Clearwater Memorial Public Library, Orofino, Idaho. [Northwest Collection]

Government Land Office, Bureau of Land Management at www.glorecords.blm.gov/PatentSearch/ [Land Patent Records Collection]

Idaho State Archives [Nez Perce County Records]

Idaho State Historical Society, Boise. [Lapwai Indian Agency Collection]

Lewis Clark State College Library, Lewiston, Idaho. [Newspaper Microfilm Collection]

National Archives, Seattle, Washington. [Record Groups 21, 75]

National Archives, www.nara.gov/cgi/bin/starfinder/15396/standard.txt

Nez Perce County Courthouse, Lewiston, Idaho. [Historical Land Records]

Nez Perce County Historical Museum, Lewiston, Idaho. [Nez Perce County Probate Book]

Nez Perce National Historic Park, Spalding, Idaho. [Archives]

Nez Perce Tribal Headquarters, Lapwai, Idaho. [Tribal Family Records Collection]

Oregon Historical Society, Portland.

Oregon State Archives, Salem.

Penrose Library Archives, Whitman College, Walla Walla, Washington. [Northwest Collection]

Tacoma Public Library, Tacoma, Washington. [Northwest Collection]

University of Idaho Library, Moscow. [Special Collections]

University of Washington Allen Library [Pacific Northwest Collection]

University of Washington Libraries [Digital Collection]

Walla Walla County Courthouse, Walla Walla, Washington. [Land and Marriage Records]

Washington State Archives, Olympia. [Eastern Washington Newspaper Collection and Frontier Justice Collection]

Washington State Library, Olympia.

Washington State University Library, Pullman. [McWhorter Collection]

Western States Historical Marriage Record Index, Brigham Young University- Idaho, Rexburg, ID: ID No. 1692, Ada County, http://abish,byui.edu/specialCollections

Notes

[1] Spelling and usage of the Nez Perce language relies, wherever possible, on Haruo Aoki, *Nez Perce Dictionary* (Berkeley: University of California Press, 1994). (Most symbols used as oral pronunciation aids have been omitted in this written work.) Names of Native American individuals are spelled as they have come down in written (English) records. They have no standardization, were usually spelled as they sounded to the writer, and are prone to great variability.

[2] Helen Phinney Peterson, "A Tale Told by Helen Phinney Peterson about William Craig," *Craig Links* 13, no. 3 (July-September 1993): 1122-23.

[3] See Appendix A, Affidavit for Settlers on Unsurveyed Lands.

[4] Peterson, "About William Craig," 1123. Fashions of Virginia's slave-owning planters at the time emulated those of French royalty.

[5] Clifford Merrill Drury, *The Diaries and Letters of Henry H. Spalding and Asa Bowen Smith Relating to the Nez Perce Mission 1838-1842* (Glendale, CA: The Arthur H. Clark Co., 1958), 308.

[6] Robin Brownstein, *Scotch-Irish Americans* The Peoples of North America (New York: Chelsea House Publishers, 1988), 24, 54-55, 70.

[7] Francis Haines, *The Nez Percés* (Norman: University of Oklahoma Press, 1955), 91.

[8] Peterson, "About William Craig," 1122.

[9] Thomas J. Beall, "Recollections of Wm. Craig," *Lewiston (ID) Morning Tribune*, March 3, 1918, p.8.

[10] *Ibid.*

[11] Peterson, "About William Craig," 1123.

[12] See Appendix A.

[13] Richard White, *"It's Your Misfortune and None of My Own": A New History of the American West* (Norman: University of Oklahoma Press, 1991), 216-17.

[14] Michael P. Malone and Richard B. Roeder, *Montana: A History of Two Centuries* (Seattle: University of Washington Press, 1976), 36.

[15] Dorothy O. Johansen, ed., *Robert Newell's Memoranda: Travles in the Teritory of Missourie; Travle to the Kayuse War; together with A Report on the Indians South of the Columbia River* (Portland, OR: Champoeg Press, 1959), 6.

[16] Beall, "Recollections of Wm. Craig."

[17] Frances Fuller Victor, *The River of the West: The Adventures of Joe Meek*, vol. 1, *The Mountain Years* (1870; repr., Missoula, MT: Mountain Press Publishing Company, 1983), 71-72.

[18] *Ibid.*

[19] Victor, *River of the West*, 1:78-79.

[20] *Ibid.*, 78.

[21] *Newell's Memoranda*, 32.

[22] Both primary and secondary narratives relating to the famed battle of Pierre's Hole are compiled in Fred R. Gowans, *Tragedy at Pierre's Hole: Revenge vs. Honor or Treachery* (Provo, UT: Mountain Grizzly Publications, 2004), 1-79.

[23] *Newell's Memoranda*, 32.

[24] *Ibid.*, 33. Never a doctor, Newell had earned the nickname after some successful field first-aid. See Francis Haines, "Pioneer Portrait: Robert Newell, "*Idaho Yesterdays* 9, no. 1 (Spring 1965): 4.

[25] Bil Gilbert, *Westering Man: The Life of Joseph Walker* (New York: Atheneum, 1983), 306.

[26] *Ibid.*, 128-29. Unless otherwise noted, information regarding the 1833 expedition to California is from this source.

[27] Milo Milton Quaife, ed., *Narrative of the Adventures of Zenas Leonard Written by Himself*, The Lakeside Classics (Chicago: The Lakeside Press, R.R. Donnelley & Sons Co., 1934), 116-17.

[28] George Nidever, *The Life and Adventures of George Nidever (1802-1883)*, ed. William Henry Ellison (Berkeley: University of California Press, 1937), 31.

[29] *Zenas Leonard*, 117. Neither Craig nor Meek spoke publicly of the trouble with the Paiutes on the California expedition; treatment of the Paiutes by the Walker party was not something about which the party boasted.

[30] Beall, "Recollections of Wm. Craig."

[31] Lafayette Bunnell, *Discovery of the Yosemite in 1851* (1888; repr. Olympic Valley, CA: Outbooks, 1977), 10.

[32] *Zenas Leonard*, 128.

[33] Bunnell, *Discovery of the Yosemite,* 10.

[34] *Zenas Leonard*, 136.

[35] A brief background on the Spanish, Mexicans, and Americans in California – and on its Indians – may be found in White, *It's Your Misfortune*, 32-3, 37, 43.

[36] *Narrative of Zenas Leonard*, 146.

[37] White, *"It's Your Misfortune"*, 65.

[38] Washington Irving, *Adventures of Captain Bonneville* (1895: Klickitat Edition, Portland, OR: Binford & Mort, Publishers, [1900]), 285.

[39] Craig, late in his life, recalled stealing "five or six hundred" horses from the "Spaniards" in California and trading most of them to Indian tribes on the way back to the Rockies. Beall, "Recollections of Wm. Craig"; *Zenas Leonard*, 158.

[40] Malone and Roeder, *Montana*, 44.

[41] *Newell's Memoranda*, 33, 43n18.

[42] Alvin M. Josephy, Jr., *The Nez Perce Indians and the Opening of the Northwest* (New Haven, CT: Yale University Press, 1965), 149.

[43] No license has been found permitting Craig to do business as a trader, but one probably existed. Since Colonial times the government had issued licenses for trade with Indians in an attempt to regulate firearms and liquor. See Francis Paul Prucha, *The Great Father: The United States Government and the American Indians* (Lincoln: University of Nebraska Press, 1984), 18-21.

[44] LeRoy R. Hafen, "Fort Davy Crockett, Its Fur Men and Visitors," *Colorado Magazine* 24, no. 1 (January, 1952): 17. Fort Davy Crockett was believed to have been on or near the present border between Utah and Colorado in what is now the Brown's Park Wildlife Refuge, but recent attempts to locate the exact site have been inconclusive. The site may have been nearer the present location of the Lodore School, which fits descriptions of it as being near the mouth of Vermillion Creek.

[45] For an excellent summary of events leading up to the armed conflict between Mexico and the Americans, see Jon Meacham, *American Lion: Andrew Jackson in the White House* (New York: Random House, 2008), 315-16, 324.

[46] Frederick A. Merk, "William Craig," *The Mountain Men and the Fur Trade of the Far West*, vol. 2 (Glendale, CA: The Arthur H. Clark Company, 1965), 108n6.

[47] Bernard DeVoto, *Across the Wide Missouri* (Boston: Houghton Mifflin Co., 1947), 353.

[48] Cornelius Rogers, *The Journey to the Rocky Mountains, The Plains and Rockies* (Boston, 1838), 75-78.

[49] A synthesis of the relationship between mountain men and Indian women during this period can be found in White, *"It's Your Misfortune"*, 46-47.

[50] For a description of traditional Nez Perce "wedding trades," see Carolyn James, *Nez Perce Women in Transition, 1877-1990* (Moscow: University of Idaho Press, 1996), 86-89.

[51] A study of the blending of Indian and European cultures in the Pacific Northwest is in Alexandra Harmon, *Indians in the Making: Ethnic Relations and Indian Identities around Puget Sound* (Berkeley: University of California Press, 1998), 14, 17, 30-31, 41.

[52] See Appendix A. See also "Affidavit of Witness for a Settler Claiming Unsurveyed Lands as Married Man," signed by Louis Raboin June 4, 1855, exhibit in *Maria Caldwell v. Martha Robie Vaughn, et al.*, Nez Perce County Records, AR 216, Lewiston, Idaho (hereafter *Caldwell v. Vaughn*).

[53] Clifford M. Drury, ed., *On to Oregon: The Diaries of Mary Walker and Myra Eells* (1963; repr., Bison Book, Lincoln: University of Nebraska Press, 1998), 98.

[54] The Certificate of Death of Mary J. Holt lists her mother as Louise Craig and her father as Charles Adams. Date of death: 2 December 1932. State of Idaho, County of Nez Perce, City of Lewiston, State File No. 82286. Copy in Clearwater County Museum, Orofino, Idaho

[55] Although the spelling in Aoki, *Nez Perce Dictionary* is "Lepwey," in the interest of clarity the current common spelling of "Lapwai" will be used.

[56] Pedigree Chart of Fermore Craig of Oregon, provided to the author in July 1997. Used with Craig's permission. Thunder's Eye was an influential man, obligated to feed many people and likely had more than one wife.

[57] *Ibid.* Kitty, wife of Robert Newell, is believed by some historians to also be a sister of Isabel (Pahtissah) Craig. See n91, following.

[58] Alan P. Slickpoo, *Noon Nee-Me-Poo (We, the Nez Perces): Culture and History of the Nez Perces,* vol. 1 (Lapwai: Nez Perce Tribe of Idaho, 1973), 58.

[59] Theodore Stern, *Chiefs and Chief Traders: Indian Relations at Fort Nez Perces, 1818-1855,* vol. 1 (N.p.: the author, 1993), 181.

[60] Victor, *River of the West*, 1:241-42.

[61] Thomas J. Farnham, *An 1839 Wagon Train Journal: Travels in the Great Western Prairies* (1843; repr.,Seattle: Pacific Northwest National Parks & Forests Association, 1983), 64.

[62] For thought-provoking discourse of the North American buffalo's place in the lives of Indians, Mountain Men and settler entrepreneurs, see Elliott West, *The Last Indian War: The Nez Perce Story* (New York: Oxford University Press, 2009), 258-63.

[63] LeRoy R. Hafen, "Mountain Men—William Craig," *Colorado Magazine* 11, no. 5 (September 1934): 174.

[64] Reuben Gold Thwaites, ed., "Part I of Farnham's Travels in the Great Western Prairies, etc., May 21-October 16, 1839," in *Early Western Travels 1748-1846*, vol. 28 (Cleveland: The Arthur H. Clark Company, 1906), 228-29.

[65] *Ibid.*, 229.

[66] See "Journal of E. Willard Smith While With the Fur Traders, Vasquez and Sublette, in the Rocky Mountain Region, 1839-1840," *Quarterly of the Oregon Historical Society* 14 (1913): 250. There were also two "half-breed" hunters, one of whom was Baptiste Charbonneau, the son of Sacajawea, who had been educated in St. Louis and then spent several years in Europe, returning in 1829 to become a well-known guide and hunter west of the Missouri. Leroy R. Hafen and Ann W. Hafen, eds., *To the Rockies and Oregon 1839-1842* (Glendale, CA: The Arthur H. Clark Company, 1955), 156.

[67] "Journal of E. Willard Smith," 261. The narration of the Craig's' trip from Fort Vasquez to Fort Davy Crockett relies on E. Willard Smith's journal unless otherwise noted.

[68] "Elijah White, Indian Agent, List of Settlers West of Rockies, 1842" http://www.oregonvos.net/~clenzen/18421st.html (5/21/2001). William Craig was listed with four children and ten horses.

[69] "Journal of E. Willard Smith," 264.

[70] *Farnham's Travels*, 250.

[71] Frank C. Robertson, *Fort Hall: Gateway to the Oregon Country* (New York: Hastings House, 1963), 216.

[72] Harvey Tobie, *No Man Like Joe* (Portland, OR; Binfords & Mort for the Oregon Historical Society, 1949), 76. Tobie believed that three daughters of Nez Perce headman Kowesote, renamed Virginia, Kitty, and Fanny, had married Meek, Newell, and Caleb Wilkins. Francis Haines maintains that Robert Newell's wife, Kitty, was the daughter of Thunder's Eye of the Lapwai Valley; Theodore Stern follows that lead. That Kitty was from the Lapwai Valley area

seems logical given the tribe's 1861 gift to Newell of land at Lewiston and the subsequent residence in Lapwai Valley of sons Frank and Thomas Newell.

[73] Victor, *The River of the West: The Adventures of Joe Meek*, vol. 2, *The Oregon Years* (1870; repr., Missoula, MT: Mountain Press Publishing Co., 1983), 258, 260.

[74] Hafen, "Fort Davy Crockett," 31.

[75] Tobie, *No Man Like Joe*, 84, 95.

[76] Drury, *Diaries and Letters*, 307.

[77] Johansen, *Newell's Memoranda*, 39.

[78] Elwood Evans, *History of the Pacific Northwest: Oregon and Washington*, vol. 1, (Portland, OR: North Pacific History Company, 1889), 219-20.

[79] *Ibid.*

[80] Victor, *River of the West*, 2:42.

[81] Robert Newell to Elwood Evans, in *Pacific Northwest*, 1:220.

[82] Victor, *River of the West*, 2:42.

[83] Robert Newell to Elwood Evans.

[84] Other than three-year-old Helen Mar, Meek's daughter by his first wife (who left him).

[85] Evans, *Pacific Northwest*, 220.

[86] See Lloyd M. Cox, *In the Days When the Rivers Ran Backwards* (Lewiston, ID: NorBon's Copy Cabin, 1995), 1-26.

[87] See Appendix A. See also U.S. Census, 1860, Washington Territory, Walla Walla Precinct. http://www.digitalarchives.wa.gov
For a discussion of early Nez Perce birthing practices, see James, *Nez Perce Women*, 19, 36.

[88] Drury, *Diaries and Letters*, 303.

[89] Kate C. McBeth, *The Nez Perces since Lewis and Clark* (1908; repr.,Moscow: University of Idaho Press, 1993), 149-51.

[90] White, *"It's Your Misfortune"*, 72.

[91] See Prucha, *Great Father*, 33, 145.

[92] Secretary of the Interior, *Report*, 1857-58, 35th Cong., 1st sess., 1858, S. Exec. Doc., vol. 12, p. 21. See also Theodore Stern, *Chiefs & Change in the Oregon Country: Indian Relations at Fort Nez Perces 1818-1855*, vol. 2 (Corvallis; Oregon State University Press, 1996), 55.

[93] Prucha, *Great Father*, 394-95.

[94] *Ibid.*, and see Josephy, *Nez Perce Indians*, 183-85.

[95] Jennifer Karson, ed., *Wiyaxayst/Wiyaakaa'awn = As Days Go By: Our History, Our Land, and Our People—The Cayuse, Umatilla, and Walla Walla* (Pendleton, OR: Tamástslikt Cultural Institute, Portland: Oregon Historical Society Press, in association with Seattle: University of Washington Press, 2006), 23.

[96] Slickpoo, *Noon Nee-Me-Poo*, 57-58. For a general understanding of religion's perceived role in wealth, see Harmon, *Indians in the Making*, 33-35.

[97] For a description of the Lapwai mission station, see Erwin N. Thompson, *Historic Resource Study, Spalding Area: Nez Perce National Historical Park* (Denver, CO: Denver Service Center, U. S. Department of the Interior, National Park Service, 1972), 13-25.

[98] *Nez Perce Country Official National Park Handbook* (Washington, D.C.: U.S. Department of the Interior, National Park Service, 1983), 67.

[99] Thompson, *Spalding Area*, Map No. 1, Historic Base Map.

[100] *Ibid.* See also Drury, *Diaries and Letters*, 249.

[101] *Spalding Area*, 25.

[102] *Ibid.*

[103] Another example of this anomaly, in this case among Puget Sound Indians, may be found in Harmon, *Indians in the Making*, 101-2. Usually Americans hoped for chiefs who were both respected by their people and able to communicate with white people.

[104] Drury, *Diaries and Letters*, 248n17, 280.

[105] Aoki, *Nez Perce Dictionary*, 91.

[106] Stern, *Chiefs & Change*, 58, quoting Clifford M. Drury, *Marcus and Narcissa Whitman and the Opening of Old Oregon* (Glendale, CA: The Arthur H. Clark Co., 1973), 395f.

[107] Fermore Craig, interview with the author, Joseph, Oregon, July 27, 1997.

[108] What motivated people to seek medical help from outsiders is explained well in Harmon, *Indians in the Making*, 39.

[109] Drury, *Diaries & Letters*, 300.

[110] *Ibid.*

[111] White, *"It's Your Misfortune,"* 72.

[112] See also Harmon, *Indians in the Making*, 47.

[113] Robert Ignatius Burns, S.J., *The Jesuits and the Indian Wars of the Northwest* (New Haven: Yale University Press, 1966), 176.

[114] *Wiyaxayst/Wiyaakaa'awn = As Days Go By*, 50-51, 64.

[115] Drury, *Diaries and Letters*, 307-09. Unless otherwise noted, the events in and around the Spalding mission are from Drury, *Diaries and Letters*.

[116] *"So·yá·po·"* is the *ni·mi·pu·tímt* term applied particularly to white Americans. The term may come from Chinook Jargon, means "crowned ones," referring to their hats, and could derive from the French word for hat, *"chapeau."* See Akoi, *Nez Perce Dictionary*, 658.

[117] Drury, *Diaries and Letters*, 304.

[118] *Ibid.*

[119] *Ibid.*, 307

[120] *Ibid.*, 307-08.

[121] *Ibid.*, 308.

[122] Francis Haines, "Tom Hill: Delaware Scout," *California Historical Society Quarterly* 11 (1946):141-44.

[123] Drury, *Diaries and Letters*, 308.

[124] *Ibid*, 309.

[125] David Lavender, *Let Me Be Free: The Nez Perce Tragedy* (Norman: University of Oklahoma Press, 1992), 110-11.

[126] *Ibid.*, 111

[127] Tobie, *No Man Like Joe*, 96.

[128] Drury, *Diaries and Letters*, 309.

[129] They were paid on May 27, 1841. See F. G. Young, "Ewing Young and His Estate,*"* *The Quarterly of the Oregon Historical Society* 21, no. 3 (September 1920) 282, 301; Ewing Young had died a wealthy man: it was to handle his possessions that a rudimentary government was set up which became the nucleus of the future government of Oregon Territory. See Tobie, *No Man Like Joe*, 96.

[130] Drury, *Diaries and Letters*, 323.

[131] *Wiyaxayst/Wiyaakaa'awn = As Days Go By*, 51, 63-64, 84.

[132] Prucha, *Great Father*, 395.

[133] *Ibid.* See also *Wiyaxayst/Wiyaakaa'awn = As Days Go By*, 51, 63-64.

[134] *Nez Perce Country*, 73.

[135] Josephy, *Nez Perce Indians*, 220-30.

[136] *Ibid.*, 221; *Wiyaxayst/Wiyaakaa'awn = As Days Go By*, 52.

[137] Harmon, *Indians in the Making*, 31.

[138] *Ibid.*, 56-57. In her study of Puget Sound Indian cultures as impacted by Hudson's Bay Company traders, Harmon concluded that Europeans applying their laws to natives often didn't send the intended message because, among indigenous people, crimes were personal problems to be worked out by individuals or families. And when immigrant settlers held rituals like trials or hangings, thinking they would impress indigenous peoples with the power of their government, the rituals were instead understood to be what they had always known--retribution for harm done.

[139] Josephy, *Nez Perce Indians*, 230-31.

[140] Drury, *Diaries and Letters*, 327-28.

[141] *Ibid.* 327, 330-31; Thompson, *Spalding Area*, 61, and see Addendum Map No. 1.

[142] See Appendix A.

[143] Drury, *Diaries and Letters*, 329.

[144] Eliza Hart Spalding to Mrs. Smith, Tualitin Plains, from Clearwater, February 14, 1842, Northwest Collection, #S-202A 5, Northwest Archives: Penrose Library, Whitman College, Walla Walla, Washington.

[145] White, *"It's Your Misfortune"*, 122.

[146] Drury, *Diaries and Letters*, 315n116, 331. Spalding noted in his diary, "... get sinnews for Craig to make mocacins for Lt. Johnson."

[147] Diary of Mrs. William Henry Gray, May 10, 1840, to September 21, 1842, William H. and Mary A. Gray Papers, MSS 1202, Oregon Historical Society, Portland (hereafter OHS), folder 11.

[148] *Ibid.*

[149] Robert H. Ruby and John A. Brown, *The Cayuse Indians: Imperial Tribesmen of Old Oregon* (Norman: University of Oklahoma Press, 1972), 185.

[150] Victor, *River of the West* 2:42.

[151] Spalding to Mr. Geiger, May 10, 1843, Henry H. Spalding Papers, MSS 1201, OHS, Folder 5.

[152] Thompson, *Spalding Area*, 75.

[153] Spalding to Ladies of the Presbyterian Church in Kinsman, Ohio, September 15, 1845, Spalding Papers, OHS, Folder 1.

[154] Thompson, *Spalding Area*, 223.

[155] Spalding to Rev. David Greene, February 12, 1846, Letters to ABCFM 1843-1848, Spalding Papers, Folder 7, OHS, vol. 248, Letter 132, 204.

[156] Archer Butler Hulbert and Dorothy Printup Hulbert, eds., "Marcus Whitman, Crusader Part Three, 1843 to 1847," *Overland to the Pacific*, vol. 8 (Colorado Springs: Stewart Commission of Colorado College; Denver: Denver Public Library, 1938), 88.

[157] *Ibid.*

[158] McBeth, *Nez Perces Since Lewis and Clark*, 156.

[159] John B. Monteith, Lapwai Agency, to E. C. Kimble, December 5, 1873, J. B. Monteith Papers, 1873-1874, MS 19, Idaho State Historical Society (hereafter ISHS), vol. 2.

[160] Many years after her death, a court found that Isabel Craig was a member and "had been substantially all of her life of the Catholic Church . . . ": "Final Decision Including Findings of Fact and Conclusion of Law, February 4, 1916," *Caldwell v. Vaughn*, 12.

[161] See Appendix A.

[162] Archie Phinney, son of Fitzhugh Phinney and Wayilatpu (Mary Lilly), grandson of Adeline Craig and Samuel Phinney. Archie Phinney, an anthropologist, worked in New York City, Phoenix, and Minneapolis and spent five years in Leningrad before returning to his people in the Lapwai Valley. He died of bleeding ulcers in 1949 at the age of 45.

[163] Hulbert and Hulbert, eds., "Marcus Whitman, Crusader," 195.

[164] 1913 Appeal of Survey, General Land Entry Files for CRAIG, William and Isabel, Donation Certificate No. 03092, Notification No. 1271, Approximate date of Entry: 9/17/1913, Serial Patent Number: 356234, *Caldwell v. Vaughn.*

[165] See Appendix A. A certified copy of the patent was obtained from the Bureau of Land Management, Eastern States, Springfield, Virginia, by descendant Gloria Manning. It would be many years before the land was officially surveyed; when that occurred the Craig claim amounted to more than 630 acres.

[166] Spalding to Rev. David Greene, August 3, 1847, Letters to ABCFM 1843-1848, Spalding Papers, OHS, vol. 248, letter 137, 240-41.

[167] Haines, "Tom Hill: Delaware Scout," 142; and see Prucha, *Great Father*, 146-48.

[168] See Appendix B for William Craig's testimony of events prior to the attack at the Whitman mission. Both "Jimmie Slickpoo's mother-in-law and Isaac Wap-tas-kune," when telling many years later about the murders at the Whitman mission, spoke of Joe Lewis as a Mormon. McBeth, *Nez Perces since Lewis and Clark*, 159.

[169] An excellent overview of the part diseases have played in the rise and fall of the world's civilizations may be found in West, *Last Indian War*, 52-58.

[170] *Wiyaxayst/Wiyaakaa'awn = As Days Go By*, 172.

[171] The account of the attack on the Whitman mission is based on Josephy, *Nez Perce Indians*, unless otherwise noted.

[172] *Nez Perce Country*, 75.

[173] The account of events after the Whitman mission attack are based on Robert Newell's *Memoranda* and companion documents unless otherwise noted.

For perspective on the economic benefits possible for settlers involved in Indian campaigns, see Patricia Nelson Limerick, *The Legacy of Conquest* (New York: W.W. Norton & Company, 1987), 82.

[174] *Oregon Spectator* (Oregon City), January 20, 1848, 1, cited in Stern, *Chiefs & Change*, 192n3.

[175] *Newell's Memoranda*, Appendix B, "Governor George Abernethy's Instructions to the Peace Commissioners," 127. This document is dated February 3, 1848, at Oregon City, citing *Oregon Spectator*, April 6, 1848.

[176] *Newell's Memoranda*, 88.

[177] Descriptions of events and the perspectives of some captors and captives following the Whitman mission attack are found in Theodore Stern, *Chiefs & Change*, 176-182.

[178] Stern, *Chiefs & Change*, 176.

[179] Catherine, Elizabeth, and Matilda Sager, *The Whitman Massacre of 1847* (Fairfield, WA; Ye Galleon Press [1981]), 80, cited in Stern, *Chiefs & Change*, 180.

[180] Stern, *Chiefs & Change*, 181.

[181] *Ibid.*, 183.

[182] J.B.A. Brouillet, "Account of the Murder of Dr. Whitman," *Indian War in Oregon and Washington Territories*, 35th Cong., 1st sess., 1858, H. Ex. Doc. 38, vol. 9, cited in Stern, *Chiefs & Change*, 185.

[183] Josephy, *Nez Perce Indians*, 263.

[184] John Baptist Gervais had been living with the Nez Perces since October 1847. Secretary of the Interior, *Report*, 1857-58, 35th Cong., 1st sess., 1858, Senate Exec. Doc. Vol. 12, p. 21.

[185] *Newell's Memoranda*, 106n8, 117.

[186] Lee to Abernethy, February 8, 1848, George Abernethy Collection, MSS 929, OHS, Folder 8.

[187] *Ibid.*

[188] *Newell's Memoranda*, 106, 117.

[189] Lee to Abernethy, February 8, 1848, OHS.

[190] "Laws of a General and Local Nature passed by the Legislative Committee and Legislative Assembly, 1843-1849 (1853)," 48, Oregon State Archives, Salem (hereafter OSA) (as quoted in Stern, *Chiefs & Change*, 186n6, and Ruby and Brown, *Cayuse Indians*, 142n40).

[191] Stern, *Chiefs & Change*, 197-99; *Newell's Memoranda*, 109; *Wiyaxayst/Wiyaakaa'awn = As Days Go By*, 82.

[192] *Newell's Memoranda*, 111.

[193] *Ibid.*.

[194] *Ibid.* See also Tobie, *No Man Like Joe*, 155-57.

[195] *Newell's Memoranda*, 112. The description of the council that follows is from Newell's Memoranda 134-39.

[196] *Ibid.*, *Newell's Memoranda*, Appendix C, Governor George Abernethy's Letter to the Great Chiefs of the Nez Perces, and Other Tribes, 128-31.

[197] *Ibid.* and n51 citing *Oregon Spectator*, April 20, 1848, for contents of Abernethy's letter.

[198] *Newell's Memoranda* 135-36.

[199] West, *Last Indian War*, 20-23.

[200] White, *"It's Your Misfortune"*, 100-101.

[201] *Newell's Memoranda*, Appendix E, Mr. Newell's Speech to the Nez Perces in Council at Waiilatpu, on the 7th of March, 1848, 137.

[202] *Ibid.,* 134.

[203] *Newell's Memoranda,* Appendix D, Report of the Peace Commissioners, 134-35.

[204] Palmer to Craig, March 10, 1848, Adjutant General's Correspondence, Oregon Military Department, OSA (hereafter AGC).

[205] *Newell's Memoranda*, Appendix D, Report of the Peace Commissioners, 134.

[206] *Newell's Memoranda*, 112.

[207] *Ibid.* 113.

[208] *Newell's Memoranda*, Report of the Peace Commissioners, 136-37.

[209] *Wiyaxayst/Wiyaakaa'awn = As Days Go By*, 81.

[210] *Newell's Memoranda,* Report of the Peace Commissioners, 137.

[211] Lee to Abernethy, February 1848, AGC, OSA.

[212] See Josephy, *Nez Perce Indians*, 276.

[213] *Ibid.*, 277. Little Chief and Frank Escaloom, who were with the Cayuse band, were said to be Nez Perce brothers related to Looking Glass. See Stern, *Chiefs & Change*, 223.

[214] The mission site was destined to become the focus of a 49-year-long bitter legal dispute known as the "Langford claim." Thompson, *Spalding Area*, 67-68, citing Craig to Spalding, May 2, 1848, *Oregon American and Evangelical Unionist* (Tualatin Plains, Oregon Territory), June 21 1848, in Elwood Evans Scrapbook, Western Americana Collection, Beinecke Library, Yale University, New Haven, CT.

The ABCFM claimed it had a legal right to the land on which the mission stood (in fact, to 640 acres). A dispute over the "Langford claim," as it became known, lasted until 1893, when federal policy mandated that the Nez Perce cede their unallotted land, which included all but two small parcels of the Langford claim, to the government. Langford was awarded $20,000 for release of his claim. But the government took the $20,000 from the monies appropriated to pay the Nez Perce tribe for their ceded land, an act that embittered many Nez Perces. See Thompson, *Spalding Area*, 120-22, 153-56.

[215] Craig to Lee on the road, May 5, 1848, AGC.

[216] Craig at Fort Walla Walla to Palmer, May 16, 1848, AGC.

[217] Craig to Col. J.W. Nesmith, May 20, 1858, Letters from Employees Assigned to the Nez Perce and Umatilla Agencies (hereafter NPUA), Washington Superintendency of Indian Affairs (hereafter WSIA), Microfilm 111, Roll 21, RG 75, National Archives and Records Administration (hereafter NARA).

[218] Clifford M. Drury, *Nine Years with the Spokane Indians, The Diary, 1838-1848, of Elkanah Walker*, (Glendale, CA: The Arthur H. Clark Co., 1976), 481.

[219] Stern, *Chiefs and Change*, 213 and citing the *Oregon Spectator*, July 13, 1848, 1-2.

[220] Josephy, *Nez Perce Indians*, 281.

[221] See William Craig Land Claim, June 19, 1848, Clackamas County, Genealogical, OSA.

[222] Ruby and Brown, *Cayuse Indians*, 71.

[223] Drury, *Nine Years*, 475n66; 481n72.

[224] Prucha, *Great Father*, 339.

[225] When gold was discovered at John Sutter's mill in Northern California, the news practically emptied the Willamette Valley of white men as they rushed south to get rich. Robert Newell was one of the gold seekers, and in 1850 he returned to the Willamette Valley with enough profit to open a general store in Champoeg. *Newell's Memoranda*, 90.

[226] For a succinct summary of Joseph Lane's Oregon Territory politics, see Robert E. Ficken, *Washington Territory*, (Pullman: Washington State University Press, 2002), 18. See also Prucha, *Great Father*, 396-97.

[227] Stern, *Chiefs & Change*, 216-17.

[228] *Ibid.*, n12.

229 *Ibid.*, 218-19, n11.

230 *Ibid.*, 220-21 and n14 ("Fifteen Cheaves Nez Perces to His Excelency, January 5, 1850").

231 *Wiyaxayst/Wiyaakaa'awn = As Days Go By*, 64, 172; Stern, *Chiefs & Change, 223*.

232 See Tobie, *No Man Like Joe*, 198-201 and nn31-38 for references to printed resources on the trial of the five Cayuse men. See also *Wiyaxayst/Wiyaakaa'awn = As Days Go By*, 172.

233 "The Whitman Massacre Trial: An Indictment is Issued," 50th Anniversary Exhibit 1-5, OSA, http://arcweb.sos.state.or.us/50th/whitman/whitmanindictment.html [4/21/2009][used with permission.]; cf. Harmon, *Indians in the Making*, 77.

234 Clackamas County U.S. District Court Case Files, *The Whitman Massacre Trial*, 50th Anniversary Exhibit, OSA, at http://arcweb.sos.state.or.us/50th/whitman/whitmantrial.html [4/21/2009][used with permission.] John McLoughlin came to the Pacific Northwest in 1824 as a representative of the Hudson's Bay Company and served from 1825 to 1846 as its chief factor at Fort Vancouver.

235 See Appendix B.

236 "More about the Cayuses," *Oregon Spectator*, June 13, 1850, 2.

237 *Wiyaxayst/Wiyaakaa'awn = As Days Go By*, 172-74.

238 Limerick, *Legacy of Conquest*, 36.

239 While the year the stone fence was first erected is unknown, building rock fences was often a stop-gap way to enclose gardens on farms in rocky terrain prior to building fences of wood. A stone fence existed on the property in 1870. See Book 13, Lessee, Samuel Phinney and M. H. Rice to J. K. Vincent, Nez Perce County, 11.

When Abel Tinkham visited Craig in 1854, there was about eight acres under tillage. See Thompson, *Spalding Area*, 76, citing Report of Lt. R. Macfeely, Jan. 20, 1854, 33d Cong., 2d sess., 1854, H. Ex. Doc. 91, 1854-5, vol. 1, 287-90. Animals and produce raised on the Craig farm in the 1850s are found in Seymour Dunbar, ed., *The Journals and Letters of Major John Owen Pioneer of the Northwest 1850-1871*, vol. 1 (New York: Edward Eberstadt, 1927), 78; James McClellan Hamilton, *From Wilderness to Statehood: A History of Montana 1805-1900* (Portland, OR: Binfords & Mort, 1957), 127-28.

240 Craig descendant Calvin Shillal described the four-petaled yellow flower design; interview with the author, April 16, 2003. A year later, Shillal drew and painted the design, using photographs of clothing worn by Craig family members as his guide, and authorized its reproduction in this work. He died in 2005 on his 49th birthday.

241 Final Decision Including Findings of Fact and Conclusion of Law, February 4, 1916, *Caldwell v. Vaughn*, 12, ISA.

242 *Ibid.*, 9, 12.

243 Craig was remembered as "... kind hearted and [with] generous impulses ...." *Idaho Tri-Weekly Statesman* (Boise), November 4, 1869, p. 2, col. 3.

244 See Appendix A. Mary Craig disappears from census records after the 1860 Walla Walla census, when she is enumerated as being fourteen years old.

245 Register of Traders' Licenses Volume 1847-1873, WSIA, microfilm, M1049, Roll 8, Target 33, Seattle Branch, NARA.

246 E. E. Rich, ed., *The Letters of John McLoughlin from Fort Vancouver to the Governor and Committee [of the Hudson's Bay Company]*, Second Series, 1839-1844 (Toronto: Champlain Society, 1943), 383-84. A bond in the amount of $2,000 was posted.

247 Stern, *Chiefs & Change*, 251.

248 Josephy, *Nez Perce Indians*, 290.

249 Clifford Merrill Drury, *Elkanah and Mary Walker: Pioneers Among the Spokanes* (Caldwell, ID: The Caxton Printers, Ltd., 1940), 231-32.

250 *Ibid.*

251 *Ibid.* See also White, *"It's Your Misfortune"*, 93, regarding treaties Anson Dart made with the Indians of western Oregon. In the early 1850s these people had agreed to give up their lands to the United States in return for reservations, only to have the treaties defeated in the U.S. Senate because Oregonians thought the reservations too close to white communities.

[252] Robert Newell, Oregon City, to Norris, October 15, 1851, Manuscript Collection, MSS 1197, OHS.

[253] Kent D. Richards, *Isaac I. Stevens: Young Man in a Hurry* (Provo, UT: Brigham Young University Press, 1979; repr., Pullman: Washington State University Press, 1993), 97, 99. Unless otherwise noted, information regarding Isaac Stevens is from this source.

[254] See Ficken, *Washington Territory*, 23n2.

[255] See Appendix A. Annie was the last child born to Isabel and William, according to the Affidavit, but there is evidence that William Craig may have fathered another son, perhaps after the 1855 Affidavit was prepared. The author was unable to find proof. However, there is a Craig connection to a young scout in "Joseph's War" of 1877, Seeyakoonilpilp (Red Spy, Red Scout).

[256] Craig to Stevens, Received March 15, 1854, Letters Received (Nez Perce), WSIA.

[257] *Ibid.*

[258] Stevens to Commissioner of Land Office, Olympia, December 28, 1853, Washington Territory Papers, #4284, Special Collections, University of Washington Library, Box 4, Folder 2.

[259] Craig to Stevens, Received March 15, 1854.

[260] See White, *"It's Your Misfortune"*, 91. Also see Prucha, *Great Father*, 400.

[261] Ficken, *Washington Territory*, 45. See also, Richards, *Young Man in a Hurry*, 190.

[262] The evolution of the reservation system is discussed in White, *"It's Your Misfortune"*, 91-92; see Prucha, *Great Father*, 392-402, for Oregon's governmental underpinnings that preceded creation of Washington Territory.

[263] George F. Weisel, ed., *Men and Trade on the Northwest Frontier as Shown by the Fort Owen Ledger*, vol. 2 (Missoula: Montana State University Press, 1955), 11-12.

[264] Thompson, *Spalding Area*, 76, citing Report of Lt. R. Macfeely, Jan. 20, 1854, House Ex. Doc. 91, 33d Cong., 2d sess., 1854, vol. 1, 287-90.

[265] Seymour Dunbar, ed., *The Journals and Letters of Major John Owen Pioneer of the Northwest 1850-1871*, vol. 1 (New York: Edward Eberstadt, 1927), 78; Craig to Stevens, Received March 15, 1854.

[266] James McClellan Hamilton, *From Wilderness to Statehood: A History of Montana 1805-1900* (Portland, OR: Binfords & Mort, 1957), 127-28.

[267] Harmon, *Indians in the Making*, 78.

[268] See Article 10 of Treaty with the Nez Perces, 1855, in Charles D. Kappler, ed., *Indian Treaties 1778-1883*, (1904; repr., New York: Interland Publishing Inc., 1972), 705. See also Deed from Wm. Craig and Wife to Samuel Phinney & Moses H. Rice, April 17, 1869, Book B (also referred to as Day Book), Nez Perce County, Courthouse, Lewiston, Idaho.

[269] *Pioneer and Democrat* (Olympia, WA), February 3, 17, 1855, cited in Richards, *Young Man in a Hurry*, 207.

[270] See John Toland, *Adolf Hitler*, vol. 2 (Garden City, NY: Doubleday & Company, 1976), 802.

[271] Justice John Marshall's decision in *Cherokee Nation v. Georgia* (March 18, 1831) as found in Prucha, *Great Father*, 208-13. See also White, *"It's Your Misfortune"*, 85-94. See also Meacham, *American Lion*, 152-53.

[272] The accepted spelling is now "Colville."

[273] A. D. Pambrun to Stevens, W.T. January 30, 1855, Miscellaneous Letters, WSIA, Microfilm 5, Roll 23.

[274] Doty to Stevens, W.T., March 4, 1855, *ibid.*

[275] William Compton Brown, *The Indian Side of the Story* (Spokane, WA; C. W. Hill Printing Co., 1961), 68-74.

[276] Letter from the Secretary of the Interior transmitting *Report of J. Ross Browne, on the Subject of the Indian War in Oregon and Washington Territories*, 35th Cong., 1st sess., 1858, H. Ex. Doc. 38, 10.

[277] Josephy, *Nez Perce Indians*, 312n24, citing Splawn, *Ka-mi-akin*, 24-26.

[278] Doty to Gov. Stevens, March 26, 1855, Miscellaneous Letters, WSIA. See also Washington State Office of the Adjutant General, *The Official History of the Washington National Guard*, vol. 2, *Washington Territorial Militia in the Indian Wars of 1855-56*, Washington National Guard Pamphlet (Camp Murry, Tacoma, WA: Office of the Adjutant General, n.d.), 206.

[279] Edward J. Kowrach, ed., *James Doty, Journals of Operations of Governor Isaac Ingalls Stevens of Washington Territory in 1855* (Fairfield, WA: Ye Galleon Press, 1978), 22.

[280] Doty to Gov. Stevens, March 26, 1855, Miscellaneous Letters, WSIA.

[281] *Ibid.* Doty noted that six days from Vancouver to Craigs' place was "very quick time."

[282] Doty to Stevens, April 21, 1855, Miscellaneous Letters, WSIA.

[283] *Doty Journal*, 22.

[284] *Ibid.*, 18.

[285] *Ibid.*, 19. See also Doty to Stevens, April 21, 1855.

[286] Doty to Stevens, April 21, 1855.

[287] *Doty Journal*, 22.

[288] *Ibid.*, 23.

[289] Stevens and Palmer to Hon. Geo. Manypenny, Commissioner of Indian Affairs, Washington, D.C., June 12, 1855, mimeographed copy in possession of author.

[290] *Doty Journal, 24-*25.

[291] Gustav Sohon Collection, Washington State Historical Society, Washington State History Research Center, 315 Stadium Way, Tacoma, WA 98403.

[292] *Doty Journal*, 26.

[293] The estimated census of tribal attendees at the treaty talks was 3,100, with the notation that the number was to be revised when the Indians reached the council grounds. See Darrell Scott, ed., *A True Copy of the Record of the Official Proceedings at the Council in the Walla Walla Valley 1855*, (Fairfield, WA: Ye Galleon Press, 1985), 29.

[294] William McKay was erroneously listed as "Wm. McCory," and Narcisse Raymond was listed as a Washington Territory interpreter but did not serve.

[295] Stevens and Palmer to Hon. Geo. Manypenny, June 12, 1855; Col. Lawrence Kip, *Indian Council at Walla Walla, May and June 1855* (1897 repr., Seattle, WA: Shorey Book Store, 1971), 4.

[296] *True Copy of the Record*, 33, 35. Unless otherwise noted, events occurring at the 1855 Walla Walla treaty council rely upon this source.

[297] *Ibid.*, 35-36.

[298] See Edward Harper Thomas, *Chinook: A History and Dictionary* (Portland, OR: Binfords & Mort, 1970), 13-14.

[299] Harmon, *Indians in the Making*, 80.

[300] Kip, *Indian Council, 9-10.*

[301] *Ibid.*, 10.

[302] Doty to Stevens, April 21, 1855.

[303] Stern, *Chiefs & Change*, 252. Interestingly, future U.S. President Ulysses S. Grant, then an officer stationed at the Vancouver Barracks, was reported to be a silent partner in the cattle operation. See Ruby and Brown, *Cayuse Indians*, 178n23.

[304] Kip, *Indian Council*, 12-20.

[305] *True Copy of the Record*, 55.

[306] *Ibid.*, 57.

[307] *Ibid.*, 58.

[308] *Wiyaxayst/Wiyaakaa'awn = As Days Go By*, 73-74.

[309] Kip, *Indian Council*, 24-5.

[310] *Nez Perce Country*, 83-86.

[311] *True Copy of the Record*, 76.

[312] That such a deal was made is the author's speculation, based on circumstances extant at the 1855 treaty grounds.

[313] *Washington National Guard*, 77.

[314] *True Copy of the Record*, 97-8.

315 Proof of Commencement of Residence and Cultivation on Land Not Yet Surveyed, forms, signed by Henri M. Chase and by William C. McKay, June 4, 1855, *Caldwell v. Vaughn.*

316 Affidavit of Witness for a Settler Claiming Unsurveyed Lands as a Married Man, signed by Louis Raboin June 4, 1855, *ibid.*

317 Certificate No. 03092, issued September 17, 1913, in Lewiston, Idaho, to William Craig and Isabel Craig, six hundred thirty and forty-four hundredths (630.44) acres, Patent Number 356234, Bureau of Land Management Serial No. IDL 0003092, General Land Office Records. See http://www.glorecords.blm.gov/PatentSearch/Detail.asp

318 *True Copy of the Record,* 87.

319 Treaty with the Walla Walla, Cayuse, Umatilla 1885, in *Indian Treaties 1778-1883,* 694; *True Copy of the Record,* 98.

320 See Lucullus Virgil McWhorter, *Hear Me, My Chiefs! Nez Perce History and Legend,* (Caldwell, ID: The Caxton Printers, Ltd., 1952, 1986), 90n9;

321 *Wiyaxayst/Wiyaakaa'awn = As Days Go By,* 75-77.

322 *True Copy of the Record,* 95.

323 *Indian Treaties,* 705. The "intercourse act" refers to the current regulations pursuant to the *Act to Regulate Trade and Intercourse With the Indian Tribes* first enacted in 1790.

324 *Doty Journal,* 28.

325 Cain to Geary, July 9 1861, NPUA. See also Josephy, *Nez Perce Indians,* 378-79, 395-96; Ronald W. Walker, Richard E. Turley, Jr. and Glen M. Leonard, *Massacre at Mountain Meadows* (New York: Oxford University Press, 2008), 47, 95-98.

326 Kip, *Indian Council,* 21.

327 William C. McKay, writing much later, recalls overhearing Stevens tell a chief that if they didn't sign the treaty they would "walk in blood knee deep." Ruby and Brown, *Cayuse Indians,* 203-04. For his theory about the possibly flawed memories of William McKay and Hazard Stevens, both of whom wrote later in life about 1855 treaty events, see Richards, *Young Man in a Hurry,* 418n23.

328 Burns, *Jesuits and the Indian Wars,* 76.

329 *True Copy of the Record,* 106.

330 *Ibid.,* 109.

331 *Ibid.*

332 *Doty Journal,* 30. Father Joseph Joset, at the time a missionary among the Coeur d'Alenes, said some years later he understood the chiefs had a plan to pretend to agree—to sign a "mock treaty"—in order to gain time and prepare for war. Ruby and Brown, *Cayuse Indians,* 205-206.

333 *Doty Journal,* 31.

334 Josephy, *Nez Perce Indians,* 338, citing in n5 Chester Anders Fee, *Chief Joseph: The Biography of a Great Indian* (New York: Wilson-Erickson, 1936), 37.

335 Charles E. Mix to Stevens, September 12, 1855, Letters from the Commissioner of Indian Affairs April 8, 1853-December 9, 1859, WSIA.

336 *Doty Journal,* 32.

337 McWhorter, *Hear Me, My Chiefs!,* 610.

338 *Doty Journal,* 75.

339 Kappler, *Indian Treaties 1778-1883,* 725.

340 Hazard Stevens, *The Life of Isaac Ingalls Stevens,* vol. 2 (Boston: Houghton Mifflin Company, 1901), 91; *Young Man in a Hurry,* 230.

341 Stevens, *Life of Isaac Ingalls Stevens,* 68-69.

342 *John Owen Journals,* 108-09. The printed version of Major Owen's journals has Benjamin Kiser written as "Benj. Ryser."

343 Richards, *Young Man in a Hurry,* 230.

344 *Ibid.,* 231.

345 *John Owen Journals,* 109.

346 Craig to Mason, August 27, 1855, Miscellaneous Letters Received April 22, 1853-April 9, 1861, WSIA. Washington Territory had its first election returns in 1853, and in 1854 passed its

first laws that established election procedures, precinct boundaries, and defined who could vote – only white male inhabitants over the age of 21 years. Governor Stevens had, in 1854, issued a proclamation that called for elections in February of 1855. See Washington Secretary of State, *The History of Voting and Elections in Washington State,* at: *http://www.secstate.wa.gov/elections/timeline/time3.htm* [7/29/2010]

[347] Stevens, *Life of Isaac Ingalls Stevens,* 108-109.

[348] *Ibid,* 116.

[349] Josephy, *Nez Perce Indians,* 341.

[350] Stevens, *Life of Isaac Ingalls Stevens,* 116-17.

[351] Albert J. Partoll, "Introduction," *The Blackfeet Indian Peace Council (1855),* 4-5. http://members.stratos.net/cpetras/blk-con.htm [11/16/2000]

[352] *Indian Treaties 1778-1883,* 736.

[353] *Blackfoot Peace Council,* 9.

[354] *Indian Treaties 1778-1883,* 739-40.

[355] *Doty Journal,* 39.

[356] *John Owen Journal,* 112.

[357] *Doty Journal,* 40.

[358] For insight into white American thinking during expansion into the Pacific Northwest, see Limerick, *Legacy of Conquest,* 36-46. Patricia Limerick looks back on the actions of missionaries, settlers and gold seekers and reached the conclusion that they were oblivious to the possibility that their behavior wasn't perfectly normal and blameless: "Whether the target resource was gold, farmland, or Indian souls, white Americans went West convinced that their purposes were as commonplace as they were innocent."

[359] Richards, *Young Man in a Hurry,* 232.

[360] White, *"It's Your Misfortune",* 101.

[361] Lucullus Virgil McWhorter, *Tragedy of the Wahk-Shum: The Death of Andrew J. Bolon, Indian Agent to the Yakima Nation, in mid-September, 1855...* (1937; repr., Fairfield, WA: Ye Galleon Press, 1968), 11-15. Unless otherwise noted, the chronicles of Bolon's murder and aftermath are based on this source.

[362] Jo N. Miles, "The Life and Death of A.J. Bolon, 1826-1855," *Pacific Northwest Quarterly* 97, no. 1 (2005-2006): 35-36.

[363] Richards, *Young Man in a Hurry,* 241.

[364] *Indian Hostilities in Oregon and Washington Territories,* 34th Cong., 1st sess., 1856, Ex. Doc. 118, 33.

[365] *Doty Journal,* 81.

[366] Josephy, *Nez Perce Indians,* 344; *Washington National Guard,* 77.

[367] *Indian Hostilities in Oregon and Washington Territories,* 33-34.

[368] *Ibid.; Doty Journal,* 40.

[369] Stevens, *Life of Isaac Ingalls Stevens,* 129. Hazard Stevens was but a boy when he accompanied his father on the treaty tour—and he recorded his memories many years later. Although his descriptions of the people, their clothing and equipment are vivid and valued for the glimpses they give us into an earlier time, other sources are more reliable accounts of the whys and wherefores of adult activities. Like Thomas Beall, Hazard Stevens was a good storyteller.

[370] *Ibid.*

[371] *Ibid.*

[372] *Doty Journal,* 41.

[373] Clifford E. Trafzer and Richard D. Scheuerman, *Renegade Tribe: The Palouse Indians and the Invasion of the Inland Pacific Northwest,* (Pullman: Washington State University Press, 1986), 36.

[374] Stevens, *Life of Isaac Ingalls Stevens,* 130.

[375] Josephy, *Nez Perce Indians,* 347.

[376] Haines, "Pioneer Portrait: Robert Newell, 2.

[377] *Ibid.,* 7.

[378] Tobie, *No Man Like Joe,* 238-40.

228

[379] Indian War Pension Papers, OHS 817-965, microfilm, reel 7, record 954.

[380] *Washington National Guard*, 64, 103.

[381] *Doty Journal*, 81.

[382] *Washington National Guard*, 129-31.

[383] *Doty Journal*, 44.

[384] Richards, *Young Man in a Hurry*, 247.

[385] *Ibid.*

[386] Trafzer and Scheuerman, *Renegade Tribe*, 69n54.

[387] Stevens, *Life of Isaac Ingalls Stevens*, 141-42; *Doty Journal*, 67.

[388] *Doty Journal*, 67.

[389] Information on the council and speeches at Craig's place in December 1855 is taken from *Doty Journal*, 68-82, unless otherwise noted.

[390] *Doty Journal*, 70

[391] *Doty Journal*, 72.

[392] *Doty Journal*, 75.

[393] *Ibid.*

[394] John B. Monteith to Edward T. Smith, March 11, 1874, Idaho Superintendency, Letters Received, Records of the Bureau of Indian Affairs Selected Documents Concerning Indian Affairs in Idaho, 1855-1906 (hereafter RBIAIS) RG 75, M234, Roll 342.

[395] For a perceptive exploration of Nez Perce motives in forming peaceful alliances with Americans—and vice versa—see West, *Last Indian War,* 20-34.

[396] *Doty Journal*, 76.

[397] *Ibid.,* 82. See *Washington National Guard*, 129, for a list of the 70 Nez Perce warriors who served as Stevens' guards under war chief Spotted Eagle. Named the "Nez Perce Mounted Volunteers, 1st Regiment Washington Territorial Volunteers" they served 36 days (December 15, 1855 – January 20, 1856).

[398] Stevens, *Life of Isaac Ingalls Stevens*, 145.

[399] *Washington National Guard*, 129-31; "Annual Report, Wm. Craig Special Agent Nez Percey 1856," WSIA, NPUA.

[400] *Nez Perce: St. Joseph's Mission Site at Slickpoo, Idaho* (Spalding, ID: U.S. Department of the Interior, National Park Service, Nez Perce National Historical Park, n.d.).

[401] *Ibid.*

[402] *Doty Journal*, 83.

[403] *Ibid.*

[404] Stevens, *Life of Isaac Ingalls Stevens*, 146.

[405] *Ibid.*

[406] *Ibid,* 147-48. See also J. Orin Oliphant, ed., "Journals of the Indian War of 1855-56," *Washington Historical Quarterly* 15, no. 1 (January 1924): 11-31.

[407] See Limerick, *Legacy of Conquest*, 39.

[408] *Doty Journal*, 85.

[409] "Journal of the Indian War of 1855-1856," 4.

[410] *Ibid.* See also *Doty Journal*, 85.

[411] Painter's Journal," 4.

[412] "Copy of P.S. of Father Cherouze," Territorial Access Project, Military Department, OSA, microfilm, reel 30.

[413] Ruby and Brown, *Cayuse Indians*, 178.

[414] "Copy of P.S. of Father Cherouze."

[415] *Ibid.*

[416] *Washington National Guard*, 55.

[417] *Doty Journal*, 85-86.

[418] [Frances Fuller Victor], *History of Washington, Idaho, and Montana 1845-1889*, Works of Hubert Howe Bancroft, vol. 31 (San Francisco: The History Company, 1890), 143.

[419] *Doty Journal*, 86.

[420] *Washington National Guard*, 57.

[421] *Doty Journal*, 91-92.

[422] *Ibid.*, 88.

[423] In his musings, Craig could not know that he would never again conduct business, nor tip a glass, with James Doty. In February 1856 Doty went on a four-day drinking spree at Steilacoom. Stevens fired him but later relented and gave him a clerking job. Doty continued drinking and committed suicide in June 1857. *Young Man in a Hurry*, 275, 427n4.

[424] Stevens, *Life of Isaac Ingalls Stevens*, 147.

[425] [Victor], *History*, 143.

[426] Trafzer and Scheuerman, *Renegade Tribe*, 61.

[427] Richards, *Young Man in a Hurry*, 258.

[428] William Simpson to Gov. Stevens, February 7, 1857, NPUA. See also *Appendix C*; and see *Washington National Guard*, 145-46, for discussion of later claims for services, horses, and audits.

[429] "Annual Report, Wm. Craig, 1856."

[430] Richards, *Young Man in a Hurry*, 260.

[431] *Ibid.* 238-39, 264.

[432] Stevens to Secretary of War Jefferson Davis, *Washington National Guard*, 77.

[433] Craig to Col. B. F. Shaw, NPUA.

[434] Limerick, *Legacy of Conquest*, 45.

[435] *Ibid.*

[436] Robert Carlton Clark, "Military History of Oregon, 1849-59," *Oregon Historical Quarterly* 36 (1935), 27.

[437] *Washington National Guard*, 143 and 63, 64.

[438] Harmon, *Indians in the Making*, 87.

[439] Stern, *Chiefs & Change*, 344 and n13; *Wiyaxayst/Wiyaakaa'awn = As Days Go By*, 44-50, 62, 83.

[440] Craig to Stevens, January 24, 1856, NPUA. There is a strategic blotch of ink on Craig's letter to Stevens that obliterates the last letters of a word beginning with the letter "d." Craig may have written "drop" or "dram."

[441] George W. Manypenny to Stevens, April 21, 1856, Letters from the Commissioner, WSIA (hereafter LFC), Microfilm No. 5, Roll 7. There were three levels of the "agent" position, depending upon the permanency of appointment and the scope of responsibilities: special agent, sub agent, and the highest, agent.

[442] W.H. Tappan to Stevens, March 3, 1856, NPUA.

[443] Manypenny to Stevens, May 5, 1856, LFC; Prucha, *Great Father*, 319-21.

[444] Craig to Stevens, February 10, 1856, NPUA.

[445] "Annual Report, Wm. Craig, 1856"

[446] *Ibid.*

[447] *Message from the President, Nez Perce 1863 Treaty Council Proceedings*, 38th Cong., 1st sess., 1864, S. Exec. Doc. T, 33 at http://members,stratos.net/cpetras/np-2-1-1.htm [3/26/2001]

[448] "Annual Report, Wm. Craig, 1856"

[449] Ravalli to Craig, May 14, 1856, NPUA.

[450] "Annual Report, Wm. Craig, 1856"

[451] *Ibid.*

[452] The names and ranks of the men in Company M are found in *Washington National Guard*, 141. Forty-three Indian men and nine white or mixed-blood men served 123 days – from March 11 to July 12, 1856.

[453] See, Henri M. Chase to James Tilton, July 31, 1856, *Washington National Guard*, 101.

[454] Craig to Stevens, March 22, 1856, NPUA.

[455] But it was not the first hanging in the region: more than forty years earlier, in 1813, at the junction of the Palouse and Snake rivers, John Clarke (an Astorian in the Wilson Price Hunt party) hanged a Palouse man accused of stealing one of Clarke's silver goblets. Many Palouse people distrusted and hated white people from that time forward. Trafzer and Scheuerman, *Renegade*

Tribe, 13-16. See also Josephy, *Nez Perce Indians*, 50, stating that the man who was hanged was a visiting Nez Perce.

[456] Chase to Tilton, July 31, 1856, *Washington National Guard*, 101.

[457] Craig to Stevens, March 22 1856, NPUA; Henri M. Chase to James Tilton, July 31, 1856, *Washington National Guard*, 101.

[458] See G. Wright, Col., 9th Inf. Comdg., to Stevens, April 20, 1856, *Washington National Guard*, 81.

[459] Wright to Curry, April 27, 1856, Doc. 7653, Ore. Military Dept., OSA.

[460] Stevens to Craig, April 9, 1856, NPUA.

[461] Umehowlish evaded Craig's men and lived to be an old man. He was baptised late in life by Henry Spalding, taking the name "Marcus Whitman." News release dated July 28, 2005, Tamástslikt Cultural Center, Pendleton, Oregon.

[462] Stevens to Craig, April 9, 1856, NPUA.

[463] Stevens to Lieut Col. Wm. Craig, April 9, 1856, Washington Territorial Volunteers papers (hereafter WTVP), box 4, folder 2, Washington State Archives.

[464] "Annual Report Wm. Craig, 1856".

[465] Tappan to Stevens, April 3, 1856, NPUA.

[466] Stevens to Wright, May 8, 1856, *Washington National Guard*, 82.

[467] "Annual Report, Wm. Craig, 1856"

[468] Angus McDonald to Craig, May 13, 1856, NPUA.

[469] George Montour to Craig, May 15, 1856, NPUA.

[470] Ravalli to Craig, May 14, 1856, NPUA.

[471] "Annual Report, Wm. Craig, 1856"

[472] *Ibid.*

[473] Craig to Stevens, May 27, 1856, NPUA.

[474] *Ibid.*

[475] *Washington National Guard*, 95.

[476] *Ibid.* 97.

[477] *Ibid.*

[478] "Diary of the Yakima Indian War kept by W.W. DeLacy, Captain, Engineers and Acting Adjutant, W.T.V. covering period June 12th to August 29, 1856," *Washington National Guard*, 105. The July 1856 Walla Walla Valley meeting of Shaw's volunteers and the Nez Perces is taken from the above source unless otherwise noted.

[479] B. F. Shaw to Stevens, July 12, 1856, Letters Received by the Office of Indian Affairs 1824-81, (hereafter LROIA), Washington Superintendency, 1853-1880 (hereafter WS), RG 75, NARA, microfilm, roll 907, Washington State Library, Olympia.

[480] Craig to Stevens, July 11, 1856, NPUA.

[481] "Account of Qr Masters Property & Clothing Issued to Officers & Men of Co. M 2nd Dept W.T. Vol. Capt. Henri M. Chase, Qr M. & Commissary, Lapwai W.T. July 31st 1856," Adjutant General's Correspondence–Incoming, Volunteer Papers, WSA, Box 5.

[482] Henri M. Chase to James Tilton, July 31, 1856, *Washington National Guard*, 101.

[483] Gov. Stevens to A. H. Robie, Dalles, June 24, 1856, WTVP.

[484] *Washington National Guard*, 141.

[485] Henri M. Chase to James Tilton, July 31, 1856, *Washington National Guard*, 101.

[486] "DeLacy Diary," *ibid.*, 110.

[487] "Annual Report, Wm. Craig, 1856."

It has been stated that the hostile Indians tried different ways to "dislodge the Nez Perces from their neutrality": Ruby and Brown, *Cayuse Indians*, 237. But the Nez Perces were not neutral—they had a formal agreement to be America's allies. In a later study, the neutrality of historians Ruby and Brown is questioned as it pertains to their documentation of the Cayuse Indians. See Eugene S. Hunn with James Sellam and Family, *Nch'I-Wána, "The Big River": Mid-Columbia Indians and Their Land* (Seattle: University of Washington Press, 1990), 211-14.

[488] Speech of the Man With the Rope in his Mouth, in Speeches of Several Nes Perce Chiefs at a Council held at Lapwai in presence of Capt. Robie July 1856, LROIA, WS.

[489] "Annual Report, Wm. Craig, 1856."

[490] Speech of The Eagle from the Light, LROIA, WS.

[491] *Ibid.*

[492] "Annual Report, Wm. Craig, 1856."

[493] *Ibid.*

[494] Stevens to Jefferson Davis, July 7, 1856, *Washington National Guard*, 97.

[495] "DeLacy Diary," *ibid.*, 110.

[496] Report of B. F. Shaw, Lt Col. Comdg Expedition to Yakima, *Washington National Guard*, 100.

[497] "DeLacy Diary," *Washington National Guard*, 114.

[498] Josephy, *Nez Perce Indians*, 371-72.

[499] Craig to Shaw, July 28, 1856, LROIA, WS.

[500] It is unknown whether his bravery was the reason for the name of Craig's whiskey keg, but there was a man named Blue John in Craig's trapping days. He was a Nez Perce warrior from the upper Clearwater who, in 1833, was killed by the Blackfeet while leading a horse-stealing raid. See Irving, *Adventures of Captain Bonneville*, 128-32.

[501] Craig to Shaw, July 28, 1856, LROIA, WS.

[502] *Ibid.*

[503] See *John Owen's Journal*, 137.

[504] Josephy, *Nez Perce Indians*, 372.

[505] Henri Chase had earlier married a daughter of Raboin.

[506] Craig to Stevens, August 8, 1856, NPUA.

[507] *Ibid.*

[508] *Ibid.*

[509] Stevens to Wright, August 3, 1856, *Washington National Guard*, 102-03.

[510] Stevens to Jefferson Davis, Vancouver, W.T., August 14, 1856, *Washington National Guard*, 103-04.

[511] "Return of Employees at Walla Walla Agency," NPUA.

[512] Joe Craig would one day be given the name of Seeyakoomilpilp (Red Spy, Red Scout, Red Courier).

[513] "DeLacy Diary," *Washington National Guard*, 115.

[514] *Ibid.*

[515] Andrew Dominique Pambrun, *Sixty Years on the Frontier in the Pacific Northwest* (Fairfield, WA: Ye Galleon Press, 1978), 101-02. As are those of Hazard Stevens, Pambrun's memories are offered with the knowledge that they were written much later than the events occurred. Many yarns that are spun have at least a nucleus—perhaps more—of truth.

[516] *Washington National Guard*, 118.

[517] Stevens to Robert McClelland, October 22, 1856, *Washington National Guard*, 118.

[518] Stevens, *Life of Isaac Ingalls Stevens*, 209-10.

[519] Pambrun, *Sixty Years*, 102.

[520] *Ibid.*

[521] Stevens to Jefferson Davis, October 22, 1856, *Washington National Guard*, 119.

[522] Pambrun, *Sixty Years*, 102.

[523] Stevens to Jefferson Davis, October 22, 1856, 119-20.

[524] Pambrun, *Sixty Years*, 104-05.

[525] Stevens to Jefferson Davis, October 22, 1856, *Washington National Guard*, 120.

[526] Josephy, *Nez Perce Indians*, 374-75.

[527] Pambrun, *Sixty Years*, 105.

[528] Richards, *Young Man in a Hurry*, 289.

[529] Return of Provisions Received and Issued in the month of September, October and November 1856 by William Craig Sub Agent Indian Department Walla Walla, NPUA, WSIA, Microfilm 111, Roll 21.

[530] See Prucha, *Great Father*, 333-34, for discussion of Commissioner of Indian Affairs George W. Manypenny's 1856 policies regarding annuity payments to tribes. Between 1853 and the end of 1856, the government had entered into fifty two treaties with various tribes; thirty two were already ratified, and those from the Walla Walla Council were among the twenty yet to be ratified by Congress.

Craig followed the current Dept. of Indian Affairs policies regarding distribution of annuities, which would actually only apply after treaty ratification.

[531] Stevens to Davis, October 22, 1856, *Washington National Guard*, 120.

[532] *Ibid.*

[533] Stevens, *Life of Isaac Ingalls Stevens*, 220.

[534] *Ibid.*

[535] For analysis of Isaac Stevens' Indian treaties, policies and behavior in Washington Territory, see Richards, *Young Man in a Hurry*, 209-10, 266, 270-75.

[536] *Ibid.*, 305-06. See also Pambrun, *Sixty Years*, 105-111.

[537] Richards, *Young Man in a Hurry*, 305-06.

[538] Stevens to Jefferson Davis, October 22, 1856, *Washington National Guard*, 121.

[539] *Ibid.*

[540] Pambrun, *Sixty Years*, 105-06

[541] *Ibid.*, 111.

[542] Stevens to Jefferson Davis, October 22, 1856, *Washington National Guard*, 121.

[543] Pambrun, *Sixty Years*, 111-12.

[544] The oath was administered in the office of a U.S. attorney in Portland, Oregon Territory – even though Craig was appointed an Indian agent for Washington Territory. From the Walla Walla Valley, Portland was easier to reach than was Puget Sound; and at that time the area was probably the scene of less conflict than was the Sound.

[545] Prucha, *Great Father*, 328-29.

[546] "Amount of Expenses by William Craig Sub Indian Agent at Portland and Dalles" (Oct. 9 - Nov. 19, 1856), NPUA.

[547] Robert Thompson and B. B. Bishop signed as sureties. Craig's $5,000 Bond and Oath of Office, October 10, 1856, NPUA.

[548] Craig at Dalles to Stevens, November 2, 1856, NPUA.

[549] Craig to Stevens, December 5, 1856, NPUA. It appears that neither Craig nor his men were issued uniforms during their service in Washington Territory's volunteer militia.

[550] General Orders No. 7: Disbandment of the Staff and Line, Olympia, W.T., October 30, 1856, *Washington National Guard*, 123-24.

[551] "Return of Employees at Walla Walla Agency," NPUA.

[552] "Amount of Expenses by William Craig," NPUA.

[553] Craig to Stevens, November 2, 1856, NPUA.

[554] Josephy, *Nez Perce Indians*, 377.

[555] Pambrun, *Sixty Years*, 113.

[556] *Young Man in a Hurry*, 313-17.

[557] To justify hanging Leschi, the Puget Sound white people decided no war had been fought. White, *"It's Your Misfortune"*, 101-102. If indeed a war had been fought between two distinct peoples, it made no sense for either side to charge Indian fighters with breaking U.S. laws. Harmon, *Indians in the Making*, 85-88, 92-94. Leschi was the victim of Isaac Stevens' ambition and Gov. Fayette McMullin's cowardice. Ficken, *Washington Territory*, 51. In March 2005, a panel chaired by Chief Justice Gerry Alexander of the Washington Supreme Court exonerated Leschi in a symbolic, potentially healing, gesture.

[558] *Young Man in a Hurry*, 310.

[559] Craig to Stevens, December 5, 1856, NPUA.

[560] *Ibid.* See also Brown, *The Indian Side of the Story*, 163.

[561] According to Josephy, in 1835 Tackitonitis, when a boy, was taken east by Whitman to learn white men's ways. Josephy, *Nez Perce Indians*, 133.

[562] Craig at Walla Walla Valley to Stevens at Olympia, December 19, 1856, first letter, NPUA.

[563] "Differences on Settlement of the accounts of I. I. Stevens, Gov & Washington Territory-2, 3, 4 Quarters 1855 and years 1856 & 1857," LFC, WSIA, Microfilm No. 5, Roll 7.

[564] Craig at Walla Walla Valley to Stevens at Olympia, December 19, 1856, second letter, NPUA.

[565] Abstract of Provision Issued Friendly Indians in the Month of December 1856 by William Craig sub Indian agent Walla Walla, NPUA.

[566] Received of A. H. Robie, Return of Provision Received and issued by William Craig Sub Indian Agent December 1856, NPUA.

[567] Return of Provisions Received and Issued in the Month of January 1857 by William Craig Sub Indian Agent Walla Walla, NPUA.

[568] Craig to Stevens, January 5, 1857, NPUA.

[569] Craig to Stevens, January 16, 1857, NPUA.

[570] PWT to Stevens, February 2, 1857.

[571] Craig to Stevens, February 6, 1857, NPUA.

[572] *Ibid*.

[573] List of Certificates Issued by Wm Craig 1857, NPUA.

[574] Craig to Stevens, February 28, 1857, NPUA.

[575] Pambrun, *Sixty Years*, 113-14.

[576] Craig to Stevens, April 20, 1857, NPUA.

[577] *Ibid*.

[578] "Reports of the Commissioner of Indian Affairs, No. 145, Report of William Craig, Sub-Agent for the Nez Perces," *Annual Message of the President and Report of the Secretary of the Interior, 1856*, 34th Cong., 3rd sess., 1857, 641-42, found at

http://menolly.lib.uidaho.edu/McBeth/governmentdoc/comag1857.htm

[579] Prucha, *Great Father*, 408.

[580] Letter from J. W. Nesmith, Sup't Indian Affairs, Oregon and Washington Territories, *Message from the President of the United States, Report of the Secretary of the Interior*, 35th Congress, 1st sess., 1857, H. Ex. Doc. 2:613.

[581] Harmon, *Indians in the Making*, 95.

[582] Richards, *Young Man in a Hurry*, 334.

[583] David Michael Goodman, *A Western Panorama 1849-1875: The Travels, Writings and Influence of J. Ross Browne on the Pacific Coast, and in Texas, Nevada, Arizona and Baja California...*, Western Frontiersmen Series 9 (Glendale, CA: The Arthur H. Clark Co., 1966), 124n14.

[584] "A Reminiscense of 1857," *The Weekly Message* (Port Townsend, WT), September 12, 1867.

[585] Goodman, *J. Ross Browne*, 9, citing 35th Cong., 1st sess., 1857, H. Exec. Doc. 38, *Letter of J. Ross Browne to the Commissioner of Indian Affairs, Reviewing the Origin of the Indian War of 1855-56, in ... Oregon and Washington*, and H. Exec. Doc. 39, *Letter of J. Ross Browne on the Conditions of the Indian Reservations in Oregon and Washington*.

[586] Letter from General Clarke to Army Headquarters, November 4, *Message from the President of the United States, Report of the Secretary of War*, 35th Congress, 2nd sess., 1858, H. Ex. Doc. 2, 2:331-32; E. J. Steptoe to Maj. W.W. Mackall, October 19, 1857, *ibid*.

[587] Beall, "Recollections of Wm. Craig."

[588] Isaac Stevens Collection, Accession No. 111, University of Washington Libraries, box No. 4, folder 117.

[589] Nesmith to Craig, December 20, 1857, Records of the Office of Indian Affairs, Letters Received 1824-1880, Oregon Superintendency 1842-1880 (hereafter LR-OS), RG 75, NARA, Microfilm M234, Roll 611, Seattle, Washington.

[590] Craig to Col. J. Nesmith, January 22, 1858, NPUA.

[591] Letters from Craig to Col. J.W. Nesmith, December 27, 1857, January 22, April 30, July 14, September 2, September 4, September 15, November 4, 1858, NPUA.

[592] Craig to Col. J.W. Nesmith, June 17, 1858, NPUA.

[593] Ficken, *Washington Territory*, 56.

[594] Brown, *Indian Side*, 341; Josephy, *Nez Perce Indians*, 379.

[595] Stevens to Jacob Thompson, Secretary of the Interior, March 29, 1858, with extracts from William Craig's letter of February 2, 1858, LR-OS.

[596] Brown, *Indian Side*, 186, citing letter written by Col. Steptoe April 17, 1858.

[597] Trafzer and Scheuerman, *Renegade Tribe*, 77.

[598] Lawyer, in a speech delivered on May 28, 1863, stated that Colonel Steptoe came into his country; "Timothy and some of my people accompanied him. The whole people of the north met him in battle array . . . ." *Nez Perce 1863 Treaty Council Proceedings*, 33. See Brown, *Indian Side*, and Trafzer and Scheuerman, *Renegade Tribe*, for other views of Timothy's involvement.

[599] Craig to Col. J. W. Nesmith, May 20, 1858, NPUA.

[600] Craig to Col. J. W. Nesmith, May 22, 1858, NPUA. Steptoe's retreat triggered the end of his military career, for within two years he resigned his commission; in 1865 he died, an ill man, at age 49. See Brigham D. Madsen, "Edward J. Steptoe," *Utah History Encyclopedia* (Salt Lake City: University of Utah Press, 1994) at http://www.media.utah.edu/UHE/s/STEPTOE,EDWARD.html [1/22/2004]

[601] Record of Appointment of Postmasters 1832-September 30, 1871 Walla Walla Co., Records of the Post Office Department, RG 28, NARA, microfilm M841, Roll 137.

[602] It was the "first home known to have been built and occupied within the . . . city," and was later acquired as a homestead by A. H. Robie; it stood on the extreme southwest corner of what was (in 1912) the Walla Walla city park. T. C. Elliott, "Walla Walla and Missoula," *Washington Historical Quarterly* 3, no. 4 (October 1912): 275-76.

[603] Postmasters of Walla Walla Washington, citing the U.S. Post Office Department, Washington, D.C., letter dated 16 November 1949, provided author by archives, Penrose Library, Whitman College.

[604] *Ibid.*

[605] Craig to Col. J. W. Nesmith, June 17, 1858, NPUA.

[606] W. W. MacKall, Headquarters, Department of the Pacific, to Colonel George Wright, 9th Infantry, Commanding Expedition &c., Fort Dallas, O.T., July 4, 1858, Message of the President of the United States to the Two Houses of Congress, 35th Cong., 2nd sess., H. Exec. Doc. 2, 2:363.

[607] For insight and analysis of traditional Nez Perce and other tribes' ways of war compared with that of the Euroamerican, see West, *Last Indian War*, 159-60; Prucha, *Great Father*, 408; Clark, "Military History of Oregon, 1849-1859," 41.

[608] Brown, *Indian Side*, 255-56, 258.

[609] Lawyer's speech at Nez Perce 1863 Treaty Council Proceedings, 28; see also, Josephy, *Nez Perce Indians*, 282.

[610] MacKall to Wright, July 4, 1858, 364. It is the only known use of U.S. uniforms by the Nez Perces up to that time: the uniform authorization read "clothing of the old pattern and condemned."

[611] Brown, *Indian Side*, 229-32.

[612] MacKall to Wright, July 4, 1858, 363.

[613] Trafzer and Scheuerman, *Renegade Tribe*, 72. See also Prucha, *Great Father*, 407.

[614] Thomas B. Beall, "Pioneer Reminiscences," *Washington Historical Quarterly* 8, no. 2 (April 1917): 84-85. The article uses "B." as his middle initial; Beall later used "J." See Beall to Brosnan, February 3, 1918, Manuscripts, Special Collections, University of Idaho. Tom Beall was a teamster and miner who spent his later years at Lewiston, Idaho.

[615] Josephy, *Nez Perce Indians*, 384.

[616] Joseph K. F. Mansfield to Bvt. Major Irvin McDowell, October 11, 1858, LR-OS.

[617] Craig to Nesmith, November 4, 1858, NPUA; Nesmith to Craig, October 24, 1858, Letter Book Relating to the Nez Perce and Flathead Agencies October 11, 1858-July 25, 1863, WSIA.

[618] Josephy, *Nez Perce Indians*, 385.

[619] General Wright served until 1864 in the Dept. of the Pacific and was with the District of California when, in 1865, he was reassigned to the Department of the Columbia. That year, when traveling by ship from California to take command of the Department of the Columbia, Wright was among the 283 people who drowned in the wreck of the ship *Brother Jonathan*. Ficken, *Washington Territory*, 79, 232n2.

[620] Craig to C. H. Mott, October 26, 1858, LR-OS.

[621] Annual Report from Craig to Col. J. W. Nesmith, September 20, 1858, LR-OS (source of all excerpts from Craig's 1858 Annual Report.)

[622] Craig to Nesmith, December 20, 1858, LR-OS.

[623] Prucha, *Great Father*, 19.

[624] *Ibid.*, 30, 98-102.

[625] According to Craig family research conducted by Gloria Manning, a number of death certificates and family histories recorded alcohol as a factor in the life or death of some Craig descendants. Letter dated June 15, 2009, from Gloria Manning in author's possession.

[626] Craig to Nesmith, December 29, 1858, NPUA.

[627] "Notes and Documents," Letter from Isaac I. Stevens to J. W. Nesmith November 16, 1858, *Pacific Northwest Quarterly* 16, no.4 (October 1940), 455-56.

[628] *Pioneer and Democrat* (Olympia, WT), February 11, 1859, p. 2, col. 3.

[629] Dennis Baird, Diane Mallickan and W. R. Swagerty, eds., *The Nez Perce Nation Divided: Firsthand Accounts of Events Leading to the 1863 Treaty.* (Moscow: University of Idaho Press, 2002), 233.

[630] Nesmith to Wm. Craig Esq Late Sub Ind Agent, January 11, 1859, Letter Book Relating to the Nez Perce and Flathead Agencies.

[631] Annual Report of A. J. Cain August 2, 1859, NPUA.

[632] A. J. Cain to J. W. Nesmith, April 16, 1859, NPUA.

[633] Notice from A. J. Cain, July 9, 1859, NPUA.

[634] The transcription of the council proceedings as submitted by A. J. Cain note "Jas. W. Craig" as interpreter. The author believes that "Jos. W. Craig" is the correct reading of the handwriting.

[635] Annual Report of A. J. Cain August 2, 1859, NPUA.

[636] McWhorter, *Hear Me, My Chiefs!*, 555.

[637] Annual Report of A. J. Cain, August 2, 1859.

[638] Ficken, *Washington Territory*, 58.

[639] A. B. Roberts, "Walla Walla Fifty-One Years Ago," *Up-To-The-Times Magazine*, January 1910, 2415.

[640] H. S. Brode, ed., "Diary of Dr. Augustus J. Thibodo," *Pacific Northwest Quarterly* 31, no. 3 (July 1940): 342.

[641] "Thibodo Diary," 343-44.

[642] Certificate of Marriage of James M. Holt and Mary Adams, by John M. Cannady, J.P., Marriage celebrated in the presence of Thomas M. Gray and Charles Addis, Territory of Washington, County of Walla Walla, at the house of Col. Wm. Craig, dated 29 January 1860, document on file at the Clearwater Historical Museum, Orofino, Idaho.

[643] U.S., Census, 1860, Territory of Washington, Walla Walla County. See also Death Certificate of Mary J. Holt cited in Chapter 1, n67. Family legend holds that Louise Craig (also known as Yahoeweyenonay and Louise Wheeler), a daughter of Lawyer and granddaughter of Twisted Hair, was a wife of William Craig when she became pregnant by Charlie Adams. JoAnn Newell Zipse, Lenore, Idaho, interviews with the author, August 15, August 29, September 21, 2002; January 6, January 13, 2003.

[644] The words were those of Elias Pierce as he recollected hearing them from Isabel Craig. It seems unlikely that the tribe ordered away anyone in the family besides William.

[645] J. Gary Williams and Ronald W. Stark, eds., *The Pierce Chronicle: Personal Reminiscenses of E.D. Pierce as transcribed by Lou A. Larrick* (Moscow: Idaho Research Foundation [1976]), ix, 47-48, 68, 70.

[646] "Memorial of the Nez Perce Indians Residing in the State of Idaho to the Congress of the United States," compiled by Starr J. Maxwell, Northwest Historical Manuscript Series (Moscow: University of Idaho Library, 2000), 86.

[647] *Pierce Chronicles*, 70.

[648] Ralph Burcham, ed., "Orofino Gold! E. D. Pierce's Own Story...," *Idaho Yesterdays* 4, no. 3 (Fall, 1960): 2-3.

[649] Pedigree Charts of Fermore Craig and Calvin Shillal. Charts were furnished the author by, and are used with permission of, Craig and Shillal. See also *Nez Perce Nation Divided*, xviii.

[650] "Married," *Oregon Statesman* (Albany), April 24, 1860, p. 2, col. 7.

[651] Carol Simon-Smolinski, "River History of Nez Perce County," *Journal of the Nez Perce County Historical Society 1*, no. 1 (Spring 1981): 9.

[652] *Sidney W. Moss v. William Craig*, "Frontier Justice": Guide to the Court Records of Washington Territory, 1853-1889, State of Washington, Office of the Secretary of State, Division of Archives and Records Management, Olympia, Washington, 1987.

[653] Burcham, "Orofino Gold!," 4.

[654] *Ibid.*, 5

[655] *Ibid.*, 9.

[656] *Ibid. "Oro fino"* (Spanish) translates to "fine gold" in the English language. Pierce may have brought the name with him from his former home in the Yreka (Scott's Valley), California, gold discovery area.

[657] The author thanks Donald S. Shannon, who spent eight years researching the attacks on the Utter and VanOrnum wagon train and their aftermath, for the following information. As most printed material reflects only the white persons' view of historical occurrences, the perspective of the Indian people is missing in this study. See Donald S. Shannon, *The Utter Disaster on The Oregon Trail: The Utter and VanOrnum Massacres of 1860*, Snake Country Series, vol. 2 (Caldwell, ID: Snake Country Publishing, 1993), unless otherwise cited.

[658] *Ibid.*

[659] "Married at Walla Walla, Mr. Charles Russell and Miss Mary Ann Sheets; Mr. Samuel Finney and Miss Adeline Craig;... Mr. Wm. J. Terry and Miss Ellen Pambrain," *Weekly Oregonian* (Portland), February 2, 1861, p. 3, col. 4, microfilm, OHS.

[660] Phinney's birthdate was August 2, 1833. See, Pension application of Samuel Phinney for service in Indian Wars 1855-1856, Indian War Pension Papers.

[661] Affidavit of Isabel Craig at U.S. Land Office, Lewiston, Idaho Territory, February 28, 1874: "...said Phinney was legally married to said Adeline on the 24th day of December A.D. 1861," Indian War Pension Papers. The correct year of Sam and Adeline's marriage is 1860.

[662] Shannon, *Utter Disaster*, 141-42.

[663] Cain to Geary, November 27, 1860, NPUA.

[664] A search of the earliest claims filed in the Pierce/Orofino Creek mining district (the first claim was filed in February 1861) reveals no claim filed by Elias D. Pierce. See *Miners Record*, Book D, March 15, 1861-June 8, 1878, Clearwater County Historical Museum, Orofino, Idaho.

[665] "News from the Nez Perce Mines," *Idaho Yesterdays* 3, no. 4 (Winter 1959-1960): 19.

[666] Gregory R. Sanford, "The Nez Perce Nation was Betrayed." *Pacific Northwesterner* 6, no. 4, (Fall 1962): 60.

[667] No records of gold claims for William or Joseph Craig have been found in the early records of the Pierce/Oro Fino Creek gold discovery. See *Miners Record*, Book D and *Index to Preemption Mining Claims*, Clearwater County Historical Museum, Orofino, Idaho.

[668] Robert G. Bailey, *River of No Return (The Great Salmon River of Idaho): A Century of Central Idaho and Eastern Washington History and Development*, rev. ed. (Lewiston, ID: R. G. Bailey Printing Company, 1947), 143-44.

[669] *Ibid.*

[670] Walla Walla correspondence, February 24, to the *Pioneer and Democrat*, March 15, 1861, p. 2, col. 3, as cited in "News From the Nez Perce Mines," *Idaho Yesterdays* 3, no. 4 (Winter, 1959-1960): 22n10, 23.

[671] "News from the Nez Perce Mines," 23.

[672] *Oregonian*, April 3, 1861, cited in *ibid.*, 23n17, 25.

[673] Thibodo to Cain, April 13, 1861, NPUA.

[674] Report of C. W. Armstrong, April 15, 1861, NPUA. Armstrong's report states that Wislaneqa was "established on the South fork of Clear Water about five miles from its mouth." At that time, the main stem of the Clearwater was referred to as the "South fork." The "mouth" referred to by Armstrong is now known as mouth of the North Fork of the Clearwater. Thus, according to Armstrong's description, Wislenéqa's village stood at the mouth of Orofino Creek (*Téwe*).

[675] *Ibid.*, 2. The federal system has been blamed for the liquor problem, which had been unsolved since earliest Colonial times. See Prucha, *Great Father*, 106-7, 115. In the case of the gold rush on the Nez Perce reservation, even a large military force would have been incapable of halting liquor at reservation borders, had there been military to deploy and had the borders been agreed upon.

[676] *Ibid.*; Tobie, *No Man Like Joe*, 115. In 1844 in Clackamas County, Marshal Joe Meek had arrested Conner for operating a still.

[677] Report of Armstrong, 3.

[678] *Ibid.*, 4.

[679] Jared S. Hurd, Clerk Register Office, to Craig, May 13, 1861, *Caldwell v. Vaughn*, Exhibits 184-104, 185-105.

[680] One of the most bitter had been the Cherokee Nation's "treaty" and "anti-treaty" factions. See Prucha, *Great Father*, 236-39. Gen. Wool's experience with the Cherokee removal influenced his sympathetic treatment of Indians in Washington and Oregon Territories.

[681] "News from the Nez Perce Mines,"26.

[682] The text of the "Articles of Agreement" is found in its entirety in *Message of the President*, 1862, 37th Cong., 3rd sess., 1862, H. Exec. Doc. 1, Pt. 2, G11, 574-75.

[683] Loose Papers Relating to Treaty Proceedings February 20, 1855-June 9, 1863, WSIA. Historians Drury and Josephy believed Thunder's Eye and Big Thunder to be the same person; pending definitive proof, the author concludes that Thunder's Eye and Big Thunder are two different people. The conclusion is based upon: (1) Sohon's 1855 sketch of Thunder's Eye showing a wrinkled, elderly man; (2) Stevens' April 1856 description of James as "an old man, 80 years old" (see Governor's Correspondence, WTVP); (3) Amos George's [Thunder's Eye the Younger] statement (below); (4) information furnished Kate McBeth and Virgil McWhorter (below).
　　In the statements compiled by Starr Maxwell and presented to Congress by Senator William E. Borah in 1911, Amos George swore that a few years after the 1855 treaty, "Chief Big Thunder, one of the chiefs, *moved to* the Lapwai Valley." [emphasis added] *Memorial of the Nez Perce Indians Residing in the State of Idaho*, 62nd Cong., 1st sess., 1911, S. Doc. 97, 49. See also McBeth, *Nez Perces Since Lewis and Clark*, 45, where her informant related that "Big Thunder a chief is buried on the top of the [Thunder] hill" in the Lapwai Valley. Thunder's Eye, according to McWhorter's informants, died while on a buffalo hunt in Montana. McWhorter, *Hear Me, My Chiefs!*, 609.

[684] *Nez Perce Nation Divided*, 168; Haines, "Robert Newell," 7.

[685] See, for example, Claim of David Diggins, J. C. Smith, William Rhodes, February 1, 1861, *Miners Record*, Book D, 51.

[686] "Bill of Sale," Shoshone County Washington Territory mining records, *Liens, Mortgages Contracts & Licenses* (1861-1863), Book A, Clearwater Historical Museum, Orofino, Idaho, 59. In January 1861, R. H. Johns sold the Comet Saloon, located on Main Street of Oro Fino City, to William M. Wilson. Johns received a promissory note for $750. The document was attested to by A. B. Power and Adam Getzelmann at "Lewiston Shoshone Co. W.T."

[687] Cain to E. R. Geary, July 9, 1861, NPUA.

[688] Notice of A. J. Cain, July 7, 1861, NPUA.

[689] *Message of the President*, 1862, 447.

[690] Cain to E. R. Geary, December 29, 1860, NPUA.

691 *Nez Perce Nation Divided*, 117.

692 *Ibid.*

693 Hutchins to Hale, July 15, 1862. Charles Hutchins, a year after the event, was relating how Craig's foresight and generosity at the 1861 annuity council likely averted war.

694 *Ibid.*

695 *Ibid.*

696 Cain was gone by September 1861. See *Message of the President*, 1862, 566.

697 Margaret Guilford-Kardell and Scott McKeown, "Hiner Miller," at http://www.joaquinmiller.com/years/1860.html [8/7/2010]

698 Henry Miller, "Letters From the Upper Columbia," Idaho Yesterdays 4, no. 4 (Winter, 1960-1961): 19.

699 See *Walla Walla (WA) Statesman*, December 20, 1861, p. 2, and January 10, 1862, p. 2.

700 Beall, "Recollections of Wm. Craig." Tom Beall's stories offer the few personal glimpses surviving about William Craig, and they are offered here for what they are: anecdotes from a good storyteller.

701 *Portland (OR) Daily Advertiser* in the *Puget Sound Herald* (Steilacoom, WT), March 7, 1861, p. 2, c. 3, as cited in "News From the Nez Perce Mines," 22, 23.

702 "Certification of Sale of one-third part of the Ferry on Snake river at 'She min a Kin' known as 'Craig's Ferry'...," (recorded April 7, 1862), *Miscellaneous Deed Records*, Book B, Walla Walla County Courthouse, Walla Walla, Washington, 223.

703 Bailey, *River of No Return*, 420.

704 James L. Huntley, *Ferryboats in Idaho* (Caldwell, ID: The Caxton Printers, Ltd. 1979), 242-43; Beall to Brosnan, February 3, 1918, Manuscripts, Special Collections, University of Idaho.

705 Bailey, *River of No Return*, 420.

706 Letter from Cain to Geary, July 9, 1861, NPUA. What Shoshone couples were doing on the Nez Perce reservation was not made clear.

707 *Ibid.* See also Walker, Turley, and Leonard, *Massacre*, 47, quoting Brigham Young's 1857 instruction to the church's southern Utah Indian mission: "Continue the conciliatory policy towards the Indians, which I have ever recommended, and seek by works of righteousness to obtain their love and confidence, for they must learn that they have either got to help us, or the United States will kill us both."

708 Cain to Geary, July 9, 1861.

709 Rumors persisted of a southern Utah massacre in 1857 in which a wagon train had been attacked and more than one hundred men, women and children had been killed by Mormon men aided by local Shoshone warriors. These stories added credence to intelligence that an alliance between Shoshone Indians and Mormons was still in the making. For scholarly treatment of the Mountain Meadows massacre using Latter-day Saints archival resources, see Walker, Turley, and Leonard, *Massacre*. See also White, *"It's Your Misfortune"*, 168, and Prucha, *Great Father*, 379.

710 Statement of Persons Employed at the Nez Perces Indian Agency this 16th day of September, 1861, by Chas. Hutchins Indian Agent W.T., NPUA.

711 *Message of the President*, 1862, 566-67.

712 *Nez Perce Nation Divided*, 169.

713 McWhorter, *Hear Me, My Chiefs!*, 100-101 and nn8, 9, citing [Victor], *History of Washington*, 238.

714 "Certification of Sale," *Miscellaneous Deed Records*, Book B, Walla Walla County Courthouse, 223.

715 Craig to Hutchins, Lapwai January 1, 1862, NPUA.

716 Hutchins to Craig, January 14, 1862, NPUA.

717 Statement of Persons employed at the Nez Perces Indian Agency the 16th day of September 1861 by Chas Hutchins Indian Agent W.T., NPUA; *Nez Perce Nation Divided*, 168.

718 Josephy, *Nez Perce Indians*, 357.

[719] Haines, "Robert Newell," 7-9.

[720] Tobie, *No Man Like Joe*, 254-55.

[721] Nez Perce 1863 Treaty Council Proceedings, 48.

[722] *Nez Perce Nation Divided*, 168. See also Prucha, *Great Father*, 138. The trust funds of the Indians had been invested mostly in southern stocks and bonds and secessionists maintained that if tribes sustained their attachment to the North, the funds would be forfeited.

[723] *Nez Perce Nation Divided*, 168, 171.

[724] *Ibid.*, 171-72. The "pair of trays" no doubt refers to a pair of threes in a hand of poker.

[725] A Democrat, Kendall was "Abraham Lincoln's most controversial territorial appointee," according to Robert Ficken, who believes Lincoln appointed Kendall to get Democratic support for the war. See Ficken, *Washington Territory*, 65; Craig to Hutchins, Lapwai June 2, 1862, NPUA.

[726] Craig to Hutchins, June 2, 1862, NPUA.

[727] Hutchins to Craig, June 3, 1862, NPUA.

[728] Hutchins to Hale, July 15, 1862, NPUA.

[729] *Ibid.*

[730] *Ibid.*

[731] *Ibid.*

[732] *Ibid.*

[733] *Nez Perce Nation Divided*, 233. Political pressures had brought about John Owen's resignation as Flathead Agent a month earlier. After his beloved Shoshone wife, Nancy, died in 1868, he began to drink heavily. Ten years later he was hospitalized with dementia and was thereafter declared legally insane. See "Fort Owen State Park," brochure, Fort Owen State Park (Missoula: Montana State Parks, Montana Dept. of Fish, Wildlife and Parks, n.d.).

[734] Anderson to Hale, August 27, 1862, NPUA.

[735] *Ibid.*

[736] *Ibid.*

[737] Anderson to Craig, September 24, 1862, NPUA.

[738] Anderson to Maj. J. S. Rinearson, September 29, 1862, NPUA.

[739] Rinearson to Craig, October 2 1862, NPUA.

[740] Craig to Rinearson, October 2, 1862, NPUA.

[741] *Ibid.*

[742] *Ibid.*

[743] Alvord to Rinearson, November 22, 1862, Fort Lapwai, Letters Received 1862-1877, RG 393, Records of U.S. Army Continental Commands, 1817-1940, NARA, MF 464/4.

[744] Lewiston (Silcott) Ferry, Reference Series 759 (Boise: Idaho State Historical Society, 1982), 3.

[745] *Washington Statesman* (Walla Walla), December 20, 1861, p.2.

[746] *Ibid.*, January 10, 1862, p.2.

[747] *Ibid.*, March 22, 1862, p. 2, col. 3.

[748] *Ibid.*, May 17, 1862, p. 2.

[749] *Message of the President*, 1862, 541.

[750] *Washington National Guard*, v.3, 207.

[751] West, *Last Indian War*, 87.

[752] Indian Appropriation Bill, *Congressional Globe*, 37th Cong., 2nd sess., 1862, p. 2094-3.

[753] *Ibid.*, 2097-3. The line of reasoning came from Agent Charles Hutchins, Craig's advocate in the fight to save his ferry.

[754] *Ibid.*, 2096-2. Finally proposed was a smaller reservation, rather than displacement to the Flathead reservation. See Josephy, *Nez Perce Indians*, 418.

[755] Richards, *Young Man in a Hurry*, 390.

[756] *Washington Statesman* (Walla Walla), October 18, 1862, p. 1, col. 1.

757 Duncan McDonald, "Indian Feeling," *New Northwest* (Deer Lodge, Montana), June 14, 1878.

758 Josephy, *Nez Perce Indians*, 412.

759 Fort Vancouver, W.T., November 25, 1862, Benjamin Alvord Collection, OHS, as quoted in Josephy, *Nez Perce Indians*, 413.

760 Aurora Hunt, "The Far West Volunteers: The Army of the Pacific and the Unsung Valor of its Men," *Montana the Magazine of Western History* 12, no. 2 (Spring 1962): 49, 60. (Congress had passed the "Volunteer Employment Act" in July 1861 to supply substitute soldiers in the West.)

761 An estimate given by Agent Charles Hutchins on June 30, 1862. See *Message of the President of the United States*, 1862, 567.

762 The personal vignette is that of Beall, "Recollections of Wm. Craig."

763 Thomas, *Chinook, A History and Dictionary*, 65.

764 Beall, "Recollections of Wm. Craig."

765 Indian Appropriation Bill, 2095-1.

766 Nez Perce 1863 Treaty Council Proceedings, 22-3. Unless otherwise noted, the 1863 events regarding the Lapwai Valley council are from the above document.

767 *Nez Perce Nation Divided*, 303, 397.

768 An overview of the government's battle against ardent spirits and Indians may be found in Prucha, *Great Father*, see especially 30, 312-14.

769 See also Clifford M. Drury, *Chief Lawyer of the Nez Perce Indians 1796-1876*, (Glendale, CA: The Arthur H. Clark Co., 1979), 173-210.

770 Report of the Adjutant-General of Oregon, 1865-66, 18, as cited in Josephy, Nez Perce Indians, 425-26.

771 "The Nez Perces Treaty," *Washington Statesman* (Walla Walla, WT), June 13, 1863, p. 2, col. 3.

772 *Nez Perce Nation Divided*, 385-86.

773 "Nez Perce: St. Joseph's Mission Site at Slickpoo, Idaho." The name "T'simslippuus" has been corrupted to "Slickpoo," a name now carried by not only a mission site but also a family.

774 Beall, "Recollections of Wm. Craig." Newell and Craig's trip to Mt. Idaho is from this source.

775 A. J. Splawn, *Ka-Mi-akin: Last Hero of the Yakimas* (Portland: Binfords & Mort for the Oregon Historical Society, 1944), 223.

776 Clark W. Durkee is reported to have lived on one route over Craig Mountain near present-day Winchester, Idaho. His cabin and outbuildings served as a stage stop. Members of the Ilo-Vollmer Historical Society in Craigmont, Idaho, believe the Durkeeville site is on McCormack Ridge Road (Fountaine Grade) on the southwest side of Mason Butte.

777 "First Poll Book of Lewiston, Idaho," *Idaho Genealogical Society Quarterly* 3, no. 1 (March 1960): 8.

778 Simon-Smolinski, "River History," 10.

779 "Nez Perces Ask Reimbursement for Palouse Country, Pierce Gold Fields," *Lewiston (ID) Morning Tribune*, February 11, 1957; Norman B. Adkison, Idaho Historian, "Nez Perce Indians' Gold Claim Based on 'Period Of Trespass' Calls Back Days of Idaho's Fabulous Mines," *Lewiston (ID) Morning Tribune*, October 19, 1958. See *The Nez Perce Tribe of Indians* v. *The United States of America*, Doc. No. 175, 27 Ind. Cl. Comm. 481, where the parties reached a compromise settlement in the amount of $3,550,000 on August 25, 1971. http://digital.library.okstate.edu/icc/727/iccu270473.pdf [8/7/2010]

780 Sister M. Alfreda Elsensohn, *Pioneer Days in Idaho County*, Vol. 2 (Caldwell, ID.: The Caxton Printers, Ltd., 1951), 206.

781 Hutchins to Hale, July 15, 1862, NPUA.

782 Dennis W. Baird, ed., *With Bird and Truax on the Lolo Trail: Building the Virginia City to Lewiston Wagon Road, 1865-1867*, Northwest Historical Manuscript Series (Moscow: University of Idaho Press, 1999), 2.

[783] "Location of Idaho's Territorial Capital," Reference Series 344 (Boise: Idaho State Historical Society, 1964), 1.

[784] Josephy, *Nez Perce Indians*, 436-37.

[785] *With Bird and Truax*, 4.

[786] "Idaho Territory, 1863-1872," Reference Series 682 (Boise: Idaho State Historical Society, 1982), 2.

[787] Hugh H. Hartman, *Founding Fathers of Boise 1863-1875* ([Boise, ID]): the author, 1989), 119.

[788] *With Bird and Truax*, 3. Unless otherwise noted, Craig's experiences with the road-building survey party are based on this source.

[789] "Distribution of Premiums to the Pupils of St. Vincent's Academy July 2d, 1866," *Walla Walla Statesman*, July 13, 1866. The academy had been in operation for two years and was turning out accomplished young women. Annie Craig was recognized for her performance in music, fancy work and embroidery. Her niece, Clara Robie, and Robert and Rebecca Newell's daughter, Martha, also attended St. Vincent's Academy: Clara earned honors in reading and Martha in arithmetic, history and grammar.

[790] *With Bird and Truax*, 14.

[791] *John Owen Journals*, 23.

[792] *With Bird and Truax*, 24.

[793] *Ibid.*, 25.

[794] Aoki, *Nez Perce Dictionary*, 1244.

[795] "The Lewiston and Montana Road," *Walla Walla Statesman*, August 10, 1866, 2.

[796] The 1863 Treaty was ratified April 17, 1867. See Kappler, *Indian Treaties*, 2:843.

[797] Harmon, *Indians in the Making*, 96-97.

[798] Records of the Roman Catholic Church, Diocese of Spokane, Register: Baptisms – Oct. 15, 1860 to Aug. 18, 1872, Bk. 2, 53.

[799] George F. Weibel, S. J., "Rev. Joseph M. Cataldo, S. J.: A Short Sketch of a Wonderful Career," reprint from *Gonzaga Quarterly*, March 15, 1928, 13-14.

[800] *Ibid.*, 13-15; Haines, "Robert Newell," 9, 14-15.

[801] Peterson, "About William Craig," 1122. Fitch Phinney was Peterson's uncle.

[802] Beall, "Recollections of Wm. Craig."

[803] Deposition of Samuel Phinney and Thomas J. Newell, May 4, 1890, *Caldwell v. Vaughn*, Exhibits.

[804] Book B (Day Book), 396.

[805] Beall, "Recollections of Wm. Craig," 5.

[806] Robert L. Holbrook, "Col. William Craig, Early Settler of Central Idaho, Paid Homage at Dedication of Memorial Stone" (unpublished, typewritten copy in possession of author), 3.

[807] "Death of An Old Mountaineer," *Idaho Tri-Weekly Statesman* (Boise), November 4, 1869, p. 2, col. 3.

[808] Finding of Fact and Conclusions of Law, *Caldwell v. Vaughn*.

[809] Haines, "Robert Newell," 15.

[810] Graves were later moved to Normal Hill Cemetery, Lewiston, Idaho, where Newell's headstone is currently found. According to "The 5th Street Cemetery Necrogeographical Study," led by Steve Branting, radar scans of the Normal Hill cemetery reveal that some headstones have been moved without exhumation of the human remains. Robert Newell's remains may therefore remain at the original cemetery. See Steve Branting, "Resurrecting a Pioneer Cemetery," *Idaho Yesterdays*, Fall/Winter 2006, vol. 47, no. 1, 28-45.

[811] For a rare account by a non-Indian trying to give Native perspective of 1862-1869 events that included the Little Crow and Sand Creek massacres, see Dee Brown, *Bury My Heart at Wounded Knee* (New York: Holt, Rinehart & Winston, 1970), 38-190.

[812] McWhorter, *Hear Me, My Chiefs!*, 111.

813 Prucha, *Great Father*, 479-83. See also White, *"It's Your Misfortune"*, 102-04.

814 See Burns, *Jesuits and Indian Wars*, 366.

815 "Saml Phinney Administrator to John W. Rice: Deed Filed for Record March 29th AD 1872 at 9 oclock AM," Book B (Day Book), 250. John W. Rice of Mt. Idaho bought three parcels totaling about 384 acres.

816 John B. Monteith to Hon. Edward P. Smith, December 12, 1873, Lapwai Agency Letters, J.B. Monteith 1873-1874, MS 19, ISHS, vol. 2. This collection contains numerous letters by Monteith regarding the Craig and Newell descendants and the status of liquor on the reservation.

817 According to family records, William Caldwell's son, Charles ("Sol"), in 1900 married Minnie Fairfield, daughter of Annie Craig and Charles Fairfield. Minnie was born December 29, 1884, in Culdesac, Idaho.

818 Petitions (undated) to Remove John B. Monteith from Office; Letter from Alonzo Leland to John Hailey, November 23, 1873; Letter from John Hailey to Commissioner of Indian Affairs, December 10, 1873, RBIAIS.

819 *Idaho Signal* (Lewiston), November 29, 1873, Vol. 2, No. 39; Hailey to Commissioner of Indian Affairs, December 10, 1873; Deposition of Thomas J. Newell with Petition, January 2, 1874, RBIAIS.

820 Affidavit of Perrin B. Whitman (179-99), February 21, 1874, Lapwai Agency Letters, vol. 2.

821 See deposition of Isabel Craig, February 28, 1874; Deed from Isabel Craig to Samuel Phinney, February 28, 1874, both Lapwai Agency Letters, vol. 2.

822 See *Caldwell v. Vaughn*.

823 Monteith to Hon. J. Q. Smith, February 29, 1876, RBIAIS.

824 *Ibid.*

825 Monteith to Hon. Edward P. Smith, July 20, 1874, Lapwai Agency Letters, vol. 2.

826 Weibel, "Rev. Joseph M. Cataldo," 19-20.

827 St. Joseph Slickpoo Ledger, Roman Catholic Church, Diocese of Boise (Boise, Idaho), p. 7-1.

828 *Ibid.*, p. 31-9; Western States Historical Marriage Record Index, Brigham Young University Idaho, ID No. 1692, 1:133. http://abish.byui.edu/specialCollections

829 Josephy, *Nez Perce Indians*, 466-67.

830 See John K. Flanagan, "The Invalidity of the Nez Perce Treaty of 1863 and the Taking of the Wallowa Valley," *American Indian Law Review* 24, no. 1 (1999-2000): 75-98.

831 Monteith to J. Q. Smith, February 9, 1877, RBIAIS.

832 Attachment A (an article from the March 31, 1877, *Lewiston Teller)* S. S. Fenn to Miller, April 20, 1877, RBIAIS.

833 Monteith to J. Q. Smith, February 29, 1876, RBIAIS.

834 Merrill D. Beal, *"I Will Fight No More Forever": Chief Joseph and the Nez Perce War* (1963; repr., New York: Ballantine Books, 1971), 42-46.

835 Josephy, *Nez Perce Indians*, 505.

836 J. Monteith, not yet 37, died in August 1879. His tombstone (a stone imbued with Nez Perce legend, moved with chutzpah to the cemetery for use as a grave marker), was located by the author on September 9, 2001, at Spalding, Idaho, and reads: "John B. Monteith born Oct. 22, 1836, Died Aug. 7, 1879."
His brother, Charles W. Monteith – who had married Perrin Whitman's daughter, Frances Alice – was then appointed agent. Charles worked to carry out the will of Eastern reformers who believed the answer to the Indian problem was to be found in enabling Indians – by force, if necessary – to become short-haired, English-speaking, landowning Christian American citizens. For discussion of the dynamics leading to the campaign (which began in 1880) to assimilate the Indians, see Frederick E. Hoxie, *Final Promise: The Campaign to Assimilate the Indians, 1880-1920* (Lincoln: University of Nebraska Press, 1984).

837 Weibel, "Rev. Joseph M. Cataldo," 21-22.

[838] L. F. McWhorter, *Yellow Wolf: His Own Story* (1948; repr., Caldwell, ID: The Caxton Printers, Ltd., 1983), 107-8 and n11.

[839] *Starr Maxwell's Memorial*, 62d Cong. 1st sess., 1911, S. Doc. 97, 48-53. Amos George had three children who were with the exiled band in Oklahoma, where one child died. The other two were returned to the Nez Perce reservation. Daughter Mary Amos died in Forest Grove, Oregon, about 1886; son Titus Amos was killed at Arrow Junction about 1895. See *Starr Maxwell's Memorial*, Exhibit 14, p. 52. Titus Amos is buried at Ahsahka, Idaho: his gravestone reads "Titus Amos, Sept. 1, 1895, 21 years."

[840] McWhorter, *Hear Me, My Chiefs!*, 280; see also McWhorter, *Yellow Wolf* for some Nez Perces' perspective on the 1877 events. See generally Josephy, *Nez Perce Indians* and, for thoughtful treatment from an historical generalist, West, *Last Indian War*.

[841] Duncan McDonald, "The Inside Story from Indian Sources," *New Northwest* (Deer Lodge, MT), July 22, 1878.

[842] *Ibid.*, February 7, 1879.

[843] Information furnished by Otis Halfmoon from Chief Joseph & Warriors Memorial Celebration, June 14-16, 1996, Lapwai Idaho Powwow Program, 16.

[844] Pedigree Chart of Calvin Shillal. According to descendant Fermore Craig, the name of a relative can be passed down to someone of the same gender after death; a man's name would normally be passed down to a male relative—a woman's name to a female relative. In the case of Seeyakoonilpilp, unmarried and without sons, a brother or nephew could be honored with his name.

[845] "Albert H. Robie," in Hartman, *Founding Fathers of Boise 1863-1875*, 119-20.

[846] C. E. S. Wood, "Private Journal, 1878," *Oregon Historical Quarterly* 70 (1969), 21n23; Pambrun, *Sixty Years*, 133.

[847] "Private Journal, 1878," 21n23.

[848] "Died: Robie—At his residence on Dry creek, Boise valley," *Idaho Statesman* (Boise), July 27, 1878.

[849] Unless otherwise noted, the author has relied upon Jon M. Skovlin and Donna McDaniel Skovlin, *Hank Vaughan (1849-1893): A Hell-Raising Horse Trader of the Bunchgrass Territory* (Cove, OR: Reflections Publishing Co., 1996), for material on Hank Vaughan.

[850] Merrill D. Beal and Merle W. Wells, *History of Idaho*, vol. I (New York: Lewis Historical Publishing Co., 1959), 438.

[851] Skovlin and Skovlin, *Hank Vaughan*, 107, 124.

[852] "The Agent's Dilemma," *East Oregonian* (Pendleton), October 13, 1885.

[853] "Henry C. Vaughn of Umatilla County Oregon and Martha A. Roby [of same county and state] were with mutual consent joined in lawful wedlock on the 7th day of October 1888 at the Courthouse of Walla Walla County . . . by authority of a License bearing date of 6th day of October A.D. 1888 . . . by Geo. T. Thompson," a probate judge. Walla Walla County Courthouse Marriage Records, 528.

[854] Skovlin and Skovlin, *Hank Vaughan*, 202.

[855] U.S., Census, 1880, Nez Perce County, Idaho Territory.

[856] Skovlin and Skovlin, *Hank Vaughan*, 146.

[857] Samuel Phinney by Tax Collector to Nez Perce Co. I.T., Nez Perce County Records, Deeds Book 38, M42B, 125, Nez Perce County Courthouse.

[858] "Sudden Death," *Nez Perce News* (Lewiston, IT), June 22, 1882.

[859] Fermore Craig and Calvin Shillal are two of those descendants. Another Craig descendant, Lydia French Johnson, contributed her memories in the 2006 Umatilla Reservation collaborative work. *Wiyaxayst/Wiyaakaa'awn = As Days Go By*, 124-27.

[860] "Nez Perce News," *Idaho Tri-Weekly Statesman* (Boise), July 8, 1886, p. 2, c. 3.

[861] Adeline's eldest son, Fitzhugh, and his wife Mary Lily, were parents at least five children, three of who lived to adulthood: Samuel, George and Archie Phinney. Archie Phinney was one of the Indian leaders who in 1944 were instrumental in creating the National Congress of American Indians, an organization designed to influence national Indian policy. For an overview of Native

Americans and their struggle within U.S. laws up to the current time, see Charles Wilkinson, *Blood Struggle: The Rise of Modern Indian Nations* (New York: W. W. Norton & Co., 2005); regarding National Congress of American Indians, see *ibid.*, 102-06.

[862] "Brevities," *Nez Perce (ID) News* (Lewiston), May 13, 1886, p. 1, col. 2.

[863] "The Excursion," *Ibid.*, col. 1.

For more copies of The Intermediary:

See www.ridenbaughpress.com

Or contact Ridenbaugh Press at stapilus@ridenbaugh.com